Hanif Kureishi

CONTEMPORARY CRITICAL PERSPECTIVES

Series Editors: Jeannette Baxter, Peter Childs,
Sebastian Groes, and Sean Matthews

Guides in the *Contemporary Critical Perspectives* series provide companions to reading and studying major contemporary authors. They include new critical essays combining textual readings, cultural analysis, and discussion of key critical and theoretical issues in a clear, accessible style. Each guide also includes a preface by a major contemporary writer, a new interview with the author, discussion of film and TV adaptation, and guidance on further reading.

Titles in the series include:

J. G. Ballard edited by Jeannette Baxter

Kazuo Ishiguro edited by Sean Matthews and Sebastian Groes

Julian Barnes edited by Sebastian Groes and Peter Childs

Sarah Waters edited by Kaye Mitchell

Salman Rushdie edited by Robert Eaglestone and Martin McQuillan

Ali Smith edited by Monica Germana and Emily Horton

Ian McEwan (2nd Edition) edited by Sebastian Groes

Andrea Levy edited by Jeannette Baxter and David James

Hanif Kureishi

EDITED BY
SUSAN ALICE FISCHER

Bloomsbury Academic
An imprint of Bloomsbury Publishing Plc

B L O O M S B U R Y
LONDON • NEW DELHI • NEW YORK • SYDNEY

Bloomsbury Academic
An imprint of Bloomsbury Publishing Plc

50 Bedford Square	1385 Broadway
London	New York
WC1B 3DP	NY 10018
UK	USA

www.bloomsbury.com

BLOOMSBURY and the Diana logo are trademarks of Bloomsbury Publishing Plc

First published 2015

© Susan Alice Fischer and contributors, 2015

All rights reserved. No part of this publication may be reproduced or transmitted in any form or by any means, electronic or mechanical, including photocopying, recording, or any information storage or retrieval system, without prior permission in writing from the publishers.

No responsibility for loss caused to any individual or organization acting on or refraining from action as a result of the material in this publication can be accepted by Bloomsbury or the author.

British Library Cataloguing-in-Publication Data
A catalogue record for this book is available from the British Library.

ISBN: HB: 978-1-4725-1334-2
PB: 978-1-4725-0915-4
ePDF: 978-1-4725-1491-2
ePub: 978-1-4725-1168-3

Library of Congress Cataloging-in-Publication Data
A catalog record for this book is available from the Library of Congress.

Series: Contemporary Critical Perspectives

Typeset by Deanta Global Publishing Services, Chennai, India

Contents

Foreword *Roger Michell* vii
Series editors' preface x
Acknowledgments xi
Contributors xii
Hanif Kureishi: A chronology xiv

Introduction *Susan Alice Fischer* 1

1   The enigma of abandonment: Rethinking Hanif Kureishi's importance for multiculturalism
    Michael Perfect 7

2   "I believe my eyes": The transformative cinema of Hanif Kureishi
    Deanna Kamiel 21

3   Culture and anarchy in Thatcher's London: Hanif Kureishi's *Sammy and Rosie Get Laid*
    Peter Hitchcock 35

4   "The suburbs that did it": Hanif Kureishi's *The Buddha of Suburbia* and metropolitan multicultural fiction
    Ryan Trimm 51

5   Hanif Kureishi's "better philosophy": From *The Black Album* and *My Son the Fanatic* to *The Word and the Bomb*
    Susan Alice Fischer 69

6   The parallax of aging: Hanif Kureishi's *The Body*
    Jago Morrison 85

7   The other Kureishi: A psychoanalytic reading of *Something to Tell You*
    Geoff Boucher 99

8 *The Last Word* on Hanif Kureishi
   Susie Thomas 115

Interview "A very serious business": Hanif Kureishi in conversation with Susan Alice Fischer 131

Interview "An extraordinary encounter": Stephen Frears in conversation with Susan Alice Fischer and Deanna Kamiel 145

References 151
Further reading 163
Index 171

Foreword

Roger Michell

I was asked to direct *Buddha of Suburbia* by the BBC in 1991. I loved the book, and knew Hanif a little from our days together at the Royal Court in the late 70s when he was an usher/reader/young writer and I a fledgling director. When the scripts arrived I ripped open the parcel with glee. But they were awful. I spent a day with the screenwriter, a likeable young man who had written episodes of *Casualty*. I presumed he'd been offered the job because he was, like Hanif, Anglo-Asian. I thought he'd missed the book by a mile. This was at the very beginning of my TV career. I agonized. The BBC assured me that yes, of course, Hanif really liked the scripts.

Miserably, I turned the job down.

A week later the BBC called back. "Hanif says he'll adapt the book. As long as we give him an office. And a secretary. Oh, and as long as he does it with you."

I'd never adapted anything in my life.

We started from scratch. We had four weeks to generate four hours of material. They gave us a tiny office in an annex overlooking Shepherd's Bush. The lino was covered in cigarette burns. Along our corridor ranged *Middlemarch*, *Clarissa*, and *Mr Wroe's Virgins* ... a sort of BBC collegiate heaven long since stamped into extinction.

Hanif strode in on the first day sporting pale green shoes, a purple waistcoat, RayBans, and a rolled-up brolly. Part dandy, part imp, part civil servant. He was puffed up with bravado. I could tell he'd been thinking about this project for the entire half-an-hour it had taken him to journey from Earl's Court. He paced the tiny room like a Hollywood tyro dictating to our utterly bewildered PA. He described a florid and fabulously expensive flashback with which he intended to begin the series. In it, from what I can remember, Haroon and his brother had the run of pre-partition Bombay. There were crowded streets, extended families, bazaars with elephants, and tramp steamers galore at the Gateway. Even David Lean would have blenched. I sat there, mouth agape, as this most famous of Anglo-Asians, this Oscar-nominated *enfant terrible* whom I hardly knew, came eventually to the end of the most expensive and pointless stage direction in the history of television.

I gingerly indicated that I could see no useful, elegant, or meaningful way of cutting back to these Empire flashbacks anywhere else in the entire four hours of the subsequent narrative. And that, anyway, the novel had the most sensational, shocking, and filmic opening and that shouldn't we maybe at least start with that? He paused, he blinked, then he sat. "Yeah," he said, "Fuck. Yeah. Fuck. I think you're right."

I think we both grew to love that little office. For him it was an escape from a miserable and chronic back problem (quite often I'd wander in to find the PA walking up and down his spine as he quaffed priceless bottles of Nigerian Guinness gifted to me by my Production Designer): from the unhappiness of directing his first and last film (*London Kills Me*): and from the loss of his beloved father: or rather, into the arms of that loss as *Buddha* is so much about fathers and sons. I'd made a big chart of the book and we'd divvy up the scenes for adaption as if we were filleting mackerel, but Hanif would become easily bored by his own prose, which he could often hardly bring himself to reread. He'd end up writing "As In Book" as in, for example, "Scene 54: INT KARIM'S BEDROOM. DAY." Then a gap. Then "As In Book."

There was a heat wave. We drank pints of black tea in melting polystyrene cups from the steamy canteen on the first floor. The fat ladies wielding the kettles were the only black faces in the building. At noon we'd eat dal and roti in a caff on the Goldhawk Rd or we'd bring it back in leaking paper bags. (Karim's younger brother's line "Yuck! Dal on my slide-rule!" is evidence of this.) Often, bored, Hanif would prowl the corridors in search of diversion. He would try to irritate the producers by standing in their doorways softly mouthing the word "wanker" over and over again as they attempted to conclude important phone calls with far-off fat controllers. Afterward they would try and engage him in intellectual conversations about literature and he would collude in pretending to know what on earth they were talking about.

He was capricious, lazy, abusive, very irritating, funny, arrogant, always well dressed, thoughtful, never late, thin-skinned, curious, affectionate. To be honest he didn't have much interest in the work in hand. For him it was like an old affair, half-forgotten. Or pulling on wet swimming trunks perhaps: just not as much fun as the first time around.

But oddly I learned immeasurably from him. I took myself so seriously then and yet was fearful too. He taught me how to bring playfulness and even carelessness into the work. That to take it all so seriously was only possible if at the same time you didn't take it seriously at all.

Since then we've made three films together (*The Mother*, *Venus*, and *Le Week-End*): that's about one every seven years. Each of them marks turning points, progressions, and even deteriorations in our own lives. We're working on a fourth one now. We remain like a grumpy old couple, bickering and snapping at each other's heels in a marriage that lurches on and will do so, I hope, until the end.

July 2013

Series editors' preface

The readership for contemporary fiction has never been greater. The explosion of reading groups and literary blogs, of university courses and school curricula, and even the apparent rude health of the literary marketplace indicate an ever-growing appetite for new work, for writing which responds to the complex, changing, and challenging times in which we live. At the same time, readers seem ever more eager to engage in conversations about their reading, to devour the review pages, to pack the sessions at literary festivals and author events. Reading is an increasingly social activity, as we seek to share and refine our experience of the book, to clarify and extend our understanding.

It is this tremendous enthusiasm for contemporary fiction to which the *Contemporary Critical Perspectives* series responds. Our ambition is to offer readers of current fiction a comprehensive critical account of each author's work, presenting original, specially commissioned analyses of all aspects of their career, from a variety of different angles and approaches, as well as directions toward further reading and research.

Our brief to the contributors is to be scholarly, to draw on the latest thinking about narrative, or philosophy, or psychology, indeed whatever seemed to them most significant in drawing out the meanings and force of the texts in question, but also to focus closely on the words on the page, the stories and scenarios and forms which all of us meet first when we open a book. We insisted that these essays be accessible to that mythical beast, the Common Reader, who might just as readily be spotted at the Lowdham Book Festival as in a college seminar. In this way, we hope to have presented critical assessments of our writers in such a way as to contribute something to both of those environments, and also to have done something to bring together the most important qualities of each of them.

Jeannette Baxter, Peter Childs, Sebastian Groes,
and Sean Matthews

Acknowledgments

Above all, I am grateful to Hanif Kureishi for his extraordinary generosity during this project, which began with his appearance at a conference on his work that Sebastian Groes and I organized at Roehampton University in 2012. He not only participated in the conference, but also shared his notebooks and films. My gratitude goes to Stephen Frears and Roger Michell, who both took time out of their extremely busy lives to discuss their collaboration with the author. I also want to thank Sebastian Groes for his collegiality and support, Nick Lavery for transcribing the interview with the author, Julia Noyce for her assistance with organizing the conference, as well as all the conference participants who helped to make it such a lively event, and the contributors to this volume who continued the conversation.

David Avital and Mark Richardson at Bloomsbury offered their full support and encouragement, as did the Series Editors Jeannette Baxter, Peter Childs, Sebastian Groes, and Sean Matthews, for which I am truly grateful.

A special thanks goes to Susie Thomas, whose work on Hanif Kureishi has been inspirational, whose feedback is always insightful, and whose friendship continues to be invaluable. I also thank those who read an early draft of my chapter at the Center for Place, Culture and Politics of the CUNY Graduate Center, where I was a Faculty Fellow during the 2011–12 academic year. I am grateful to my students at Medgar Evers College with whom I discussed some of Kureishi's work.

I especially want to thank my friends: Gregory Woods, who first suggested we see *My Beautiful Laundrette* all those years ago, and Chantal Brotherton-Ratcliffe and Frances Tomlinson, who generously hosted me in London while I was working on this book. Most of all I am grateful to *all* my family, and especially to Michele Gregory whose love, laughter, and patience have sustained me during this project.

Contributors

Geoff Boucher is a senior lecturer in literary studies at Deakin University in Australia. He is the author of a number of books on culture and psychoanalysis, including *Žižek and Politics* (2010) and *The Charmed Circle of Ideology* (2008). His most recent works are *Understanding Marxism* (2012) and *Adorno Reframed* (2012).

Susan Alice Fischer is a professor of English at Medgar Evers College of The City University of New York, where she is the Cross-Cultural Literature Coordinator and teaches British literature, contemporary London literature, and literary theory. She is editor of *The Literary London Journal* (www.literarylondon.org) and co-editor of *Changing English: Studies in Culture and Education*, both peer reviewed. She has written extensively about contemporary women's London narratives and other contemporary British fiction.

Stephen Frears is the director of Hanif Kureishi's screenplays *My Beautiful Laundrette* (1985) and *Sammy and Rosie Get Laid* (1987). His many other titles include *Prick Up Your Ears* (1987) and *Philomena* (2013). He has been nominated for numerous awards, including a BAFTA nomination for *Dirty Pretty Things* (2002) and Oscar and Golden Globe nominations for *The Queen* (2006). He won the 2004 BAFTA TV Award for Best Single Drama for *The Deal* (2003).

Peter Hitchcock is a professor of English at Baruch College and The Graduate Center of The City University of New York. His books include *Dialogics of the Oppressed* (Minnesota, 1993), *Oscillate Wildly* (Minnesota, 1999), *Imaginary States* (Illinois, 2003), and *The Long Space* (Stanford, 2010).

Deanna Kamiel is the director of documentary studies at The New School in New York and an assistant professor in the School of Media Studies at The New School for Public Engagement. A Canadian, she is a documentary filmmaker with a career in public broadcasting at the CBC in Toronto and at PBS in Minneapolis and New York. Recipient of a Guggenheim fellowship, she previously taught in the conservatory film program at Purchase College, State University of New York. Currently she is at work on a film about newsstands and the information future. In Manhattan, her film *Nuclear Outpost* screens as part of The Museum of Modern Art's permanent digital collection.

CONTRIBUTORS

Roger Michell is the director of the BAFTA-nominated television version of *The Buddha of Suburbia* (1993) and of Hanif Kureishi's screenplays *The Mother* (2003), *Venus* (2006), and *Le Week-End* (2013), in addition to many other titles, including the recent *Hyde Park on Hudson* (2012). Nominated for numerous awards, he won the 1996 BAFTA TV Award for Best Single Drama for *Persuasion* (1995), a Locarno International Film Festival Award for *Titanic Town* (1998) and the 2000 Empire, UK, Award for Best British Director for *Notting Hill* (1999).

Jago Morrison is a specialist in contemporary and postcolonial writing at Brunel University (UK). His publications include *Contemporary Fiction* (Routledge, 2003), *Scandalous Fictions: The Twentieth Century Novel in the Public Sphere* (with Susan Watkins, 2006), *The Fiction of Chinua Achebe* (Continuum, 2007), *The Post-War British Literature Handbook* (with Katharine Cockin, 2010), and *Chinua Achebe* (Manchester University Press, 2014). In association with the think tank Demos, he published the policy report *Coming of Age* with Philip Tew and Nick Hubble in 2011. A major new study, *Ageing in Contemporary Fiction*, is forthcoming from Routledge in 2015.

Michael Perfect is an assistant professor of English Literature at Bilkent University in Ankara, Turkey. His main research and teaching interests are in twentieth- and twenty-first-century literature and culture. His book *Contemporary Fictions of Multiculturalism: Diversity and the Millennial London Novel* was published by Palgrave Macmillan in 2014. He has also published journal articles and book chapters on contemporary British literature and postcolonial studies, and has taught at the University of Cambridge—where he obtained his PhD in 2011—as well as in London.

Susie Thomas is the author of numerous essays on Hanif Kureishi as well as editor of *Hanif Kureishi: A Reader's Guide to Essential Criticism* (Palgrave Macmillan, 2005). She is the book reviews editor for *The Literary London Journal* and Director of AHA London, an academic program of the University of Oregon. She has published articles on British authors from Aphra Behn to Martin Amis, and some of her articles appear on www.londonfictions.com.

Ryan Trimm is an associate professor of English and Film Media at the University of Rhode Island (USA), where he is chair of the English Department. His work focuses on uses of the past in contemporary Britain. He has published in journals such as *Critique*, *Cinema Journal*, *Novel*, and *Literature Interpretation Theory*, as well as in several well-received collections.

Hanif Kureishi: A chronology

1954 Hanif Kureishi, born in Bromley, Kent, UK, on December 5

1970s Studies philosophy at King's College London

1976 *Soaking the Heat*, Royal Court Theatre, London

1980 *The Mother Country* (performed at Riverside Studios; receives the Thames Television Playwright Award); *The King and Me* (premieres at Soho Poly Theatre); *You Can't Go Home* (BBC Radio)

1981 *Tomorrow Today!* (Soho Poly Theatre); *Outskirts* (premieres at The Royal Court Company's Warehouse Theatre, London; wins George Devine Award); *Borderline* performed at the Royal Court Theatre, London (after being performed by Joint Stock Theatre Group; Methuen publishes play); London Theatre Critics' Most Promising New Playwright of the Year for *Borderline* and *Outskirts*

1982 Writer in Residence, Royal Court Theatre

1983 *Birds of Passage* (first performed at Hampstead Theatre; published by Amber Lane Press); Calder publishes *Outskirts and other Plays*

1985 *My Beautiful Laundrette* (dir. Stephen Frears); receives Evening Standard Award for Best Film

1986 Faber and Faber publishes "The Rainbow Sign" with the screenplay of *My Beautiful Laundrette*

1987	*My Beautiful Laundrette* nominated for Oscar for Best Writing (Screenplay Written Directly for the Screen); wins National Society of Film Critics Award for Best Screenplay; *Sammy and Rosie Get Laid* (dir. Stephen Frears)
1988	*Sammy and Rosie Get Laid: The Script and the Diary* (Faber and Faber)
1990	*The Buddha of Suburbia* (Faber and Faber); receives the Whitbread First Novel Prize
1991	Writes and directs *London Kills Me*; screenplay published by Faber and Faber
1992	Faber and Faber publishes *Outskirts and Other Plays*
1993	*Buddha of Suburbia* (dir. Roger Michell) (BBC)
1994	*Buddha of Suburbia* nominated for BAFTA film award for Best Drama Serial
1995	*The Black Album* (Faber and Faber); author co-edits *The Faber Book of Pop* with John Savage
1996	*My Beautiful Laundrette and Other Writings* (Faber and Faber)
1997	*Love in a Blue Time* (Faber and Faber); *My Son the Fanatic* (dir. Udayan Prasad), based on a short story of the same title published the same year
1998	*Intimacy: A Novel* (Faber and Faber); *My Son the Fanatic* nominated by British Independent Film Award for Best Original Screenplay by a British Writer of a Produced Independent Film; screenplay published by Faber and Faber
1999	*Sleep with Me* (premieres at the Royal National Theatre; published by Faber and Faber); *Midnight All Day* (Faber and Faber)
2001	*Intimacy* (dir. Patrice Chéreau); Berlin Film Festival prizes Blue Angel and Golden Berlin Bear awarded to director; *Gabriel's Gift* (Faber and Faber)

2002	*The Body and Seven Stories* (Faber and Faber); *Collected Screenplays: My Beautiful Laundrette, Sammy and Rosie Get Laid, London Kills Me, My Son the Fanatic* (Faber and Faber); *Dreaming and Scheming: Collected Prose: Reflections on Writing and Politics* (Faber and Faber)
2003	*The Mother* (dir. Roger Michell); nominated for European Film Award for Best Screenwriter; screenplay published by Faber and Faber
2004	*My Ear at His Heart: Reading My Father* (Faber and Faber); *When Night Begins* (premieres at Hampstead Theatre; published by Faber and Faber)
2005	*The Word and the Bomb* (Faber and Faber)
2006	*Venus* (dir. Roger Michell); nominated for Best Independent Film Award for Best Screenplay; screenplay published by Faber and Faber
2007	*Venus* wins Humanities Prize in Feature Film Category; "Weddings and Beheadings" shortlisted for the National Short Story Competition; author awarded Chevalier de l'Ordre des Arts et des Lettres in France
2008	Author awarded Commander of the Order of the British Empire (CBE) for services to literature; *Something to Tell You* (Faber and Faber)
2009	*The Black Album: Adapted for the stage* (premieres at the National Theatre, London; published by Faber and Faber)
2011	*Collected Essays* (Faber and Faber); *Collected Stories* (Faber and Faber)
2013	*Le Week-End* (dir. Roger Michell); screenplay published by Faber and Faber; appointed professor at Kingston University, London
2014	*The Last Word* (Faber and Faber)

Introduction

Susan Alice Fischer

Since his stunning Academy Award-nominated film, *My Beautiful Laundrette* (1985), Hanif Kureishi has been recognized as a major figure who has both documented and shaped contemporary British culture. His first novel, *The Buddha of Suburbia* (1990), has been studied at schools and universities around the world and remains a key work in redefining our sense of what it means to be English. The author of numerous novels and screenplays and countless short stories, essays, and plays, Kureishi has engaged with many of the preoccupations of contemporary culture in ways that are bold, honest, fearless, and funny.

My Beautiful Laundrette brought postcolonial relations and race, class, and sexuality to the forefront, something that continued in *Sammy and Rosie Get Laid* (1987) and *The Buddha of Suburbia*. Writing in opposition to all that Thatcherism stood for in his early career, Kureishi has never sought the easy answers that some critics of his later work have often seemed to desire. In response to the Rushdie affair, Kureishi wrote *The Black Album* (1995). He continued his exploration of why some young Muslim British men become religious extremists in *My Son the Fanatic* (1997). While some have criticized his portrayal of Muslim characters in a context that is increasingly Islamophobic, Kureishi has been equally scathing in his appraisal of the ways that the West has—with its colonial, imperial, and racist legacies—provided a context for extreme religious positions, as can be seen in his essays, such as those collected in *The Word and the Bomb* (2005).

Some have seen Kureishi's work after *The Buddha of Suburbia* and *The Black Album* as a depoliticized move toward a more personal and individual focus. While critics have had no trouble recognizing his exploration of the radical possibilities of love in such works as *My Beautiful Laundrette* and *The Buddha of Suburbia*, once he moves away from the obviously transgressive same-sex or cross-cultural couplings, some seem to resist recognizing that Kureishi is still raising larger cultural issues despite using characters that are often white, middle-class, heterosexual, or middle-aged. For instance in *The Mother* (2003), May discovers she has subordinated her own desires—including her sexuality—to others because of expectations of womanhood and motherhood, but by contravening societal norms about motherhood (which needn't be taken literally or prescriptively), she reaches out to life's possibilities. Similarly, Leo/Adam in *The Body* (2002) develops a critique of the cult of youth, which makes aging invisible. Presenting transgressive behavior and unconventional "odd couples"—a hallmark of Kureishi's work, as Susie Thomas (2005: 132) has noted—forces us to see the humanity of the other and to question conformist ideas around gender, sexuality, ethnicity, class, and age.

Throughout his work, Kureishi tackles uncomfortable topics and the messiness of human interactions without absolutist answers. In *Sleep with Me* (1999), Kureishi's interest in human relations is compellingly put forward when one character notes that "there's only one subject, what it is to be a human being, living with other people" (95). That play and his novel *Intimacy* (1998) explore the experience of a middle-aged man leaving his partner of many years and their children for another woman, while *Gabriel's Gift* (2001) looks at the possible dissolution of a family from the perspective of a gifted child whose wish for his parents' reunion comes true. Written in different genres and from diverse points of view—children, parents, white, and Asian characters—such work includes *The Mother*, a film about a mother who has an affair with her daughter's lover; *Venus* (2006), about a relationship between an elderly man and a very young woman; *The Body*, a novella about an aging man trading in his body for a newer model; a moving memoir of his father, *My Ear at His Heart: Reading My Father* (2004a); and *Something to Tell You* (2008), a novel about a psychoanalyst coming to terms with his own sense of guilt.

His short fiction has run the gamut from stories about parents and children ("Hullabaloo in the Tree" (2010[2002])), to relationships between older men and younger women ("Four Blue Chairs" (2010[1999a])), to feeling like a disgusting outsider when meeting one's much younger lover's parents ("The Tale of the Turd" (2010[1997])), torture ("Weddings and Beheadings" (2010[2006])), racism ("We're Not Jews" (2010[1995])), and appropriation of another's voice ("With Your Tongue Down My Throat" (2010[1987])). His essays have engaged with a wide range of contemporary issues, from those emerging in the wake of the Rushdie affair and 7/7 (as in *The Word and the Bomb*) to the importance of children's creativity and the perils of conformism ("The Art of Distraction" (2012)). True to his beginnings in playwriting, with such works as *Outskirts* (1992[1981]), Kureishi has continued to write for the stage, with plays such as *When Night Begins* (2004b) about the complications of abusive relations and contrasting narratives of the past, and the 2009 production of *The Black Album*.

His work in screenwriting also continues apace, most recently with the 2013 release of his fourth collaboration with director Roger Michell, *Le Week-End*, about a middle-aged couple reviving their love by recovering the anarchic. Appropriately for an author who has had so much to say about contemporary culture, his most recent novel, *The Last Word* (2014), continues to argue for the centrality of the writer, artist, and intellectual in shaping contemporary culture.

While highlighting his significance for redefining national identity, the essays in this book move beyond pigeonholing Kureishi as a "postcolonial" writer and reevaluate the critical claim that his later work has undergone a depoliticizing shift. The collection thus challenges the view that an English writer of Asian descent must always address issues of "ethnic identity"—or indeed that such questions can't be addressed when the characters are white. While Kureishi's work has changed the perception of what it means to be English, a single-minded focus on this important aspect of his work overlooks the breadth and depth of his contributions to contemporary culture, including his work's stylistic concerns. Often what has been lost in the critical discussion of his work are the nuances of his literary language and style, as well as his psychological and philosophical insights as he raises broadly defined ethical positions about wide-ranging contemporary concerns. For instance, while the postcolonial implications—and other power dynamics—are clear in such stories as "With Your Tongue Down My Throat," as is his postmodern resistance to the notion of a fixed self, it is also equally clear that such work is stylistically interesting, as are his playful experiments with intertextuality, in such work as "The Penis" (2010[1999b]), which evokes Gogol's "The Nose," not to mention the wit and satire of much of his work. Not fitting comfortably within any one category is part of what makes Kureishi who he is as a writer and also what makes his work so compelling.

This book approaches Kureishi's work from a range of perspectives. It includes Roger Michell's touching and funny foreword about his four film collaborations with Hanif Kureishi and an interview with the author himself. Stephen Frears, director of Kureishi's first two screenplays, reminds us in his interview of the transformative power of that early work.

The critical essays begin with a reassessment of Hanif Kureishi's work and critical approaches to it. Following an overt focus on contemporary political issues in his earlier work, Kureishi has sometimes been criticized for later taking a more "personal" turn. Michael Perfect argues that trying to squeeze Kureishi's *oeuvre* into the categories of "Asian British," "postcolonial," "ethnic," or "postethnic" fails to do justice to its complexity. Instead, Perfect jettisons the attempt to see Kureishi's body of work as "representative" and proposes the concept of abandonment as a more fruitful way of examining it.

The essays that follow are arranged to reflect the chronology of Kureishi's work from his first film *My Beautiful Laundrette* to his most recent novel, *The Last Word*. Deanna Kamiel and Peter Hitchcock examine Kureishi's first two films—*My Beautiful Laundrette* and *Sammy and Rosie Get Laid*, respectively—within the context of Thatcher's Britain and, more specifically, the London of the 1980s. Drawing upon film scholarship, Kamiel argues that the astonishing force of Kureishi's first film disrupts the vision of Britain that Thatcher promulgated, transforming our sense of Britain to include the diverse and transgressive. She adds that in *Venus*, Kureishi continues to provoke through startling new images, focusing this time on aging. Hitchcock looks instead at the way *Sammy and Rosie Get Laid* presents London as an ideological battleground during the turmoil of the Thatcher years. He argues that despite refusing facile answers, ultimately Kureishi's film finds a space for hope. Both authors suggest that with his first two films Kureishi bested Thatcher in what Kamiel calls her "war of representation."

Ryan Trimm shifts the focus from central London to the suburbs in his exploration of *The Buddha of Suburbia*. Claiming that the novel overturns the more traditional dichotomy of city and country by relocating the diversity often associated with the city in the suburbs, he argues that Kureishi introduces the "multicultural suburban novel" and thus "remaps" Englishness with respect to the Windrush Generation's "multicultural metropolitan novel." Trimm identifies a "restlessness" indicating the protagonist Karim's fluid sense of identity, something that he notes in *The Black Album*, in which Shahid also journeys from the suburbs to the city.

My own contribution examines *The Black Album* and the film *My Son the Fanatic* as Kureishi's responses to the Rushdie affair and looks at similar preoccupations in his essays in *The Word and the Bomb*. Bringing together contemporary manifestations of extreme religion and extreme capitalism to highlight the worst of two clashing and destructive worldviews, Kureishi attempts to locate constructive spaces between these poles in which "a better philosophy" might be found through the radical possibilities of both love and ongoing cultural debate.

In his contribution, Jago Morrison takes issue with critics who have seen *The Body* merely as a rewriting of the Faust narrative or as exemplifying the author's "creative exhaustion." Drawing upon Žižek's notion of the "parallax view," according to which the same object appears different when viewed from varying angles, Morrison uncovers the complexities of the novella, highlighting its criticism of contemporary culture's preoccupation with youth and "the politics of looking."

Also reevaluating approaches to Kureishi's recent work, Geoff Boucher conducts a psychoanalytical reading of *Something to Tell You* to examine how, despite a focus on interiority, the novel still engages with larger questions of the human condition and contemporary British culture. Boucher suggests that, by positing the figure of the psychoanalyst as protagonist and "cultural hero," Kureishi's text reclaims the political through the personal and the intimate.

Finally, Susie Thomas reminds us that while the critical focus on the content of Kureishi's work attests to its engagement with important contemporary issues, critics have largely overlooked the stylistic features that make it both so compelling and so effective. Beginning with the types of "self-subverting sentences" the author constructs—from his most famous "born and bred, almost" in *The Buddha of Suburbia*—Thomas considers the other aspects of Kureishi's style that allow the rich ambiguity of his work to emerge in his major novels, including his most recent, *The Last Word*.

While it is impossible to provide a comprehensive look at such a prolific creative force as Hanif Kureishi in the short space of this introduction or in the eight essays—however insightful—that follow, one can only hope that this volume opens new avenues for understanding his work. While this book was underway, both *Le Week-End* and *The Last Word* came out. No doubt, by the time of its publication, Kureishi will have already moved in new creative directions, making it ever more unimaginable to have a "last word" on his work.

1

The enigma of abandonment: Rethinking Hanif Kureishi's importance for multiculturalism

Michael Perfect

Chapter Summary: Critics have often attempted to emphasize Hanif Kureishi's importance for debates about multiculturalism by endowing his work with representational status; he has, variously, been labeled a "British Asian," a "postcolonial," an "ethnic," and a "postethnic" writer. This has often led to a failure to recognize the multiplicity of his writing and to engage fully with its complexities. Indeed, criticism of Kureishi has often been at its most confused when it has attempted to account for his entire *oeuvre*, and there has been much anxiety over the issue of who or what his writing finally "represents." Critically examining the theoretical contexts within which Kureishi has been read, this chapter argues that it is not productive to think of him as a "representative" writer of any sort. It explores the notion of abandonment in Kureishi's work, theorizing it as a new means of understanding the importance of his writing for contemporary debates about multiculturalism.

Keywords: Multiculturalism, representation, postcolonialism, ethnicity, postethnicity, abandonment

Throughout his career, Hanif Kureishi's writing has frustrated critical attempts to identify its significance for multiculturalism. For a quarter of a century Kureishi has been a key figure in debates about contemporary British literature, culture, and identity, and yet critics have often attempted to emphasize his importance for such debates by endowing his work with representational status. This has often led to a failure to recognize the multiplicity of his writing and to engage fully with its complexities. Criticism of Kureishi has often been at its most confused when it has attempted to account for his entire *oeuvre*, and there has been much anxiety over the issue of who or what his writing finally "represents."

Focusing primarily on Kureishi's fiction but with some reference to his work in other forms, this chapter argues that it is not productive to think about Kureishi as a "representative" writer of any sort and theorizes a new way of understanding the significance of his work for debates about multiculturalism. It argues that the notion of abandonment—while not necessarily the major theme of Kureishi's *oeuvre*—offers a way of thinking about his importance for debates about multiculturalism without taking authorial ethnicity as its starting point and without taking Kureishi to be a "representative" writer.

Reading Kureishi as "representative"

During the 1980s Kureishi was widely considered to be a "minority writer" whose plays and films explored and celebrated "minority culture." Although his work enjoyed some mainstream recognition—perhaps most notably, the Best Original Screenplay Oscar nomination that *My Beautiful Laundrette* (1985) received—it was perhaps only recognition at all in that Kureishi was recognized as "an important minority writer" or an iconic "representative" of minority culture. While this was always a rather clumsy account of his early work, in 1990 Kureishi published his first novel, *The Buddha of Suburbia*, to massive critical acclaim and immediately established himself as a *major* writer in the contemporary canon of British literature. The success of Kureishi's subsequent work has both cemented his place in the canon and reinforced his status as a crucial figure in debates over ethnic and cultural diversity in Britain.

Since 1990 Kureishi has, variously, been read as an "ethnic" writer, as a representative of "the British Asian experience," as a "postcolonial" writer, and as a "postethnic" writer. Interestingly, when Kureishi has written about issues other than ethnicity—most notably, in the late 1990s, his work shifted its primary focus to the issue of gender—critics have often sought to maintain the notion of his being representative by describing his work as having come to represent postfeminist masculinity rather than postcolonial ethnicity. Keenan Malik said of *Intimacy* (1998), for example, that "[the novel] speaks to, *and for*, a lost generation of men: those shaped by the sixties, disorientated by the eighties and bereft of a personal and political map in the nineties" (Malik 1998, my emphasis). Upon the publication of *Something to Tell You* (2008), Kureishi's first novel in a decade, critics were quick to declare that it marked a "return to the territory of his first and still best-loved novel, *The Buddha of Suburbia*" (Mars-Jones 2008). *Something to Tell You* does, indeed, deal with ethnic and cultural diversity in a much more explicit way than anything Kureishi wrote in the decade that preceded it, and his most recent novel *The Last Word* (2014) is a work that takes not just a migrant but also a "postcolonial writer" as one of its major characters (one that seems to have been loosely based on V. S. Naipaul). While a great deal of Kureishi's recent writing in other forms—such as, for instance, film scripts *The Mother* (2003a), *Venus* (2006), and *Le Week-End* (2013)—has had very little to do with, or to say about, multiculturalism, Kureishi is still known predominantly for his fiction, and there is perhaps a danger of his most recent novels being taken as a confirmation of Kureishi's status as, ultimately, a representative "ethnic" writer.

The label most commonly attributed to Kureishi has been that of "postcolonial." In 1998, Kenneth Kaleta published the first critical overview of Kureishi's work, entitled *Hanif Kureishi: Postcolonial Storyteller*. Convincingly enough, Kaleta argues that, having produced plays, film scripts, novels, and short stories, Kureishi is best considered a "storyteller" rather than, for example, a novelist or playwright. Crucially, however, Kaleta offers no justification for "postcolonial," and the term does not even appear in the volume's index. The assumption made throughout is that Kureishi is a "postcolonial" writer; indeed, that this is so obvious as to not require any critical qualification whatsoever. While I certainly do not want to suggest that Kureishi's work cannot usefully be read within postcolonial interpretive frames, I do want to contend that critics have often been too quick simply to assume that Kureishi is best considered "postcolonial."

Critics have often attempted to strengthen the case for Kureishi as a postcolonial writer by comparing him to Salman Rushdie. That Kureishi's second novel, *The Black Album* (1995), explores events surrounding the fatwa pronounced on Rushdie in 1989 following the publication of *The Satanic Verses* the previous year has been repeatedly used by critics to forge connections between the two writers. However, the comparison has often been a rather forced one. Bart Moore-Gilbert, for example, observes that the work of both writers alludes to Rudyard Kipling, and suggests that this is an "area in which Rushdie's influence on Kureishi can be detected" (Moore-Gilbert 2001: 127). The assumption made here is an odd one; it seems much more likely that the two have both been influenced by, and have engaged with, Kipling, not that Kureishi's interest in Kipling is symptomatic of his being first influenced by Rushdie. The implication is that Kureishi is imitative to the point of actually taking up Rushdie's literary influences, and that Rushdie has been a formative, primary influence on him.

Critical comparisons between Kureishi and Rushdie have often led critics to attempt to account for the general absence of postmodernist or magical realist aesthetics in the former's work. For example, worried by the realist narrative mode employed in *The Black Album*, Maria Degabriele (1999) tries to reinvest the novel with a sense of formal subversiveness by suggesting that it is a parody of *The Satanic Verses*. Although she rightly observes that both novels offer parodic accounts of the transcription of divine instruction into religious text—Kureishi's treatment of Riaz's poems is a clear example of *The Black Album* poking fun at the notion of religious texts representing divine will—Degabriele gives no justification for considering Kureishi's novel as a parody of Rushdie's. Also comparing the two novels, Frederick M. Holmes goes to great lengths to account for what he sees as the puzzlingly traditional realist narrative frame that *The Black Album* employs, finally suggesting that Kureishi's "frustrated desire for solidity and significant purpose ... led him to seek a compensatory stability in the aesthetic realm. Such a hypothesis would account for the conservative, rather old-fashioned novelistic form of *The Black Album*" (Holmes 2001: 309). Notably, both Holmes and Degabriele make a comparison between Rushdie's Saladin Chamcha and Kureishi's Shahid Hasan, but it is one that is, again, strained, even false. Holmes mistakenly calls British-born Shahid a "migrant" (296) and an "immigrant" (298), and while we might consider him a migrant from the suburbs to the city, he is certainly *not*, as Holmes suggests, a South Asian (im)migrant to Britain. Here, the attempt to locate *The Black Album* within a postcolonial interpretive frame affords the critical conflation of characters whose cultural heritage is very different indeed under the category "postcolonial subject." The key point here is that critical eagerness both to liken Kureishi to Rushdie and to read him as a postcolonial writer has often led to critical confusion over his work.

That Kureishi's writing does not tend to go about *obviously* destabilizing its own representations by deploying glaring metatextuality or magical realist aesthetics has perhaps meant that critics have tended to read it as presuming to be representative, and Kureishi has often been attacked for his pretensions or his failings as a representative of some form by critics, the British media, and by those who know him. It has repeatedly been implied that his work is somehow representationally deceptive, and the critical assumption that underlies such a complaint is that Kureishi is, or at least should be, a writer of representational status; that his experience either has a particular, sociohistorical significance—namely, that it warrants narrative representation and that this is (or at least should be) the specific value of his work—or that his experience is not as significant as his work attempts to suggest. The former has led to Kureishi being criticized for failing to represent adequately—or, perhaps more accurately, for failing to take up the task of representing—the experiences of ethnic minorities in contemporary multicultural Britain, and the latter to his being condemned as a self-exoticizing performer of cultural alterity.

The comparison between Kureishi and Rushdie is useful here for the distinctions that it allows to be made between the two. Contemporary criticism has questioned the appropriateness of considering "cosmopolitan" writers such as Rushdie as representatives of third-world nations, and has done so with much justification. The status of cross-cultural commentator to which Rushdie has, for more than three decades, aspired (and has, largely, been successful in achieving for himself) is vulnerable to critique chiefly because of his pretensions to represent, in terms of both standing for (performatively) and speaking for (politically), India and Indianness while enjoying a Western, metropolitan lifestyle and writing exclusively in a language that is not spoken by the vast majority of Indian people. While it is clearly of major cultural, political, and literary significance, Rushdie's work is often difficult to defend against accusations of self-exoticization and often "performs" Indianness for a Western literary mainstream (see Huggan 2001; Wachinger 2003). Kureishi's work, it might be said, tends to shy away from the kind of representational status that Rushdie's has tended to court.

Far from being representatively "ethnic" or representing a generalized postcolonial condition, Kureishi's writing, as Mark Stein observes, often acts out the tensions between "conforming to ... [and] parodying the sometimes constricting expectations directed towards post-colonial literature" (Stein 2004: 118). As a way out of taking Kureishi's work as postcolonial, Stein advocates reading it as "postethnic," which he formulates as follows:

> In my usage, the term *postethnic literature* characterizes writing that shows an awareness of the expectations that so-called ethnic writing faces; I apply it to texts working through these expectations and going beyond them. "Postethnic," then, does *not* try to *transcend* the "ethnic." Instead, it disputes the confinements of the very category. (Stein 2004: 112, emphasis in original)

Stein makes a case for reading *Intimacy* as "postethnic," and his case is rather useful in situating the novel within Kureishi's *oeuvre* (particularly in relation to his earlier work). However, it is much more problematic to argue that that whole *oeuvre* itself could be described as "postethnic." The risk here, as with the postcolonial, is that readings of Kureishi's work become predisposed toward searching for particular types, and strategies, of resistance—in this case, resistance against "the regime of ethnicity" rather than the regime of imperialism. While critics have been quick to group together *Intimacy* and the work that immediately followed it, *Gabriel's Gift* (2001), as texts that marginalize ethnicity, in many ways the two novels are probably as dissimilar as any two works that Kureishi has produced; although both deal with the break-up of a family, tonally they are at opposite ends of the spectrum of his *oeuvre* and their endings are almost antithetical. To group *Intimacy* and *Gabriel's Gift* together within Kureishi's *oeuvre* is to do so on the grounds of their relative lack of "ethnic" markers in comparison to his earlier work and, so, to identify ethnicity—even in absence—as somehow of foremost significance in anything that Kureishi writes. As such, laudable critical attempts to move beyond reading Kureishi's work as "ethnic" have, paradoxically, often ended up privileging the very factor they have sought to transcend.

Interestingly, in the last decade, Kureishi has produced three film scripts that do not feature any characters from ethnic minorities, a memoir that delves deeply into his South Asian ancestry as well as the experiences of his father as an immigrant to England, a novel that supposedly revisits "the territory of ... *The Buddha of Suburbia*" (Mars-Jones 2008), a stage adaptation of a novel that has questions about ethnicity at its very center, and a novel that takes a prominent "postcolonial writer" as one of its major characters (respectively, *The Mother* (2003a), *Venus* (2006), *Le Week-End* (2013), *My Ear at His Heart: Reading My Father* (2004), *Something to Tell You* (2008), *The Black Album: Adapted for the Stage* (2009), and *The Last Word* (2014)). To argue that these works are all "postethnic" would be to expand the notion to the point of meaninglessness. Indeed, attributing any one signifier to the entirety of Kureishi's *oeuvre* is a critical *cul de sac* and hinders attempts to identify its significance.

Abandonment: Rereading the importance of Kureishi's work for multiculturalism

Abandonment and departure are often portrayed as necessary for personal development and maturation in Kureishi's work. Both the young protagonists of *The Buddha of Suburbia* and *The Black Album*, for example, leave their family homes in the suburbs of London to live in the center of the city, and if both novels might usefully be considered within the literary tradition of the *Bildungsroman*, in each case it is in the metropolis that maturation occurs, with the leaving behind of the suburbs reflecting the leaving behind of adolescence. In the final stages of the former novel, it is only after Karim and Charlie have left London for America that they are able to achieve the success and celebrity that they have aspired toward. In turn, the act of returning often goes hand in hand with a sense of defeat and disillusionment. Whenever Karim returns to the suburbs to visit family members, he is struck by both the ugliness and the cultural parochialism of the area, and in the final chapter of the novel, on his first day back in England following his (mis)adventures in America, he describes London with the kind of weary disgust with which he previously referred to the suburbs:

> I walked around central London and saw that the town was being ripped apart; the rotten was being replaced by the new, and the new was ugly. The gift of creating beauty had been lost somewhere. The ugliness was in the people, too. Londoners seemed to hate each other. (Kureishi 1990: 258)

Karim's sense of being alienated in a place in which he was once at home, whether it be the suburbs or London, offers a striking contrast to the sense of excitement that he describes upon arriving somewhere new, whether it be London or America.

In *The Black Album*, which Kureishi wrote after the death of his own father—a period during which, he has said, his life "was falling apart" (quoted in Kumar and Kureishi 2001: 126)—Kureishi examines the feelings of abandonment following the death of a close family member. At the beginning of the novel, we learn that Shahid's father has died and that he has spurned the chance to take over the family business in order to study at university. Moreover, the death of his father seems to be instrumental in his search for ideological groundings. Much humor arises from Shahid's attempts to conceive of his elder brother, the shameless and extravagantly self-absorbed Chili, as a fatherly role model, and it is in the absence of paternal guidance that Shahid begins to experiment with both lecturer Deedee Osgood's hedonistic liberalism and the fundamentalist Islam of Riaz and Chad. Kureishi's portrayal of the experience of being abandoned through the death of a loved one is at once tender in its evocation of pain and loneliness but also determined in its affirmation of the possibilities that such abandonment affords.

Intimacy deals candidly with the feelings of guilt that accompany the decision to abandon, rather than the experience of being abandoned by, one's family. While the novel is certainly rather bleak in tone, there is a determination to affirm the possibility of a kind of existential rebirth following abandonment; Jay is convinced that he can "become someone else" (Kureishi 1998: 101) by being "loyal" to himself (Kureishi 1998: 42). "Yes, it is an adolescent cry," he says; "I want more. Of what? What have you got?" (Kureishi 1998: 98). As with Deedee and Riaz in *The Black Album*, Jay's friends Victor and Asif serve as opposing ideological influences in the novel, the former encouraging his departure from the family home and the latter advocating loyalty to his (Jay's) partner and family. Although he wavers momentarily at times—not least when kissing his children goodbye—Jay remains determined to leave, and the novel does not so much examine the problems of choosing value systems and allegiances, as does *The Black Album*, but the problems of following through on such choices. Crucially, Jay's awareness of the permanence of his decision—his adamance in the first line of the novel that he is "leaving and not coming back" (Kureishi 1998: 3)—is the source not only of pain but also of rejoicing. Ultimately, the novel subverts the assumption that to abandon a relationship is to concede defeat; rather, Jay's departure constitutes his rebirth (albeit a painful one) while his return would signify defeat.

There is a sense in which *Gabriel's Gift* is the antithesis of *Intimacy*, and it is the only work in Kureishi's *oeuvre* in which a final act of return—the eventual return of Gabriel's father Rex to the family home—is a cause for celebration. The thematic parallels with *Intimacy* are obvious, and there are certainly moments in the narrative that recall the earlier novel; at one point, Rex muses that the man Christine is seeing will "take" Gabriel, and we are easily reminded of Jay imagining another man taking his place in the household and becoming closer to his children than he is. However, it is made clear that Rex has not vacated the house of his own volition but has been ousted by Gabriel's mother Christine, who is tired of his laziness and ineptitude, and his departure is certainly not akin to the existential scream of *Intimacy*'s Jay. In this sense, Rex's departure is not an act of willful abandonment at all, but it does afford the novel's exploration of fifteen-year-old Gabriel's confused sense of abandonment. Kureishi has stated that *Gabriel's Gift* began as a children's book; apparently, "David Bowie wanted a book that he could illustrate" (which perhaps explains the Lester Jones character), but it "became more of an adult book" as he wrote (quoted in Monteith et al. 2004: 100). Indeed, there are residual elements of a children's story in the narrative, which in many ways seems to be uneasily suspended between children's book and literary novel. However, this sense of formal awkwardness reflects Gabriel's own feelings of awkwardness, and Kureishi's experiment with form constitutes an inquiry into what "form" a person might take following abandonment.

Characters from Kureishi's earlier novels make cameo appearances in *Gabriel's Gift*. *The Buddha of Suburbia*'s Karim Amir and Charlie Hero turn up in Speedy's restaurant, both jaded and pettily competing with each other for popular recognition. *The Black Album*'s Deedee Osgood is also mentioned; we discover that she has become a therapist, written a self-help book and, apparently, seduced young guitarist Carlo Ambler (she is also mentioned, albeit again rather incidentally, in *The Body*). Significantly, in revisiting these characters, Kureishi shows that each has abandoned, or been abandoned by, the people and lifestyles with which they were left at the close of the earlier novels. Deedee has clearly parted from Shahid (seemingly so that she can seduce the even younger Carlo), and has also abandoned her career as a university lecturer. In the case of Charlie and Karim, return is again portrayed as signifying defeat; their return to London from America seems to be symptomatic of their descent into middle-aged exhaustion and creative bankruptcy.

The Body (2002) again explores abandonment and seems to confirm the permanence of a decision to leave. In many ways, the story seems to rewrite *Intimacy*, in which Jay declares "I am not leaving this unhappy Eden only because I dislike it, but because *I want to become someone else*" (Kureishi 1998: 101, my emphasis). The name Adam certainly gestures toward Edenic parallels, and Adam's decision to abandon his body and life and pursue the pleasures of youth—and, in particular, sexual liberty—are very much evocative of Jay's narrative. Certain passages describing Adam's euphoria in his new body seem to actually respond to Jay's anxieties over his bygone youth. For example, concerned by the ongoing deterioration of his body, Jay is dismayed by the unresponsiveness of his penis when he tries to masturbate and by "how weak the ark of [his] urine is" (Kureishi 1998: 111). Waking up in his new body, however, Adam "touche[s] his new penis and bec[omes] as engrossed in it as a four-year-old," and says of urinating "when I peed, the stream was full, clear and what I must describe as 'decisive'" (Kureishi 2002a: 36). Perhaps the crucial difference between Jay and Adam is that, from the beginning, Adam plans to return to his life and partner while Jay is determined not to. While *The Body* isn't particularly concerned with making the transplantation of old mind into new body credible, the prospect of the return to normality is made to seem even more unlikely; once Adam abandons body, family, and life, his intentions to return to them are little but whimsy. Jay repeatedly expresses anxiety over how he and his family will change following his departure (in particular, its effect on his relationship with his children); he questions whether he would ever be able to return and imagines someone claiming the domestic role and the partner that he is abandoning. By relocating these concerns within the genre of science fiction, *The Body* seems to reconfirm the finality of willfully leaving one's life and family. Even though, unlike Jay, Adam only wants "to become someone else" temporarily, he is finally "condemned to begin again, in the nightmare of eternal life" (Kureishi 2002a: 126), and in reaching this near-paradox *The Body* seems, like *Intimacy*, to assert that abandonment occasions both pain and the joy of newness. When Adam does return to his home, and finds it easy to use his attractive new body to seduce his unknowing wife, he very nearly (he does not actually have sex with her) becomes both cuckolded and cuckolder. He is simultaneously delighted at being able to kiss his wife again and horrified by her infidelity, and this paradoxical moment (which perhaps only science fiction could allow) offers a shrewd remark on the impossibility of returning to one's life unchanged having decided to abandon it.

With the film script *The Mother*, which he wrote in 2003 (and which was filmed by Roger Michell the same year), Kureishi again reflects on abandonment in the form of death, examining the effects of bereavement on a family. Widowed when her husband has a fatal heart attack, aging housewife May—whose name, tellingly, implies possibility, but indecision as well—stays with her daughter in London and comes to rediscover her latent sexuality by having an affair with Darren, a man who is much younger than her and who is seeing her daughter. In a conversation with Darren shortly before their first sexual encounter, May tells him about a man she had a brief affair with:

> A few years ago, an intelligent man who lived nearby, an antique dealer, started to like me. Twice he took me into his bed. … I planned to go away with him. I would go to my husband and explain. But I never saw the man again. I couldn't upset anyone. (Kureishi 2003a: 60–1)

Shortly afterward, about to embrace Darren for the first time, May says "I should have been doing this... before..." (Kureishi 2003a: 61). Kureishi seems to agree, and while his treatment of May is highly empathetic, her earlier inability to leave her husband for fear of causing "upset" ultimately results in a great deal more upset; she loses Darren, is cast out by both her son and daughter, and returns from London to the suburbs. This return is, again, one that seems to signify defeat and disillusionment. However, the film ends on an optimistic (if rather ambiguous) note as, in the final scene, May "walks up the street, trundling her suitcase behind her" (Kureishi 2003a: 103). Where she is going remains unclear, but she seems to finally be making the departure that she did not dare make while her husband was still alive; indeed, May finally moves beyond the indecision implied by her name and begins to fulfill the sense of possibility that it suggests. Beginning as a portrait of a woman who has been abandoned through the death of her husband, ultimately *The Mother* examines a postponed and overdue act of abandonment and the repercussions of being, in the words of *Intimacy*'s Jay, "loyal to the idea of loyalty itself" (Kureishi 1998: 56).

As a memoir, *My Ear at His Heart* (2004) is another formally distinct work in Kureishi's *oeuvre*. Its narrative is occasioned by Kureishi's discovery of the manuscript for a novel that his (now deceased) father wrote, a novel that is itself a thinly disguised memoir. Of his father's preferred literary style, Kureishi says "he always used realism as his preferred form; he disliked the arts being 'experimental,' as though different ways of writing implied different ways of living" (Kureishi 2004: 94). Although careful to shield his father's writing from criticism, Kureishi concedes that his father's material "isn't always coherently organised" (Kureishi 2004: 20), and although it "is written in the third-person," "An Indian Adolescence" "switch[es] occasionally, by 'mistake,' into the first"

(Kureishi 2004: 18). In turn, the narrative of *My Ear at His Heart* repeatedly betrays anxieties over its own formal discipline or lack thereof, and at one point Kureishi jokes that what he is writing "feels like a cross between lovemaking and autopsy" (Kureishi 2004: 114). If the finished book can reasonably be described as a memoir, there is the sense throughout the narrative that, while writing, Kureishi has little sense of its eventual form; *My Ear at His Heart* is not a playful experiment with form, as we might describe *The Body*, but a struggle to find a form in which to speak at all.

Kureishi's first major work to deal explicitly with race and ethnicity since *The Black Album*, *My Ear at His Heart* again has abandonment as one of its major themes and explores the effects of leaving behind cultures, places, and ways of life as well as people; there are particularly poignant moments when Kureishi describes his extended family's eagerness to "return" to their new homeland Pakistan, a country they had never been to, following Partition. Kureishi's father's abandoned manuscript, "An Indian Adolescence," is an account of a life, country, and culture that have been left behind and, implicitly, of the tensions between feeling guilty for having left and being proud to have become "successful" in doing so. In turn, *My Ear at His Heart* itself becomes an account of Kureishi's own youth in middle-class suburbia (it could even, perhaps, be titled "An English Suburban Adolescence"), and of his abandoning it. While the narrative deals candidly with Kureishi's feelings of grief following his father's death—indeed, his sense of abandonment—it also explores the ways in which, by becoming a successful writer, Kureishi fulfills his father's aspirations for him but also leaves behind his father as well as a particular culture and way of life, and the book is a testimony to both the intimacies and the divisions between father and son.

In *Something to Tell You*, Kureishi's first novel in a decade, abandonment is again a major theme. Early on in the novel, narrator Jamal Khan remarks that "people couldn't do anything well if they weren't lost enough, if they couldn't feel abandoned" (Kureishi 2008: 18–19), and over the course of the novel we learn that Jamal himself has often both been abandoned and has abandoned others. While his father left the family when Jamal was very young, even more traumatic was the experience of being abandoned by his first love, Ajita, when he was a student. After he learns that she is being raped by her father on a nightly basis, he and his two closest friends, Valentin and Wolf, decide to administer a violent warning to him in order to stop the abuse. Surprising him in his garage at night, they strike him a number of times and Jamal threatens him with a knife. Later, Jamal learns that Ajita's father died of a heart attack, and following the "murder" (which is never solved), Ajita disappears from Jamal's life. Devastated by Ajita's disappearance (as well as that of Valentin and Wolf after the three decide that it is safer for them to be apart), Jamal sinks into an intense and lengthy depression. Utterly isolated and harboring a secret that is "turning [his] soul septic" (Kureishi 2008: 67), he suffers from "hallucinations, panic attacks, inexplicable furies, frantic passions and dreams" (Kureishi 2008: 62). After he begins seeing a psychoanalyst, Jamal not only begins to work through his own problems, but also discovers a career; as so often in Kureishi, it is Jamal's traumatic experience of being abandoned that affords his self-discovery. Moreover, even though he continues to long for Ajita, after she returns later in the novel he finds that "reality had alleviated my fantasies of her" (Kureishi 2008: 336). Like so many of Kureishi's middle-aged male narrators, Jamal has left his wife and child. The pain of this separation is a major theme in the novel, but again the implication is that this act of abandonment is ultimately something positive; Jamal has a strong relationship with his son and, in the novel's closing pages, declares that he is "not ... finished with love" (Kureishi 2008: 345). *Something to Tell You* does, indeed, seem to suggest that people "cannot do anything well" unless they feel abandoned.

In Kureishi's recent work, the attempt to find literary forms in which to examine the anxieties associated with the reconfiguration of identity—and, more specifically, an individual's role within familial, domestic, social, and political systems—following abandonment not only reflects those very anxieties but actually performs them. Kureishi's ongoing struggle with literary form is indicative of, but is also part of, an inquiry into what "form" a person might take following the traumatic yet transformative experiences of leaving or being left. Moreover, Kureishi's writing abandons consistency itself, and as each text engages with, and yet refuses, previous texts there is certainly a sense in which, in Karim Amir's words, Kureishi's *oeuvre* is "discovering [it] self through what [it] reject[s]" (Kureishi 1990: 255).

Finally, it is also of significance that, in recent years, Kureishi's work has shown a renewed tendency toward encouraging creative collaboration; *Something to Tell You* and *The Last Word* are the only major new works that he has produced in more than a decade that have not involved the creative input of others. As drama, his earliest work required, by its very nature, the contributive and often drastically alterative involvement of figures such as director, producer, and actors, but in the late 1980s Kureishi expressed some concern over the degree to which his material—and, in particular, its social and political emphases—was being modified at the hands of others (especially in the case of his collaboration with Stephen Frears on the filming of *Sammy and Rosie Get Laid* (see Kureishi 2002b: 127–99)). This might be seen as foundational in his shift to novel writing in the early to mid-1990s with *The Buddha of Suburbia* and *The Black Album*. That he made his directorial debut with the film script *London Kills Me* in 1991 is perhaps also indicative of his preferring to maintain creative authority over his work during this period.

However, in 1997 Kureishi rewrote the short story "My Son The Fanatic" as a film script to be directed by Udayan Prasad, and in 2001 collaborated with Patrice Chéreau on the filming of *Intimacy*. *Gabriel's Gift* was, originally, to be illustrated by David Bowie. In *The Mother* and *Venus*, Kureishi produced his first original screenplays in years, both to be directed by other people; the 2009 stage adaptation of *The Black Album* was directed by Jatinder Verma. While *My Ear at His Heart* is, ostensibly, a very private, individual reflection, in a sense it is a collaboration with Kureishi's deceased father: "I am now [my father's editor], of course," Kureishi writes; "*the two of us working together again as we did in the suburbs, me typing upstairs, him downstairs*" (Kureishi 2004: 20, my emphasis). Over the last decade and a half Kureishi has rediscovered a willingness to grant others contributive access to his work. Apparently happy to allow his writing to be quite literally formally transformed, his choices about literary form seem actually to invite such transformation. In surrendering his writing over to the creative discretion of others, then, Kureishi increasingly *abandons* his work in the sense of relinquishing control over it.

That accounts of Kureishi's *oeuvre* have often failed to recognize its complex multiplicity is symptomatic of the critical construction of Kureishi as a "minority," "postcolonial," "ethnic," or "postethnic" author. If Kureishi's importance for debates about contemporary multiculturalism is to be identified, this cannot be achieved through simply asserting that his writing resists the regimes of colonialism, ethnicity, or monoculturalism. Kureishi's work is *not* representatively "ethnic," "postcolonial," or "postethnic." Rather, if his *oeuvre* is discovering itself through what it rejects—indeed, through what it *abandons*—then it might be said that his work ultimately *represents* the contention that this is also the way in which a contemporary, multiethnic, multicultural society should develop and discover itself. More central to Kureishi's work than the figure of the postcolonial migrant who abandons a particular place and culture is the notion that *all* individuals—and indeed *cultures themselves*—must remain on the move, developing through a process of continual abandonment. In this sense, Kureishi's work is not so much concerned with exploring individual migrations *between* cultures as with suggesting that the experience of living *within* a contemporary multicultural society should, in itself, be a kind of migration. Kureishi has argued that

> if there is to be a profusion, or multi-culturalism, of voices, ... then the possibility of dispute and disagreement is increased. The virtue and risk of real multi-culturalism is that we could find that our values are, ultimately, irreconcilable with those of others. (Kureishi 2003b)

Kureishi's work insists on inconsistency, and if critics have found his *oeuvre* to be irreconcilable to itself, this is because it is itself an inquiry into irreconcilability—into the necessity and possibility of abandonment amid a profusion of voices.

Acknowledgments: Another version of this chapter first appeared in my monograph *Contemporary Fictions of Multiculturalism: Diversity and the Contemporary London Novel* (London: Palgrave Macmillan, 2014).

2

"I believe my eyes": The transformative cinema of Hanif Kureishi

Deanna Kamiel

Chapter Summary: A direct challenge to the reigning paradigm of English heritage cinema, the 1985 film *My Beautiful Laundrette*, authored by Hanif Kureishi, drew international acclaim for its satire of the Thatcherite free-enterprise project and its creation of a new British social iconography. It also drew critical abuse at home from the conservative media establishment for departing from what Raymond Williams (1983) described as Margaret Thatcher's "from-the-top imagery of a nation," her grandiose vision of England's imperial past. Ironically, this war of representation between the state and the artist focused on the aesthetics of cinematic imagery. With the director Stephen Frears, Kureishi's *My Beautiful Laundrette* had constructed a vision of Britain that had not been seen before—multiracial, mixed, class diverse, sexually transgressive—the state of the nation as a collage of difference. This chapter explores the content of that collagist imagery and, as Sukhdev Sandhu (2003) writes, the "startling act of transformation" it performed upon the cultural body politic.

Keywords: *My Beautiful Laundrette*, *Venus*, Stephen Frears, Junichiro Tanizaki, Andre Bazin, Jean-Luc Godard, narrative space

"There must be a fresh way of seeing Britain"
(HANIF KUREISHI, "THE RAINBOW SIGN", 1986: 34)

In the year 2012 Margaret Thatcher returned to the public arena after an absence of twenty years. The British prime minister who famously declared "There is no such thing as society" did not return in her prime, however, as warrior woman for free-market capitalism, but in her dotage, assailed by dementia and Alzheimer's. Nevertheless, her return was noteworthy because it took the enduring cinematic form of the magisterial actress Meryl Streep, whose Oscar-winning portrayal of an elder infirm Thatcher in the film *The Iron Lady* brought the great dismantler of the social project back into view.

In cinematic terms, Thatcher made her return as a conflation of two icons—Margaret the prime minister and Meryl the actor—both elided to construct a singular new iconic image. If we apply the film theory terms of French critic André Bazin to this Thatcher/Streep elision, or fusion, we could say Thatcher has been "embalmed" and "mummified" for eternity in the guise or mask of the beauteous Streep. For it was Bazin in his canonical essay "The Ontology of the Photographic Image" who attributed the power of the camera image to a "mummy complex": "namely, the preservation of life by a representation of life"—"man's primitive need to have the last word in the argument with death by means of the form that endures" (Bazin 2005[1967]: 9–10).

It is worth considering then what constitutes an enduring image—and, in the Bazinian name of preservation and representation, to appreciate its power. The decade of the 1980s, the era during which Margaret Thatcher refashioned Britain's national identity from social-democratic to "the most open right-wing government for half a century" (Williams 1983: 8), offers a defining example. In 1985 the small television film *My Beautiful Laundrette*, authored by Hanif Kureishi and directed by Stephen Frears, achieved tremendous international acclaim for its irreverent satire of the Thatcherite free-enterprise ideology and its transformative view of race, class, and sexuality in contemporary Britain. The film tells the story of the renovation of a failing South London laundrette by two social outliers, one a member of a gang of white-skinhead racists, the other a young Asian Briton, son of an unemployed socialist journalist, both looking for a way up in the world. Central to the film's plot is the love affair between the two young men. As Julian Henriques observed, the narrative structure pivots on the idea of contradiction, "the multiple contradiction of a love affair between two men, two races and two politics" (Henriques 1987: 19).

In cultural history, *My Beautiful Laundrette* ranks as a phenomenon, a political and social landmark, and as one of the first great films of the independent cinema movement, breaking new ground "in critical thinking about representation and cultural diversity" (Geraghty 2005: 5). Critically and commercially successful, it launched the international careers of Kureishi, Frears, and actor Daniel Day-Lewis, repositioned the career of the great Indian-born British actor Saeed Jaffrey, and provided a first major box office success for the producers Tim Bevan and Sarah Radclyffe and their then fledgling company Working Title Films.

Yet, at home, it drew critical fire from the British conservative media establishment for departing from what critic Raymond Williams described as Thatcher's preferred "from-the-top imagery of a nation" (Williams 1983: 10), her grandiose vision of England's imperial past that she deployed effectively to sustain the Falklands War and determined to preserve in perpetuity as her archetypal image of Britain. A gay interracial romance and a load of working-class dirty laundry did not suit her iconographic agenda. In deference to Thatcher, *The Sunday Times*, her ally on the ideological right and fervently protective of her enterprise program, ran a prolonged campaign of abuse against *My Beautiful Laundrette* and several other oppositional indie films, pointing to their "general disgustingness." A notorious piece by Oxford historian Norman Stone (1988), titled "Through A Lens Darkly," took Kureishi and Frears, as well as directors Derek Jarman and Lezli-An Barret, to task for failing to adhere to the then reigning paradigm of English heritage cinema exemplified by middlebrow quality films like *A Room With A View* (1986) and *A Passage to India* (1984), films which Kureishi trenchantly described in a response in *The Guardian* as "the overdressed British abroad": "glamourised travesties of novels by the great E. M. Forster, the sort of meaningless soft-core confection that Tory ladies and gentlemen think is Art" (Kureishi 1988: 19).

Although much of the conservative attack could be attributed to propaganda masquerading as film criticism, at heart was a fierce struggle over representation. Which vision of England would prevail? Interestingly, this war of representation between the policy of the state and the imagination of the artist focused on the aesthetics of cinematic imagery. On the one hand, the gilded prestige cinema of *A Room With A View* (1985) with its nostalgic display of elite period artifacts and "visually pleasing iconography" (Hill 1999: 99). On the other, the cocksure dissident cinema of *My Beautiful Laundrette* with its more formally challenging techniques of collage and juxtaposition, as Sukhdev Sandhu describes, "evoking the congestion and collision of metropolitan life" (Sandhu 2003: 253). What drew conservative ire—and Stone's accusations of "messy," "desultory," and "ragged"—Sandhu rightly locates in a screen grammar of collagist montage, a film language closer to Eisenstein or Chaplin than to David Lean, "showing how London exists and thrives through the repeated jamming together of disparate groups" (Sandhu 2003: 255). "Juxtaposition and collage," writes Sandhu, "are the ideal aesthetic modes for incarnating this higgledy-piggledy commotion of a metropolis" (Sandhu 2003: 259).

Aesthetics, then, is the issue. But as Susan Sontag memorably wrote, issues of aesthetics and style are often "a front behind which other issues, ultimately ethical and political, are being debated" (Sontag 1961: 18). *My Beautiful Laundrette* struck a nerve. It appeared on the cultural horizon in the fall of 1985, when the Conservative Party was at its most triumphal, as a direct challenge to Thatcher's entrepreneurial values and, imagistically, as a stunning riposte to Thatcher's messianic attempts to control the look and packaging of the national brand.

With *My Beautiful Laundrette*, Kureishi constructed a vision of Britain that had not been seen before—multiracial, mixed, class diverse, sexually transgressive—the state of the nation represented as a collage of difference. The content of that collagist imagery, its contrapuntal play between realism and surrealism, coupled with the film's central irony—the inversion of the social hierarchy through the business model of a launderette where, against stereotype, the solution to post-empire socioeconomics becomes "the brown man's burden" (Kureishi 1995: 15)—performed what Sandhu calls "a startling act of transformation" upon the body politic that brought fringe minority culture center screen (Sandhu 2003: 255).

Although Margaret Thatcher warred victoriously on many fronts—the Falklands, the trade unions, the welfare state—she failed in this battle for the cultural imaginary. With the worldwide release of *My Beautiful Laundrette*, the signifying image of Britain was irrevocably altered by a shop-front tenderly lit in blues and pinks and a kiss over spin-dryers between a white punk drug-dealer and a gay Pakistani-English businessman. Thatcher lost the war of representation to a new mythos and a new iconography which, unlike her own romantic illusions of Britain's past, was inspired by the reality of Britain's vital present.

She also lost it to something new in British postwar cinema, something more than style, a sensibility and mode of address that film historian Dudley Andrew calls *"optique,"* a term he applies to films that establish an imagistic "rapport" with their culture (Andrew 1985: 320), offering "ocular mechanisms of perspective" that connect with the politics and history of their time (Andrew 1985: 19). He cites by example the poetic realist films of Jean Renoir and Marcel Carne. Made during the popular front era of 1930s France, these films address their audience in the tone and temper of their historical conditions. Perhaps the same could be said of the films of Fellini and the postwar *auteur* Italian cinema that revolutionized Italy's self-image and redeemed its national identity after the devastating era of Fascism. Such films, says Andrew, "are entrances to a different way of being a spectator … different enough to tempt us to construct the spectator to which they are addressed" (Andrew 1985: 23).

"I am a spectator," he writes, "ready to become another spectator" (Andrew 1985: 23).

How does a film derive such influence, change the way we see, humor our worldview? In a television interview I did some years ago for PBS with the filmmaker Jean-Luc Godard, I made the mistake of attributing the power of his work to his signature theoretical complexity. "But no," he said. "My films are no more complex than a Steve McQueen picture. A Steve McQueen picture, yes." (He refers to the American actor Steve McQueen of *Bullitt* (1968) and *The Getaway* (1972).) He added: "To make a good picture is to offer images the audience feel they are seeing for the first time. An image is when we see for the first time. When we believe our eyes. I *still* believe in my eyes" (Kamiel 1980).

Godard's trust in the image we see "for the first time" is an elegant measure of the transformative power of cinema, one that particularly applies to the films written by Kureishi. His screenplays engender images that have transformed the social iconography of a nation, changing the face of British identity from monocultural to mixed, giving us new images that radically alter our perspective. To look closely at the content of those images—the places and locations, the narrative spaces they inhabit—is to explore a new *optique*, a screen consciousness in which we see something new that we believe. Certainly, this is the vocation of cinema—the production of new images that cause us to believe. But the idea that we *believe* links again to a tenet of Bazin's: his faith in the innate realist function of photography, which he applies to all films, whether fiction or documentary. In a 1947 essay, he observes that "in a certain sense, cinema cannot lie ... to the extent that it has come to satisfy the dream desire of the masses" (Bazin 2008[1947]: 40). Films are true, then, because they are true to our dreams, and thus know us in ways we may not know ourselves. At times, he adds, they may even "wake us" from our dream. Dudley Andrew puts it in a slightly different way, saying certain filmmakers "create as well as display a culture's imagination" (Andrew 1985: 25).

Similarly, in *My Beautiful Laundrette*, Kureishi created a vision of London, latent and alive in British consciousness, but not yet realized or "displayed" on screen. His anticipatory vision—part-observation, part-imagination—was an implicit counter-image to Margaret Thatcher's, subverting her brutal business model with his own neon fantasy of a small service shop. In Kureishi's own words, this construction of London, though an act of cultural representation, was also an act of imagination. As he told Colin MacCabe in a 1999 interview, the London he writes about is "in his head":

> London was always a place that I imagined. ... I was born in the suburbs, in a place called Bromley ... and we could get to London quite easily on the train—but it was a big jump. ... So for me London became a kind of inferno

of pleasure and madness. It's a playground, a place where I can imagine, where I can play. (MacCabe 1999: 37)

The imagined spaces of Kureishi's London playground, often hallucinatory and expressionist, represent a departure from traditional British realist form and are presented, usually within the same single sustained shot, in contradiction to the film's otherwise realist conventions. Hybridity, then, as theorist John Hill points out, is both a thematic and formal strategy in this film about multiracial in-betweenness and mixing up (Hill 1999: 216–17). Like Fellini and the Italian Neorealists who created a cinema of reconstruction after the catastrophe of the Second World War, Kureishi reconstructed cinematic London after the catastrophe of colonialism.

Such reconstructions, born of historical necessity, inform all modes of art, but in film the effect is particular and connects, as Walter Benjamin wrote, to the camera's "cathartic" and "unconscious" properties (Benjamin 2008: 22). Referring to film as mass culture's "most powerful agent," Benjamin described it as a technology capable of shattering tradition while at the same time "cathartically" renewing humanity in crisis (Benjamin 2008: 22). In Kureishi's case, the crisis at hand was the 1970s England of his youth with its bursts of fascistic violence from the white supremacist National Front. Throughout *My Beautiful Laundrette*, Kureishi makes constant reference to this period, largely through the relationship between Johnny and Omar. Although the two were friends as children, Johnny later marched in the streets in the hate demonstrations against Pakistani immigrants. His participation shocked Omar and his parents. At a crucial point in the film, that sense of shock is reconstructed, as it were, during a quiet scene between Johnny and Papa, Omar's father. Papa has come late to the celebration party for the newly transformed launderette. All the celebrants have left, except Johnny. Papa takes Johnny by the hand, affectionately. The two share a medium shot, standing and facing each other, warmly and intimately, in the frame. Papa kids Johnny about the fancified laundrette. "I thought I'd come to the wrong place," he says. "That I'd suddenly found myself in a ladies' hairdressing salon in Pinner, where one might get a pink rinse. Do you do a pink rinse, Johnny?" Then he pauses, looking at Johnny all the while. Suddenly he says: "Or are you still a fascist?" (Kureishi 2002[1985]: 67). The moment is unexpected. Shattering, to use Benjamin's term. The camera acts for us, creating, as Benjamin wrote, the necessary catharsis. Papa is now no longer in the shared frame. He is alone in a close-up, on a bench, gazing up at the off-screen Johnny. Johnny too is now alone in his frame as the camera cuts to him, and at the same time moves in. However, the camera move is not a simple zoom. It is a dolly move. As it tracks closer to Johnny, the plane of the film space contracts and we feel the weight of accusation.

Johnny is off-guard, speechless, moved. Something has changed, and we are renewed.

As Kureishi describes in an essay of 2009, "Newness in the World," the fascist politics of the 1970s National Front occurred as a reaction to postwar Britain's "huge, unprecedented social experiment": "The project was to turn—out of the end of the Empire and on the basis of mass immigration—a predominantly white society into a racially mixed one, thus forming a new notion of what Britain was" (Kureishi 2011[2009]: 114).

Mass immigration from Africa, the Caribbean, and the Asian subcontinent caused not just "a mere confrontation with simple racism, the kind of thing I'd grown up with, which was usually referred to as 'the colour problem'" (Kureishi 2011[2009]: 114). It was of a far greater dimension, an historical event of magnitude that led to massive social transformation. As Benjamin states in "The Work of Art" essay, a transformation of such magnitude generates concurrently a transformation in human perception. Benjamin's ultimate example of perception transformed was the "adventure" afforded the mass audience through film language:

> Clearly it is another nature which speaks to the camera as compared to the eye. ... The camera, with all its resources for swooping and rising, disrupting and isolating—it is through the camera that we first discover the optical unconscious, just as we discover the instinctual unconscious through psychoanalysis. (Benjamin 2008: 37)

Benjamin's "optical unconscious" is vitally on display in *My Beautiful Laundrette*'s romantic scenes, where the camera indeed swoops and isolates, yet at the same time maintains fluid forward motion, thus surprising us in the manner of a dream as juxtaposed behaviors occupy the same frame: violence and sexual attraction, for example, or estrangement and intimacy. Also, juxtaposed backgrounds—dark alleys and sudden color-saturated mists—optically involve us in a kind of aesthetic dialectic. In this way Kureishi's London playground, convincing "first time" imagery in the Godardian sense, makes waking dreamers (and dialecticians) of us all.

When he first read the screenplay for *My Beautiful Laundrette*, Stephen Frears said he saw immediately how radical a film it was. "The sexual anarchy came out," he said in an interview four years after making the film, "and the sexual was as radical as the rest of it" (Friedman and Stewart 1994: 226). Frears described the famous tracking shot which puts in motion the film's set of personal and political transformations to come:

> It begins with a window shot. You see Johnny, while Omar is sitting in the car, thirty to forty feet away. Then he gets out of the car (in a single sustained tracking shot) and he walks over to Johnny. I realized someone

was crossing over from alienation ... written by someone with a white English mother and a Pakistani father. It's about the journey from one side to another ... crossing over and integration through separation. (Friedman and Stewart 1994: 226)

The journey described in this strategic shot illustrates the key aesthetic approach to *My Beautiful Laundrette*'s cinema, the way in which, says film scholar Christine Geraghty, "utopian possibilities are presented through the organisation of film space" (Geraghty 2005: 45). The film's politically and erotically charged mise en scène constructs a screen experience of oneiric visual pleasure through a distinctive use of narrative space that, says Geraghty, "has the effect of transforming mundane settings into symbolic locations" (Geraghty 2005: 55).

The scene of the laundrette's final transformation is a prime example. On the evening before the grand opening, a high-angle camera places us outside the shop at roof level, next to Johnny (Daniel Day-Lewis) on a ladder putting the final touches to the new neon sign. The top half of the frame glimmers in the light of a few twinkling white bulbs as Johnny descends the ladder, with the camera, tracking on a crane, keeping pace. As we glide toward the sidewalk below, we see Omar (Gordon Warnecke), in a suit, and two gang members, Genghis and Moose, gazing upward at Johnny's progress. Finally, Johnny reaches ground level, hoists up the bottom panel of the laundrette sign, and signals to Moose for help in carrying it back up the ladder. Moose pauses, torn between loyalties: whether to support the gang, or Johnny and Omar's new enterprise. But the momentum of creation wins out. As Walter Benjamin (2008) might say, "the natural use of productive forces" is unimpeded—and up they go to finish the job. The camera positions us just behind Johnny and Moose so that when the completed neon sign lights up, we experience the spectacle of final transformation by inhabiting their shared space. The entire scene is a single-shot vertical camera move of just fifty seconds' duration, yet it traverses a space of history that spans generations.

According to John Hill, the heightened setting and symbolic treatment of the laundrette renders it less a "real" laundrette than a sort of imagined space in which personal desires and social tensions are worked out. "It is a space," he says, "which opens up the possibility for new forms of social connection and ... socially transgressive desires" (Hill 1999: 218). Referring to the erotic relationship between Omar and Johnny, Christine Geraghty remarks on the film's sexualized space, on the space defined not only by the camera frame but also, profoundly, by the interior space within the frame formed by the physical distance separating the two young men, a space of "sexual excitement" and, worth noting, a space only the camera's optical unconscious can locate (Geraghty 2005: 55). It is also a politically contested space. Frears himself points out that it is a space created and, until *My Beautiful Laundrette*, hidden by colonialism:

> Nobody had any idea that this world existed. Nobody had ever done this before. Nobody had ever written from that perspective before. That someone could be so confident about it, make the jokes, be so on the inside. It was astonishing because Hanif got it so right. (Friedman and Stewart 1994: 233)

Equally "right" in *My Beautiful Laundrette* is the speed at which possibilities are realized within a unified narrative space, the velocity in film time of political and sexual collision. The scene in which Omar and Johnny first kiss is an example. In one seamless continuous tracking shot we see the two emerge from a car, walk down an alley, and seemingly, spontaneously, begin a kiss which enfolds into darkness as the embrace becomes passionate. Suddenly they break apart, disturbed by a gang of lads kicking and banging dustbins at the edge of the frame—an edge which, until now, has not been evident. Yet the two moments—one erotic, the other violent; one dark, the other glaring with light—take place within the same photographic space.

"Such a mise en scene," says Geraghty, "works not at the level of contemplation and ambiguity but in the context of engagement and surprise. ... This film, with its serious political and social intentions, becomes a celebration of cinema itself as a utopian space, a site of transforming and life-enhancing activity" (Geraghty 2005: 59). It is also a kind of evocation of Benjamin's conclusion in "The Work of Art: Second Version": that as a culture we have the political choice to use the productive forces of technology artfully to act on our desires and transform our relations with each other; or to express our passions through the technological apparatus of war (Benjamin 2008: 42).

The achievement of *My Beautiful Laundrette* is that an imagined story in an imagined city, full of spectacle and artifice, satire and fantasy, stylization and surrealism, could feel, as Frears says, so *right*, and that when it appeared on television and later in theaters worldwide, it could also be seen—within the British tradition of television as social criticism—to be "an accurate account of what it's like to live in Britain" (Friedman and Stewart 1994: 224). As Godard might say, we were offered a new image of Britishness, and we believed what we saw.

It bears mentioning that *My Beautiful Laundrette*, considered by Charlotte Brunsdon as "perhaps *the* London film of the 1980s" (Brunsdon 2007: 75), has been intensely analyzed in contemporary critical discourse, and its qualities of transformation and transcendence have been eminently discussed by numerous film scholars, among them Sukhdev Sandhu, Christine Geraghty, Charlotte Brunsdon, Tim Corrigan, and John Hill. A less discussed but equally radical London film of Kureishi's is *Venus*, released in 2006, starring Peter O'Toole (Kureishi 2006a). Directed by Roger Michell, the film won O'Toole a best actor Oscar nomination.

The provocations in *Venus* differ from those in *My Beautiful Laundrette*, focusing more on age and class than on race. But once again Kureishi offers a vision that counters conventional perspective and demonstrates the writer's power to reimagine a familiar landscape—in this case, the landscape of old age—to transformative effect. Like *My Beautiful Laundrette*, *Venus* too constructs an enduring new image of its subject and, in many ways, is itself about the phenomenon of endurance—in the Bazinian cinematic sense as well as the physical and metaphysical sense.

The usual Kureishi dialectics are present. The mordant perversities of an old guy/young girl relationship propel the narrative and provide the necessary conflicts and comic ironies. The perversities are partly inspired by one of the film's sources, the novel *Diary of A Mad Old Man* by the Japanese master Junichiro Tanizaki (1965), about a dying man infatuated with his son's wife. In *Venus*, the dying man is a once renowned actor, Maurice (Peter O'Toole), now geriatric, half-forgotten, impotent, and ravaged by prostate cancer. Nevertheless, he is infatuated by a young working-class girl, Jessie (Jodie Whittaker) whom he names "Venus" and is determined to seduce. He has a passionate dilemma. His sexuality is alive only in the abstract, yet he must find a means to give it enduring death-transcendent form. This quixotic mission is the film's central imperative: giving form—a cinema of the real—to an *idea* of desire. Sexual fulfillment is not possible; therefore the idealization of it becomes all the more compelling. This is a love story that places its romantic hero at considerable disadvantage. Yet, true to the Kureishi mode of dialectical irony, this is less an impediment than an inspiration. Maurice begins his charm offensive accordingly:

> "I will die soon, Venus. Can I touch your hand?"
> "That's one chat-up line I haven't heard," says she.
> "I'm impotent, of course," says he.
> "Thank Christ," says she.
> "But I can still take a *theoretical* interest," says he. (Kureishi 2006b: 59–60, emphasis added)

It is a funny line and a pivotal word—"theoretical." Articulated by O'Toole in Shakespearean cadence, it is a service to satire, *and* to the writer's selection of the word, the absolutely right word—"theoretical"—to represent the dilemma of thwarted desire. It is also a word that suggests the existential dilemma embodied by cinema, Andre Bazin's conviction that the filmic image is about dying as much as it is about living, and that in its attempt to create a living record of a dying presence, it offers an enduring means of preservation through representation.

Like *My Beautiful Laundrette*, *Venus* too engages us in a politics of representation; but here the transformative imagery aims not at the state of the nation, but at the erotics of old age. The effect, however, is equally startling, as the film gives us a set of images meant to defy our view of "what it is we love about the other" (Kureishi 2006b: xiv; also collected in Kureishi 2011[2006]). It plays with our ideas of pleasure and perversion, tantalizingly constructing a reality true to its original inspiration, the idea of "the persistence of desire," expressed by Tanizaki's 74-year-old dying protagonist. "Even if you're impotent you have a kind of sex life," he writes in his diary (Tanizaki 1965: 5). Like death, impotence is not a discouragement to a true believer. There is an association here again with Bazin, whose faith in the power of photography is equally optimistic. "The making of images," he writes, "is no longer a question of survival after death, but of a larger concept, the creation of an ideal world in the likeness of the real" (Bazin 2005[1967]: 10).

In *Venus*, Maurice is given just such an ideal world, a reimagined London, a pleasure dome decreed in his likeness, in which he can play out his perverse fantasy of infatuation: perverse not because of his impotence and age, but because we do not, as a rule, cheer for a dirty old man. But in Kureishi's *Venus*, Maurice is an exemplary dirty old man, an illuminating guide to the real turbulence of old age, as opposed to its anodyne placid brand image.

Incontinent, ever fearful of "old man smell," and perennially tilted against the force of gravity as he strides unsteadily through his London of erotic delights, Maurice pursues the object of his desire with unrelenting skill—undoubtedly he is, or was, an expert—devising strategies to keep his Venus close. Every encounter is a negotiation—a pair of earrings in exchange for a kiss on her neck, a tattoo in exchange for a whiff of her finger scented by the journey from between her legs. But when his hand on her breast proves a breach of contract and gets him an elbow to the stomach, she, Jessie/Venus, reminds us that seduction, for her, is a game in which neither party is passive. Although *Venus* is a story of masculine despair, Jessie is the film's real political subject. She occupies a space in the film that is shared equally with O'Toole's Maurice, not as a "love interest," but as a co-conspirator.

Her power as a subject in her own right is expressed in a scene midway through, where we see her seated side by side with Maurice in the back seat of an enormous chauffeur-driven limousine. Her position, physical and political, is emphasized within the space of the frame by director Roger Michell's use of an extreme wide-angle lens that satirically expands the already expansive interior geography of the car. The satire develops as Jessie, impressed by the luxe car, says to Maurice: "You must be really famous." And O'Toole replies to deadpan effect: "Oh I am, I am" (Kureishi 2006b: 61). Then, as if to underscore, sardonically, the moral high ground the film will eventually bequeath her, Jessie asks the chauffeur to open the car's roof panel and proceeds to stand up on the seat and stick her head out the top. Her reward is a triumphant panorama of the London cityscape. O'Toole's reward is an equally triumphant panorama up Jessie's skirt.

In the terms of the film, this is a fair exchange. Everyone wins. But in terms of the film's organization of cinematic space, the balance tips in Jessie's favor. For Jessie's view of the London skyscape is an exclusive one, normally unavailable to someone of her class and social background. By endowing her with this otherwise inaccessible perspective, the film accords her a privileged position—in Andrew Higson's terms, "a position of visual mastery [that] is also a position of class authority" (Higson 1996: 151).

Jessie's class status is not insignificant in *Venus*. In the screenplay's introductory essay, Kureishi refers to her as a member of an invisible demographic, "a new scapegoat":

> I noticed that young working-class women—slags, mingers, munters, dogs, chavs—are easy targets, perfectly representing our greed, lasciviousness, immorality. Condemned for the pursuit of pleasure, and regarded only as consumers without inner texture, they are one of the few groups who can be satirized without complaint, damned for their stupidity and inarticulacy; a group with no lobbyists and little power. (Kureishi 2006b: xv; also collected in Kureishi 2011[2006])

Unprotected by political correctness, he told CBC Radio in Canada, "they are generally despised"—a sociopolitical offense Kureishi takes personally: "My family having moved to Britain from India, I was generally abused and spat on by society as a kid. I'm interested in people who occupy that position" (Wachtel 2006).

Similar to Kureishi's childhood experience, the major characters in both *Venus* and *My Beautiful Laundrette* occupy positions on the social margins. All are vulnerable to abuse and bias, yet they prevail. Such is the alchemy of transformation in the Kureishi universe. In *Venus*, even as his illness advances, Maurice makes strides in his erotic campaign. The film's pleasure principle works inversely, paradoxically. As Maurice's health declines, his desire—in defiance—ascends. These opposing forces are expressed by the film's imagery. Maurice's physical decline is presented to us as a gleeful excess of medications, leaking catheters, rectal probings, and presurgical pubic shavings. The film's surface reality is a procedural of disintegration. Yet even as we are repelled, we laugh, we are charmed, and we begin to discern the literary qualities of the film. That Maurice's erotic ambition is not a contradiction of aging but a legitimation. The more he suffers, the more he has reason to desire. It is a triumphant rebuke to the insult of old age, an insult Maurice refuses to acknowledge. The pursuit of pleasure is his finger to the humiliation of decay. Edward Said calls this "untimely behaviour," a refutation of accepted notions of aging (Said 2004: 3).

The emblematic scene in *Venus* puts this idea into play. It takes place at the National Gallery where the transformative site is an idealized one: a painting, the Rokeby *Venus* by Diego Velazquez, his only surviving nude. Here, gazing at the voluptuous canvas, Maurice and Jesse behold their mythic counterparts, Venus and Eros. Within the space of the camera frame, the two couples mirror each other in a transference of desire. It is a consummation, of sorts. Eventually, she, Jessie, will enter the ideal world of the painting, actually and symbolically, and mature into confident sexual womanhood. He, however, will die. But, *theoretically*, he will no longer be impotent for he has created an image of his desire—to recall Bazin—"in a form that endures" (Bazin 2005[1967]: 10).

The enduring image—the image that endures as an index of our earthly presence—is, ultimately, the film's underlying subject and the solution to Maurice's mortal dilemma, foretold at the start of the film. *Venus* begins with three subtle shots—two landscapes and a face. First is a seaside beach—an ocean expanse fills the frame. Next is a painting of a seaside beach, mounted on a wall. Finally, there is a medium close-up of Maurice, in pajamas and robe, drinking tea, gazing out from the center of the frame, unblinking. This formal progression from place, to painting of a place, to a place that resides as an image in the mind's eye, announces the film will be a retreat—from the actual to the imagined.

The territory of the imagined is a privileged space in the cinema of *Venus*, and, indeed, throughout Kureishi's body of work. It is here where new ideas can be entertained and new realities expressed. It is also a contested space where the artist and the state most often conflict, proving that words and images matter. For Margaret Thatcher, it was a space she presumed to dominate, attempting to impose upon the collective imagination of a nation an image of past imperial glory that was false. It was a decadent vision, illusory and dishonest. It could not endure. It was displaced, subversively, by an image of a small neon laundrette, a place not real, yet true. In the end, it was not a fair fight, this battle of representation for the cultural imaginary between the prime minister and the artist. For like all great artists, Kureishi recognizes that the imagination is a free zone and cannot be owned or colonized. It is a sovereign space, a space where transformation can occur, making subversives and radicals of us all.

3

Culture and anarchy in Thatcher's London: Hanif Kureishi's *Sammy and Rosie Get Laid*

Peter Hitchcock

Chapter Summary: This chapter looks at Hanif Kureishi's extraordinary identification with London in terms of both urban content and imaginary representation. The chapter addresses the provocative ways in which Kureishi redraws London's cityscape as a ground for politics in his confrontation with Thatcherism in *Sammy and Rosie Get Laid* (1987), the second of two film collaborations with Stephen Frears. It focuses on how Kureishi imagines social change given the aura of violence and instability that pervades his text, in which postcolonial London is not only "calling," but burning. While the terms of urban upheaval have certainly changed from the conditions remarked upon by Matthew Arnold in *Culture and Anarchy* (1869), the meaning of Kureishi's film for our understanding of modernity is similarly salutary. Kureishi finds both tenderness and hope in what London can become even as he offers a city that in its neoliberalism and postcolonialism defies all hints of nostalgia or easy solutions.

Keywords: *Sammy and Rosie Get Laid*, Thatcherism, anarchy, postcolonialism, nation

I don't think London bears any resemblance to England. It's a right crummy place without London. I think if England didn't have London, it'd be a fucking dump.

(HANIF KUREISHI, "LOOSE TONGUES AND LIBERTY" 2003)

One of modernity's trusted truths is that the city undoes them, and this poignant paradox allows for London's permeable identities and complex contradictions. Such persistent self-canceling is a marked feature of the urban and reveals creative destruction as part of the everyday in London, from its circulation of people and capital to the electronic billboards of Piccadilly Circus that pixellate the present and then dissolve it. Yet modernity has also fostered the idea of the city as a consolidating device that reflects the nation as an agglomeration of national ideals or as a projection of national identity. However obtuse the notion of a "spirit of nation" might be, it becomes distilled and revered in its urban centers, especially in the capital. The association of London with the nation thus becomes as easy as it is automatic. As Disraeli once quipped, London was a nation, not a city.

London is its own truth, and the essence of nation is somehow secured by constantly restating that. The capital functions as the institution of state and statehood, as the bureaucratic infrastructure that holds whatever is imagined or real together. London therefore demands a careful grooming of its otherwise wild and anarchic inclinations so that these do not compromise its overall aura of permanence. A capital is not just a symbol of state continuity, but a confirmation of its physical presence. While the evidence of this projection is reserved primarily for the tourist class to observe and digitally preserve, many of the longer-term denizens of the contemporary city follow other fantasies of belonging and alternative logics of community existence. For them the monuments of state are marble, good for sleeping on, or, as we shall see below, occasionally need decapitating.

Hanif Kureishi is by now so identified with London that his work is symptomatic of its globality and worldliness and of modernity's crisis of community. If, as Kenneth C. Kaleta (1998) has argued, Kureishi is a quintessentially "postcolonial storyteller," then it is precisely because of the ways he reconfigures the cityscape as a ground for politics in the wake of Empire and provocatively remaps the past. This urban focus enables the modern city to become the space of postcolonial possibilities. Thus, rather than seeing Kureishi only as "an Englishman born and bred, almost" (Kureishi 1990: 3), such doubt about identity creates London as urban space in which such stories about identity can be told. The specificity of Kureishi's cityscape is initially marked by a particular politics focused on displacing a regressive ideology of urban "renewal" that in the 1980s was known simply as Thatcherism. (This ideology had many components, one of which included "cleaning up" the city center to draw in corporations and the revenue streams associated with them.)

If, as some have suggested, Kureishi's more recent tales of the deeply personal and individualistic appear to lack the political élan of his earlier work, this may in part be due to a kind of consensual introjection of Thatcher-like policy across the political spectrum. However, as Bart Moore-Gilbert (2001) points out, this has not dulled Kureishi's interest in the texture of ethnicity and race in contemporary British life. Here, though, I am interested in Kureishi's urban engagement with Thatcherism in which postcolonial London is not only "calling," but burning.

Kureishi's emergence in the 1980s was at once exceptional and mainstream. He was born and bred in Britain, but had many of his interviewers asking him about India, or Pakistan. He was painted as an *enfant terrible* or Mr Anti-Establishment of English letters, yet appeared in hardly revolutionary Gap ads; his writing was full of the angst of indeterminacy in contemporary identity discourse, but he cheerfully sent it all up as the latest form of cocktail party polemics. He produced nuanced critiques of the corrosive effects of Thatcherism, yet his career could also be read as consonant with that very spirit of individual enterprise and populism so skillfully employed in Tory England to deride and fool whatever was left of opposition in British political life. This contradictory construction of selves is reflected in his fiction and screenplays, which have been praised for addressing the diasporic subjects of contemporary Britain, yet damned because these subjects are often portrayed as being as corrupt and reprehensible as their white counterparts. Such an anarchic implosion of opposites would seem to mark Kureishi as postmodern *avant la lettre*. But here I wish to address the ironic ambivalences of one text in particular—*Sammy and Rosie Get Laid* (1987)—both as an instance of London's peculiar ground for storytelling and as an anarchic symptom of the city's ability to mark its exceptionalism, especially as it stages the terms of a counter-critique about Thatcherite versions of what Stuart Hall called "authoritarian populism" (Hall 1988: 150) and that garnered mass support for a right-wing agenda.

Thatcherism also has a form of spatial logic, but if it were a building plan then its architects must have had an awful sense of humor. Whatever the patina of reason applied, the somewhat more fluid wash of contradiction dissolved its easy itemization: monetarism, free enterprise, small government, market forces, privatization. Neoliberalism desires free trade, but in its Thatcherite neo-Conservative inspiration this necessitated resolute government intervention to ensure that "free" meant access to other people's markets, not a dissolution of still cherished business subsidies and donor protections. Thatcher's own pronouncements often smacked of typical petty-bourgeois double-think tinged with a rather obvious nostalgia for British brutishness of the 1950s or before. This "before" can mean "before," for instance, immigrants arrived in Britain following decolonization that for vampiric imperialists amounted to a veritable stake in the heart of Empire. It could mean "before" Britain's military, bereft of numbers and the basic iron arrogance of colonialism, tripped down the table of world powers (the Suez Crisis of 1956 provides a critical symptom). It could mean "before" those "nasty" continentals started suggesting national sovereignty might have to be supplemented by regional "European" protections, a common market, and a more supine sense of autonomy. It could certainly mean "before" labor established itself as a significant social force, one that in 1972–4 in the form of the National Union of Mineworkers took on the whole establishment and brought the Conservative Party and Edward Heath to their knees.

But Thatcher applied her authoritarian doctrine to another crucial "before." This was a "before" culture. This "before" was needed to counter a successful strand of British sensibilities that harangued and ridiculed her regime for its blindness to the patent inequalities that riddled British society in the 1980s. This "before," one must surmise, yearned for the muddled consensus-building of the early 1950s and the mind-numbing conformism of the period when greengrocers, like her father, and their daughters felt at home in the world of Englishness as a posited norm, and the government could be expected to protect "England's green and pleasant land" of Blake's "Jerusalem." This "before" fostered its own mythological forebears, troping on the Second World War, as well as the First (the "Great War"), as moments of classless solidarity and indomitable spirit, perky enthusiasm, and ingenious (and acceptable) improvisation. Holding together such a myth required major ideological suture and the odd strategic misadventure (the Malvinas/Falkland War of 1982). But Thatcher clung to this double displacement, rather than facing unpleasant realities, such as the race and class riots of 1981 and the miners' strike of 1984–5, that suggested the New Jerusalem never existed, and what did exist was burning.

Great swathes of British culture were dedicated to unmasking the very mythology on which Thatcher's worldview was based, and Kureishi himself was such a demythologizer. The "before" was, in fact, irretrievable, and the "now" featured other Britains and other Britons, disjunctive reminders that, whatever was timely in Thatcherism, much of it was empty of contemporary resonance except in small enclaves of the Heritage industry and in stereotypic self-ethnography worthy of the tourists' gaze. Thatcherism was paradoxically at the cutting edge of the disappearance of its subjective ground, presiding instead over its ghostly remainder. The English "Two Tone" band The Specials had a hit about Thatcherland called "Ghost Town," and at the heart of the desolation depicted, one senses Thatcher herself as its presiding specter.

The ghost town contrasts sharply with the urban renewal propagated by Thatcher during the boom years. London's "inner city" for Thatcher meant immigrant enclaves whereas "the City" itself could depend on its association with finance and capital accumulation. From the early years of her first administration, Thatcher's London was a battleground between her capitalist vision and the poverty that it encouraged. She fought the Greater London Council (GLC) and any of its supporters in order to free up more land for private development. Its leader, Ken Livingstone, resisted Thatcher at every turn, even going so far as to provide a huge banner hung opposite Parliament to remind MPs of the latest unemployment figures (in 1986 Thatcher had the GLC abolished). Thatcher's London also represented a sharp contrast between the Englishness of "before" and the myriad constructs of Englishness that the city embraced. The notorious "sus" law (revived from a nineteenth-century Vagrancy Act), by which "Suspect Persons" could be detained and questioned on the suspicion that they were likely to commit a crime, was largely aimed at policing such difference by harassing inner-city African Caribbeans and South Asians. The ominously named "Special Patrol" often spearheaded such racially motivated enforcement. It was this pattern of harassment and Thatcherism's dismissive understanding of poverty and unemployment that led to the riots of 1981 in which postcolonial enclaves like Southall and Brixton became hotbeds of urban resistance and anti-Thatcher sentiment.

Kureishi's London does not simply observe and reconstruct this schism. Growing up in the middle-class London suburb of Bromley, Kureishi did not experience the same racial and economic exclusion (though he clearly encountered racism in the suburbs, as he recounts in "The Rainbow Sign" (Kureishi 1986)). What is notable, however, is how Kureishi's convictions about English hybridity and multiculturalism integrate the outbreaks of social strife in London noted above in order to provide a broader, more vibrant, and certainly more menacing articulation of a city straining to reinvent itself. Thus, Kureishi's anti-Thatcher work, particularly the two films with Stephen Frears, My *Beautiful Laundrette* (1985) and *Sammy and Rosie Get Laid* (1987)—and to a lesser extent, *The Buddha of Suburbia* (1990), *London Kills Me* (1991), and *The Black Album* 1995)—do not emerge on the basis of a particular political platform so much as instantiate the confusions and contradictions of Kureishi's multicultural viewpoint, a kind of cartographic synthesis of London variations. If he ultimately eschews the ghost town correlative, however, this does not mean his work has no space for ghosts. For even as an ardent individualist, and realist, Kureishi understands the nature of the pall cast over British society in the present and the traces of the past that slip through its shimmering topography, and this provides a provocative contrast to the specter of Thatcher herself in what one recalls of the 1980s.

To say that Kureishi is a Londoner is not only to remark on his fashionable insiderism, but also to note the very uncertainty on which London identity rests. Trying to capture the city's fluidity realistically, as Kureishi often has, results in a kind of excess that questions what makes up the city. The fantastic, magical realism, and the gothic, for instance, attempt to absorb this excess as the ground for representation (by drawing the remainder into proximity one opens up the possibility of the uncanny), but realism, by contrast, measures its insufficiency either through a highly developed forgetfulness or through the irruption of symptoms that counter its otherwise secure sense of representation. This is the difference between the London of Salman Rushdie's Chamcha and Gibreel (*The Satanic Verses*, 1988) and the London of Sammy and Rosie (*Sammy and Rosie Get Laid*), or Omar and Johnny (*My Beautiful Laundrette*). And yet both writers pick away at what puts together Englishness in the national imaginary so that "London" itself signifies the exorbitant, the megalopolis that can no longer hold to the nation-state idea in any obligatory manner. As Kureishi comments, "I was brought up in London. It's my city. I'm no Britisher, but a Londoner" (Kureishi 1988: 75). Or, as Sammy, Kureishi's doppelgänger puts it, "We love our city and belong to it. Neither of us are English, we're Londoners you see" (Kureishi 1988: 33). Kureishi's London is the mise en scène of a cunning misfit between identity and place, a spatial dislocation that fosters a specific critique of Thatcher's ideology of Englishness.

If Thatcher finds culture her bugbear during her administrations, much of Kureishi's writing at the time underlines why. Again, this is not just because Thatcher's worldview dared to ride roughshod over more egalitarian visions of Englishness but because Kureishi strove to articulate the difference of London—a world of alternative lived relations beyond her front door on Downing Street. Sukhdev Sandhu has suggested Kureishi was chiefly responsible for bringing Asian cultural difference to the forefront of popular consciousness in Britain in the 1980s, and there is much to recommend this view, although it has to be said that Kureishi's London, in particular, is a little more frantic and edgy than the everyday struggles of many Asians in London generally imply. Partly this is because of a generational difference (a critique that indeed could be extended to Thatcher's preconceptions) but it also says a great deal about Kureishi's pop cultural idiosyncrasies and his obvious skills in humor. The depth of his London is achieved less by plot and description—especially in *Sammy and Rosie* where chaos seems to sanction an aversion to basic story—and more by timing: comic timing and the timing of popular London references.

I want to focus on Kureishi and Frears's second film collaboration (after *My Beautiful Laundrette*), *Sammy and Rosie Get Laid*, which premiered in London in January 1988, mainly because this second film intensifies the tendencies present in the first and also provides a unique perspective on the "actual existence" of London under Thatcher. With his profile significantly raised by an Oscar nomination for *My Beautiful Laundrette*, Kureishi offers a new screenplay that initially shows renewed confidence in the politics of irony. The narrative represents a London that is both more anarchic than that of *My Beautiful Laundrette* and pointedly more anti-Thatcher in its social message. The film begins with a voice-over of Thatcher's 1987 acceptance speech, after her third election for a further five years in office (the inclusion of the voice-over was suggested by Frears (Kureishi 1988: 126)). Thatcher admonishes her audience that "No one must slack" and that "We've got a big job to do with some of those inner cities." This is quickly juxtaposed in the film with images of police-state tactics and a cunningly stylized riot suggesting that not only is the political vision of Thatcherism misguided, but also that its social effects threaten to tear the nation-state apart.

Beyond the ominous warnings of the opening, Kureishi's screenplay again explores what the political dogma of Thatcherism has done to British conceptions of self in the 1980s, particularly in relation to new and recent immigrants. Indeed, in this regard, the film is an important correlative for some of the major debates about race and culture in England at the time (see, for instance, Rutherford 1990). In the anarchic cultural surface of *Sammy and Rosie Get Laid*, a film that takes anarchy as its aesthetic content, we can trace an attempt to break from the old order of culture *and* anarchy (actually the culture versus anarchy thesis of Matthew Arnold, formulated in mid-Victorian England to combat the rise of the working class) toward an identity politics significantly apposite to the dislocations and shifting allegiances of what it means to be living as a Londoner in the 1980s.

Because this has simultaneous implications for the question of national allegiance, especially under Thatcherism, *Sammy and Rosie Get Laid* is an allegory about the inscription of anarchic ideas into an identity debate too often weighed down by the lingering essentialism of the white man in his castle. It is a film that, to borrow from Homi Bhabha, announces the possibilities and contradictions of self and community in the modern "dissemiNation" State, a place where state stability is threatened by the plethora of new meanings migration and diaspora provide (Bhabha 1990: 291–322). Rather than a base for centered subjectivity, the film suggests that the nation-state has become an arena of intense and, indeed, anarchic contestation over the meaning of Englishness, Britishness, and nationhood. Although not the convenient stage on which this theory is played out, *Sammy and Rosie Get Laid* nevertheless provides a cinematic practice through which to focus on the state of the dissemiNation and the Kureishi phenomenon, or "Kureishi's England" as one commentator terms it (see Walters 1990).

The tableau seems tame enough: the viewer is presented with a few days in the life of Sammy (Ayub Khan-Din) and Rosie (Frances Barber), a trendy, politically correct couple ensconced in one of the many rundown neighborhoods of South London. Their marriage is open, hence the "laid" of the title, and the film explores their latest affairs with indiscreet charm (Sammy's "lay" is an American photographer, Anna (Wendy Gazelle), Rosie's is Danny (Roland Gift)). Sammy is visited by his Indian father, Rafi, who is on the run from those he politically repressed or brutalized back home (though why such a figure commands Sammy's continuing allegiance is never adequately explained). Rafi, brilliantly played by Shashi Kapoor, also takes time to visit an ex-lover, Alice (Claire Bloom), allowing for an inspired split screen sequence in which all three interracial couples can be seen making love at the same time. Besides fucking however—and an earlier title for the screenplay was "The Fuck"—none of these relationships leads anywhere, and the film ends with Rosie and Sammy on the point of breaking up, and Rafi dead by his own hand.

But the relationships, such as they are, are not the focus of this narrative. What is riotous is not so much the couples' coupling, but Britain disintegrating, a country straining to breaking point under the weight of postindustrialism and the "homecoming" of postcolonial dislocations. This is not to downplay the racial divisions of the couples but is, instead, to read them in terms of UK race relations as a whole at the time. *Sammy and Rosie Get Laid* records the living legacies of Thatcherism and what makes and unmakes it.

In the film, only the anarchic community is lent any credence, and the only activism celebrated is rioting. Under the surface of Thatcherism, with its new ownership philosophies and moribund attempts at renewed Britishness, boil effervescent counter-cultures, the realities of ethnic and racial diaspora, and the cut-and-paste polemics of postmodern style. For Kureishi the watchword is "chaos" (a term that litters his screenplay and is at the heart of his aesthetics of anarchy), not a conscious form of resistance so much as a condition of transition with no guarantees. For Frears this has plenty of artistic potential, but the risk is that the necessities of form will overly stylize what is in essence a threat to more popular film formulae, at least of the prepackaged corporatist variety. It is unsurprising that two of Frears's early Hollywood "successes," *Dangerous Liaisons* (1988) and *The Grifters* (1990), both made a virtue of stylization, even as they framed some outrageous versions of decadence or moral decline. *Sammy and Rosie Get Laid*, with tighter purse strings and less studio oversight, provides a greater opportunity to celebrate chaos as a reality to ponder (indeed, on this level, *Sammy and Rosie Get Laid* is closer in its rawness to other Frears's movies, *Prick Up Your Ears* (1987) and *The Hit* (1984)). Paradoxically, and somewhat conveniently, the aesthetics of anarchy—which means both visualizing breaking the rules and breaking the rules of visualizing—resist their own representative claims leaving the heart of this narrative studiously incomplete. Yet there remains a tension between the anarchic content of this film and its formal conventions, and this is worth further comment.

On several occasions in the film, anarchy is figured not just by a community of anarchists of which Danny, for instance, is a part, but literally as excess. Early on while Rosie is visiting Danny (in her underwear covered only with a coat) and Sammy's father is in bed, Sammy is in the living room enjoying himself. While listening through headphones to music of something Kureishi calls "noble" (Shostakovich, he suggests), Sammy is taking Thatcherite multitasking to a new level by masturbating with a porn magazine propped against his knees, snorting a line of coke, eating an enormous hamburger and sucking on a milkshake and a beer. In part, this is simply an extension of what Sammy means by "cosmopolitan," but it is simultaneously a remark on "Pomo Sapiens" and Kureishi's conception of the Londoner as intensely pleasured within time/space compression. Interestingly, Art Malik, who was the original choice for Sammy, objected strongly to this scene (which was a major factor in his being dropped for the less experienced but more enthusiastic Ayub Khan-Din (Kureishi 1988: 70)). Rafi, awakened by his dream of fire engulfing Rosie's photo of Virginia Woolf (which epitomizes his otherwise displaced fear of women and an ambiguous relationship to British tradition), looks out the window to see half the street in flames and a riot in progress. With his headphones still on, Sammy cannot hear his father's remonstrations and is discovered in the condition described above, funny and futile. A psychoanalytic approach might carelessly assign the reinscription of the law of the father with Rafi's appearance, but typically there is no condemnation, no reproach, just an urgency to move to the next scene of excess—an anarchic overload of the senses.

Such anarchic extravagance can be seen in the riot itself, a mêlée of gaslit proportions and a representation of an England still redolent of postimperialism. The disturbances begin as a response to the "accidental" shooting of a black woman by the police in the film's opening sequence (an incident based on a real-life counterpart, the 1985 police shooting of Dorothy "Cherry" Groce while they were searching for her son). The justification for what follows may seem extraordinary, but police brutality and harassment (again, one thinks of the "sus" law) often led to inner-city conflict in Britain in the 1970s and 1980s (Notting Hill, Lewisham, Bristol, Brixton, Toxteth, Moss Side, Southall, Handsworth—among others (see Solomos 1988, for instance)). *Sammy and Rosie Get Laid* is not, however, a documentary of British race relations, but it does offer a refraction of them. (For a more self-conscious and incisive film of British race relations, see Black Audio Collective's *Handsworth Songs* (1986), which was shot against the background of actual disturbances in Handsworth, Birmingham.)

Even the staging of the riot is a gloss on racial inequities and the justifiable antipathy to the police. In his diary Kureishi notes: "The kids in the mob are locals, not extras. These kids refuse to sit in the caravan with the actors in police uniform in case their friends think they're fraternizing with the police" (Kureishi 1988: 89). And later: "On some takes the kids playing rioters continue to attack the extras in uniform after we've cut. Some of the extras playing police threaten to go home if this doesn't stop" (Kureishi 1988: 96). In the script, the rioters answer the excessive violence of the police in killing an innocent woman by indulging in some rough stuff of their own, belting the coppers whenever they can. But when it comes to performing this, the extras act out a very real hostility to the actors playing the roles of the police, even when the cameras stop rolling. The effect approaches *cinema verité*. Frears adds his own touches, plunging Rafi and his son into the center of the fray while continuing their dialogue, almost matter-of-factly. With an eye for irony, Frears also has Rosie passing Anna on the street while on her way to see her lover. Anna is photographing the riot, not only in its immediacy, but also by setting up shots of posing rioters with stolen boomboxes and bricks in hand. When Anna is asked why she lives in England she says, "It's photogenic": she is working on an exhibit called "Images of A Decaying Europe."

Not long after, Sammy spots Anna in the riot and introduces her to Rafi. As bricks fly through the air and Molotov cocktails explode against cars, Anna turns to Rafi and blurts like a tour guide, "Welcome to England. I hope you enjoy your stay!" This wit is not lost on Rafi, who writes a postcard home saying only, "Streets on fire—wish you were here!" The joke, however, is a cruel one for Sammy who, at one moment, agrees with Rosie's idea that the riots are "an affirmation of the human spirit" and, in the next, bemoans the fact that this affirmation also destroys his car. The staged riots are a strange blend of this offhand humor and heartfelt realism. The latter is underscored by shooting the revolt in London streets rather than a studio (Kureishi locates this scene in North Kensington, but according to the credits it takes place a half mile away in Kensal Town where the local police agree—without seeing a script—to block off some streets for the filming of "scuffles," as producer Tim Bevan had described them (Kureishi 1988: 89)). Just as in many of the actual "race riots," the groups of rioters are multiracial with their solidarity also marked by the working-class neighborhoods in which they live. This does not ameliorate the race question, the mistreatment of inner-city South Asians and African Caribbeans in particular, but underlines the racism depicted and the reactions to it can be linked to a broad set of social problems in which race is crucial.

Given the complex social issues involved, it is not surprising that the question of rioting itself is seen as problematic. As Danny, the black anarchist, explains to Rafi:

> For a long time, right, I've been for non-violence. Never gone for burning things down. I can see the attraction but not the achievement. OK. After all, you guys ended colonialism non-violently. You'd sit down all over the place, right? We have a kind of domestic colonialism to deal with here, because they don't allow us to run our own communities. But if full-scale civil war breaks out we can only lose. And what's going to happen to all that beauty? (Kureishi 1988: 21)

This is as close as the movie comes to proselytizing (in fact, the screenplay has other examples that were later dropped). It is the acuteness of Danny's dilemma rather than his preachy tone that comes through strongest. Should the anarchist match the violence of the State? It is an important question within anarchist theory but Kureishi, even with his familiarity with anarchist ideas from Winstanley through Godwin, only hints at a possible response. One feels that the beauty at stake is the same that made the laundrette "beautiful," the beauty of making spaces collective. As such, the anarchists portrayed in the film are not violent either in the riot, where they provide a musical accompaniment, or on the day when the local Conservative Party MP and a property developer conspire to have their camp under the flyover where they are staying bulldozed. On the latter occasion, only Rafi offers any resistance, urging the others to fight "the fascist bastards." Indeed, it is appropriate that Danny saves his "political" conversation for Rafi because Rafi embodies many of the possible contradictions that beset anti-(domestic)-colonialism in Danny's London.

Rafi's rise to political importance in India has often been achieved at a severe cost to those he would claim to represent. Sammy and Rosie have either overlooked this in the past or rather incredulously forgiven him. Rosie's friends Rani and Vivia, however, dig up information about Rafi that foregrounds his sordid career. It is a history of corruption, torture, and political repression. When Rosie confronts Rafi, he is indignant: "Our government awoke the down-trodden and expelled Western imperialists! I nationalized the banks! I forged links with the Palestinians!" When accused of murder he becomes even more defensive:

> A man who hasn't killed is a virgin and doesn't understand the importance of love! The man who sacrifices others to benefit the whole is in a terrible position. But he is essential! Even you know that. I come from a land ground into dust by 200 years of imperialism. We are still dominated by the West and you reproach us for using the methods you taught us. I helped people for their own good and damaged others for the same reason—just like you in your feeble profession. (Kureishi 1988: 29)

For Rafi, the postcolonial subject is not only marked by imperialism, but also convinced of the virtues of its methodology. But Rafi's position is challenged in the narrative not so much by Rosie's somewhat awkward English ethics, as by the ghost of one of Rafi's victims, a ghost who subverts his logic of violence and exacts a high price for Rafi's state terrorism.

The ghost is Frears's most obvious attempt to challenge the formal realism of Kureishi's script. He pops up all over the place: in the taxi that picks up Rafi from the airport, under a street lamp outside Sammy and Rosie's flat, in the basement of Alice's house, and in Danny's caravan. Apart from the image of the ghost's mutilated face we are also presented with what seems like his body parts: a finger turns up on Rafi's plate, and hair, blood, and bone fill a sink that Rafi tries to wash in. Sometimes he is seen by other characters, such as Sammy, but generally he is Rafi's specter. Indeed, the ghost seems nothing less than Rafi's cultural unconscious, a double who signifies a victimhood that has been compensated or rationalized by Rafi's political career as victimizer. This splitting, or doubling, is the narrative's boldest stroke for it suggests that the decolonization of the mind is not just a question of practical politics but remains a battleground of the psyche. In one of Rafi's nightmares the ghost places a blindfold over Rafi's eyes, and then a cap bundled with electrodes onto his head. The ghost electrocutes Rafi and the screen is filled with sparks and screams. This is the second meaning of anarchy: the purging of the master and his discourse. It is also, in no small way, the spirit of London's excess, the conscience of its role as Empire's heart. As Yeats says of "melancholy London," "I sometimes imagine that the souls of the lost are compelled to walk through its streets perpetually. One feels them passing like a whiff of air" (Yeats 1986[1888]: 43).

Eventually, what kills Rafi is not the presumption of authoritarian populism, but miming the brute authority of the élite, a reinscription of hierarchy after colonialism that his unconscious self, the subaltern within, must remedy. It is highly appropriate, then, that this return occurs in London—the seat, as it were, of South Asia's psychic trauma of colonialism. The resurgence of British essentialism is both a racist reaction to the ethnic diversity within Britain and an attempt to deny the legacy of that racism abroad. *Sammy and Rosie Get Laid*, while certainly not an analysis of the causes of this situation, romps among its various effects in London with alternating glee and gloom.

We have noted so far that anarchy erupts over much of the content of this Frears–Kureishi collaboration, and in part it is a tribute to and product of the clash of their respective skills and worldviews. Yet this is far from saying that this is an anarchist film, for at no point does the film attempt to subvert the governing precepts, or authority, of conventional cinematic narrative. Now this might seem unduly harsh (after all, why should Frears risk an even smaller viewership by being more experimental or avant-garde?), but the point is that the traditional time and space of *Sammy and Rosie Get Laid* hems in the disruptive potential of its content, elevating the acceptability of the film while undermining its transgressions. True, we have noted the representative claims of the ghost moving in and out of shots—the omnipresent Id of colonial and postcolonial violence whose agony is not assuaged by Rafi's suicide. But overall, the formal compulsions of the narrative begin to pick away even at its innovative content. Consider, for instance, that Danny's caravan, set in a wasteland, is covered with quotations from T. S. Eliot's *The Waste Land* (1922). Ostensibly, this might seem a wonderful comment on the decline of contemporary London, "the unreal city, under the brown fog of a winter dawn"; however, the implications for the film's polemic are questionable. On one level, there is an irony in emblazoning an anarchist stronghold with an arch-conservative's pièce de résistance, but on another, there is a second irony that *Sammy and Rosie Get Laid* repeats the contradiction that is its inspiration. Terry Eagleton's comment on Eliot's poem could just as well be leveled at this film: "*The Waste Land*'s fragmentary content listlessly mimes the experience of cultural disintegration, while its totalising mythological forms silently allude to a transcendence of such collapse" (Eagleton 1976: 148). In this sense the film runs the risk of many artistic attempts at épater les bourgeois, that is, of reproducing the very ideology with which it would take issue (invocation as inadvertent endorsement). This takes us back not only to Eliot, but also to Arnold, his noble precursor, whose cultural praxis provides a benchmark for culturalism as a form of ideological contradiction.

Arnold's definition of culture as the "study of perfection" is proposed against the perceived dissolution of British society in the 1860s, whether through Nonconformism, or more violent outbreaks of popular dissent seen in Birmingham, London, Chester, and Manchester. The "sweetness and light" of culture, a veritable poetry of the soul, describes a passion for science and a passion for doing good, and "the best that has been thought and said in the world." Eschewing the burdens of petty sectarianism or class warfare, culture emerges as the process of civility, of right reason, a linchpin of the State:

> Thus, in our eyes, the very framework and exterior order of the State, whoever may administer the State, is sacred; and culture is the most resolute enemy of anarchy, because of the great hopes and designs for the State which culture teaches us to nourish. But as, believing in right reason, and having faith in the progress of humanity toward perfection, and ever labouring for this end, we grow to have clearer sight of the ideas of right reason, and of the elements and helps of perfection, and come gradually to fill the framework of the State with them, to fashion its internal composition and all its laws and institutions conformably to them, and to make the State more and more the expression, as we say, of our best self,

which is not manifold and vulgar, and unstable, and contentious, and ever-varying, but one, and noble, and secure, and peaceful, and the same for all mankind,—with what aversion shall we not *then* regard anarchy, with what firmness shall we not check it, when there is so much that is so precious which it will endanger! (Arnold 1971[1869]: 170–1)

Arnold's peroration against anarchy is worth quoting at length because of the way he insists on making the State and culture expressions of one another: anarchy is abhorrent because it upsets the happy metonymic substitutions of State and culture. Culture must conspire with the State to deal firmly with anarchy because the latter threatens an intuitive definition of perfection. This "clearer sight" has a singular vision of the State and culture as saviors and healers, which, far from abolishing social inequalities, ideologically justifies a ruling bloc containing those who have convinced themselves, if not others, that they exude "right reason" and "best self."

Consider, the voice-over that accompanies the eviction of the anarchists from their camp to the strains of "I vow to thee my country": "Where there is discord, may we bring harmony; where there is error, may we bring truth; where there is doubt, may we bring faith; and where there is despair, may we bring hope." This is Thatcher once more (perhaps channeling Disraeli more than Arnold), convinced that her philistinism will ceremoniously harmonize the disruption Thatcherism itself is condemned to sow. Like Arnold's definition of culture, Thatcherism purports to harmonize without the apparent meddling of big government, and armed with this alibi, State control becomes more secure, better equipped to mete out "firmness" to those who would dare challenge its hegemony.

Perhaps *Sammy and Rosie Get Laid* fails in that it sends too many mixed messages and is indecisive precisely where it should have shown more courage. But it is an artful piece of protest nevertheless because ultimately it resists the homogenizing hysterics of "Britishness" (Arnold's "best self"), the old dogma of a desperate nationalism, and revels in the undecidability of the moment without giving up on the promise of the next one. London, however restless, cannot make this view its own aesthetic of ambivalence because it produces and is produced by more than culture's difference (and perhaps less than anarchy's abandon). Thus, while Sandhu is right to say that "in Kureishi's London young people are always on the move ...they hustle and circulate" (Sandhu 2003: 253), their mobility speaks more to their youth than it does to the time and space in which it occurs. One leaves Kureishi's London with a memory of vital vignettes rather than that of a city linking them. (The appropriately titled *London Kills Me* betrays what happens when Kureishi himself attempts to forge those connections, although most of the difficulties arise from Kureishi's decision to direct his screenplay.) *Sammy and Rosie Get*

Laid, like *My Beautiful Laundrette*, ends on a note of irrepressible optimism. Kureishi's script says of the departing anarchists: "The convoy is leaving the waste ground and heading for the road. The kids remain defiant, cheerful and rebellious, like the PLO leaving Beirut. Some of them sit on the top of the moving caravans, playing music as they go" (Kureishi 1988: 56).

Such an image has not, perhaps, outlasted Thatcher's, but that is not to say Kureishi's London against Thatcher cannot prove inspirational, or, indeed, that London's culture of anarchy, London's Kureishi, does not continue to separate itself from Thatcherism (even as Ken Livingstone, former head of the GLC under Thatcher and more recently, as Mayor of London, pushed redevelopment projects that were not unlike the tear-down mentality of his former nemesis).

In July 2002, a theater producer, Paul Kelleher, took a cricket bat to Thatcher's statue on display at the Guildhall Art Gallery in London, decapitating the Iron Lady (now rendered in Carrara Italian marble, like Michelangelo's "David"). When accused of criminal damage, Kelleher said that if it pleased the court, he could outline all of the criminal damage caused by Thatcher in her eleven-year reign. True to London's undecidability, the jury could not reach a verdict at the first trial. True to the Establishment's ardent sense of democracy, Kelleher was tried again and sentenced to three months in jail in 2003. Once re-headed, Thatcher's statue took its place in the Members' Lobby at the Houses of Parliament where she not only towers above luminaries like Disraeli and Churchill but, because she is carved in bright white marble and not cast in bronze, she can linger, ghostlike, for centuries to come. Just as London has space for Kureishi's bold presencing of postcolonial hybridity, so the city has a corner for Baroness Thatcher's likeness, and even surreptitious cricket bats.

4

"The suburbs that did it": Hanif Kureishi's *The Buddha of Suburbia* and metropolitan multicultural fiction

Ryan Trimm

Chapter Summary: Multicultural British fiction is associated with central urban areas, especially London. Linking new British ethnicities and cities unintentionally echoes tension between the purportedly organic English countryside and cosmopolitan openness. National identity apparently resides in "natural" and unified roots, while migration and urban alienation render cities places of transit, diversity, and newness. The multicultural suburban novel initiated by Hanif Kureishi upends this contrast: *The Buddha of Suburbia* (1990) locates complex, mobile ethnicities and sexualities in quotidian, domestic spaces. Gone are immigrant ghettos, bedsits, and tourist topographies of previous multicultural fiction for places all-too-ordinary, suburban locales reorienting the division between English countryside and diverse urban center. This suburban stress remaps Englishness. Distinctions between old and new, between Commonwealth and English ethnicities no longer hold, but rather roil in a mêlée. Consequently, identities and places are fluid, generating a "new breed as it were," undoing old taxonomies of English and alien, city and country.

Keywords: Suburbs, national identity, multiculturalism, London, race, home, urban

Hanif Kureishi's 1990 novel *The Buddha of Suburbia* initiates a new line of fiction: postimperial metropolitan novels revolving around suburban characters who navigate a contingent and uneasy path through a Britain of fast-changing politics and demographics. The suburbs here revise the traditional relation of country to city with the pastoral signifying the national, the urban the modern and cosmopolitan. The suburbs in contrast are an in-between space, one caught between "nature and community" (Ball 1996: 20) in an attempt to give large swathes of homeowners a little taste of the country through possession of their own gardens (Williams 1973: 297). As a result, suburbia crosses associations, offering to the masses their own connection to the very soil of the nation, and thus comes to be seen as the country's heart. As Dominic Head suggests, "suburbia is Middle England" (quoted in O'Reilly 2009: 2). Such links position the suburbs as a signifier for bourgeois stability and settlement—ultimately, for national domesticity. Consequently, if "newer" Britons had previously been linked with migration, with their arrival in urban centers and the subsequent struggle to establish roots, then their situation in suburbia suggests a more grounded residence.

Yet *The Buddha of Suburbia* seizes on such associations only to unsettle them. Karim Amir, the novel's biracial protagonist, is firmly situated as "native," as English (though a "funny kind") and suburban (Kureishi 1990: 3). However, for the novel, suburbia is only the point of departure, and habitation morphs into a restive rootlessness. Indeed, the stumbling and evolving trajectory of Karim's progress reworks the idea of being settled itself. Although Karim finds home a problem, his peregrinations begin from a position of already dwelling in Britain (having in fact been born there). His flight out of the suburbs betrays a restlessness, one less about race, migration, or newness—themes driving previous postimperial metropolitan novels—than about a deracination marking fissures in English spaces themselves. Race certainly affects Karim's world. However, though numerous interlocutors assume old associations of racial difference and migrancy with regard to Karim, the novel disrupts those links: his only migration is from settled suburbs to central London. The novel thus rewrites expectations of home, indigeneity, and identity, offering a more provisional and contingent sense of self and settlement. Consequently, even the very language must change: traditional associations of identity and place (such as "native" and "home") suggest a more anchored and established vision of identity than that on offer in the novel. A critical vocabulary of the contingent, such as "settling," "dwelling," and "habitation," more accurately conveys this evolving, fluid sense of identity in the novel. Indeed, the novel uses the suburbs to signal a change, as descendants from the "New Commonwealth" have now more fully settled and have made more "native" spaces their own. However, this transformation also signals an uprooting of the idea of home itself, for the home is no longer something anchored, but marked by a certain, if limited, mobility. Karim thus moves beyond the exiled alienation of early migrant fiction for a paradoxically settled rootlessness: firmly in Britain, but no longer secured within a single abode.

The novel thus marks a shift from the line of earlier postimperial metropolitan fiction inaugurated by George Lamming (1954) and Sam Selvon (1956), moving from stories of uprooted immigrants arriving in Britain to accounts of an uprooting internalized within the nation, one where the second generations of migrant families prefigure a broader, unsettled identity. By offering differences and feelings of displacement that start at home, the novel reveals not an organic, unified nation remapped by immigrants, but one in which movements of settled citizens manifest a fluid situation of competing elements. Kureishi's novel then disrupts postwar literary associations regarding residence. The suburbs in *The Buddha of Suburbia* mark the settlement of new Britons; however, this residence reveals not an agglomerated nation, but one in which difference becomes the site for staging new and contingent selves. Karim's mobility stems from dissatisfaction with the stolid settledness of the South London suburbs, a frustration propelling him to perform ironic versions of this identity as his path out. However, such movement does not leave the suburbs behind so much as inscribe a fluid metropolis for Karim, one with many shelters but no concrete residence.

Problems of residence and home are a central tension in postwar British fiction. The deprivations of the Second World War, the loss of housing stock from bombing, the influx of refugees and new Britons, all forced the issue of dwelling and the domestic. Thus, both "native Britons" and newer citizens scrambled to secure a domicile. Consequently, a major fault line in postwar British fiction might be framed around contrasting articulations of residence. On the one hand, stand representatives of the country-house novel, including fiction such as Evelyn Waugh's *Brideshead Revisited* (1945), L. P. Hartley's *The Go-Between* (1953), Nigel Dennis's *Cards of Identity* (1955), and Kazuo Ishiguro's *The Remains of the Day* (1989). In these novels, traces of previous fiction (such as E. M. Forster's *Howards End* (1910)) help to foreground the country house as the assumed locus of the Condition of England. Consequently, such country-house novels seize on postwar concerns with residence and settling, one frequently oriented around questions of who owns (or runs) the country house. By locating the place of domesticity in a pastoral setting, the frame, if not the final articulation, of the nationalized home is rurally situated. Britain—and more particularly England—is thus associated with the familiar (and often conservative) chain of associations belonging to Little England: traditional, pastoral, bound by certain class relations, and threatened by cities and modernization. Consequently, many of these novels look to the countryside—and country house—as the citadel of national values and identity in a fast-changing Britain.

In contrast are novels centered around an urban setting, city scenes in which immigration and "new Britons" figure prominently: George Lamming's *The Emigrants* (1954), Sam Selvon's *The Lonely Londoners* (1956), Colin MacInnes's *City of Spades* (1957), V. S. Naipaul's *The Mimic Men* (1967), Buchi Emecheta's *Second Class Citizen* (1974), and, perhaps most iconically, Salman Rushdie's *The Satanic Verses* (1988). The focus on London shifts the traditional architecture of identity and social structure toward more fluid characterizations of subjectivity. Rather than appealing to stability or a once-anchored self now uprooted, these urban selves are inhabited as a never-fixed mobility. The cosmopolitan settings, where migrant communities are provisional and still partially oriented toward points of origin, accentuate this fluidity and provide a stark contrast to the tightly woven tapestry once firmly enclosing characters in British provincial novels (such as George Eliot's *Middlemarch* (1874)). Further, these two lines of fiction are also articulated around distinct temporalities: on the one hand, novels appealing to a lingering past of tradition, toward given frames of identity (even if in crisis); on the other, fiction that, in emphasizing the disestablished, foregrounds the new, the evolving, in the form of transitory and migrant selves.

Because this second line of fiction entails displaced characters on the move, the question of residence is often manifested through the theme of hospitality, a welcoming that is itself transient and uncertain, given the lack of settled spaces. As a consequence, staying with others in these novels is a necessity, a hosting emphasizing contingent residence. Characters move from host to host, from place to place. There is not a rooted place of return, for roots seem not yet possible. Post-Windrush fiction, as represented by Lamming, Selvon, MacInnes, and Emecheta, accordingly stresses shuffling between living quarters. In such works, place is always complex for the characters, residence never certain, and being uprooted a continuous experience. These novels all center on migrants, those who have made the journey to Britain to settle. Consequently, they inevitably underscore an ongoing sense of, if not displacement, then an inability to settle fully just yet. Rushdie's *The Satanic Verses* differs somewhat in this regard as the novel offers us a settled character (Chamcha) complete with home and wife. Significantly, however, the projections imposed by the British upon his very skin generate upheavals ending with his return to India by novel's end.

In all such novels, the problem of home is heightened through the magnetism exercised by London on these migrants. London, as imperial and social capital, has very particularly drawn these new citizens and composes a very specific type of topography for them. Selvon's lonely Londoners stand out in this regard, for their London consists of iconic central tourist spaces (Piccadilly Circus, Waterloo Station, Green Park) and anonymous and isolating locales (bedsits, buses, trains). With such a geography, it is hardly surprising that roots cannot yet be sunk: no one can claim cold temporary lodging and busy sightseeing spots as home. Indeed, the loose narrative structure of many of these novels—*The Lonely Londoners*, *The Emigrants*, *City of Spades*—reflects this rootlessness: a wide cast of characters drift in and out of narrative focus, plots are episodic and thematic rather than linear. Such narratives cannot yet suggest how migrants could move from being guests dependent on the hospitality of others to being fully settled in their own right. The concern expressed in *The Satanic Verses* with "how newness enters the world," though, foregrounds an ambivalence in this unsettled state (Rushdie 1988: 8). Migrants and their families at once represent the new, an eruption of a force for transformation. However, if the new is associated with migrants, with "new Britons" in urban spaces, such an advent unfortunately echoes claims of an older, established identity anchored in the countryside, in areas and among those who are seemingly untouched by postwar movements.

Consequently, old and new remain separated, not only temporally but also spatially across country and city with little hope of forging a national identity to bridge such a gulf. Such linking of hospitality and newness might unfortunately suggest—or fail to disprove—that those who are "guests" will forever remain so, that the unclaimable spaces through which such characters maneuver will in fact remain unclaimed. Indeed, this experience is echoed in A. Robert Lee's observation that multicultural British fiction alters its characterization of the metropolitan center from the first generation of Sam Selvon and George Lamming to that of subsequent black British writers: "living in London was felt as part of a wider experience of travel and adventure [for early generations of black British writers]; for a later generation, England is felt as a place of oppression and restriction" (quoted in Thompson 2005: 122). This second phase clearly signals the tensions of settling in: doing so comes at a cost, affixes an identity and place, adheres selves to a social topography that situates, but also solidifies.

Against such literary historical antecedents, *The Buddha of Suburbia* stands out for its urban geography and by initiating a new mode in metropolitan multiculturalism. In contrast to the migrant fiction preceding it, Kureishi's novel centers on the suburbs and a flight from these comparative hinterlands, a focus reframing the problem of settlement. This emphasis is most striking in the first half of the novel, "In the Suburbs," which situates Karim Amir and his evolving cast of family and friends in southeastern ring communities such as Orpington and Bromley. These spaces are all too quotidian and settled (for Karim, this is precisely the problem), bypassing the alienated topography of Selvon for houses, back gardens, and local pubs. As critics such as James

Procter argue, this new emphasis on London's suburban spaces signals a growing establishment. Procter notes that this shift in place marks a change in tone: "the geography of suburbia ... foregrounds the privileging of an aesthetics of distance, artifice, self-consciousness and irony" (Proctor 2006: 155), a transformation working to "provincialize" London (160) and articulate "the 'hereness'" of black Britons (156). As A. Robert Lee suggests, such vocalization "speaks out of, and to, the absolute centre of 'England,' changing the 'script' of what it means to be English" (quoted in Thomas 2005: 62). The tonal shift depends greatly on having achieved and claimed the very metropolitan spaces that had earlier drawn characters in Selvon and Lemming to the capital. Now that central London has been occupied, now that there is a movement from migrant to urban dweller, the shift to the suburbs is accompanied by a sardonic distance from the magnetism of the metropole that had once been the impetus inward. This centrifugal stage ironizes the preceding centripetal one. Like Selvon's and Lemming's characters, Karim is still drawn to the center; however, he already begins in the greater metropolitan area of that magnetic pole. His grand journey is not across the globe but merely across town: from the satirized suburbs to a center that, though still alluring, is often undercut by the same biting wit.

Center, though, is a relative and relational term, one often homogenizing important differences and distinctions within this realm: "The country (in the sense of 'nation') became metaphorically the city (the new 'metropolis'), while a significant portion of the rest of the world became a new version of 'country'" (Ball 1996: 8). The center then is not stable but can take on new dimensions as the sphere around it alters. Significantly, though the center might remain central, it is not characterized by homogeneity: center here is at once Britain itself, particularly its countryside and its putative possession of a core identity, and the metropolitan center, a cosmopolitan heart gesturing outward toward a larger world. Karim's journey to this heart ironically takes him further from the quintessential national core in the countryside. Ball suggests that London is now marked by great diversity, that its postcolonial makeover renders it a liminal space, one signaling racial and geographical "in-betweenness"; consequently, "Kureishi's 'London' can be called a semi-detached signifier: it is and is not Britain; it is and is not the world" (Ball 1996: 9). However, it is more accurate to suggest that London is altered, not by being decentered, not by being detached from Britain, but by having that center reconstituted, by remapping its centrality—or, perhaps more exactly, by foregrounding differences encompassed by that axial point. As a result, it is more precise to indicate that the diversity of London is concealed by talk of its centrality, a diversity only growing with the circumference of the circle it organizes. This altered centrality is conveyed by Karim's summary of the attractions of London:

There was a sound London had. It was ... people in Hyde Park playing bongos with their hands; there was also the keyboard on the Door's "Light My Fire". There were kids dressed in velvet cloaks who lived free lives; there were thousands of black people everywhere, so I wouldn't feel exposed ... (Kureishi 1990: 121)

London's magnetism here attracts through its encompassing diversity and cultural distinctiveness, elements no longer bound to a restricted catalog of putative Englishness as seemingly the case in the suburbs, at least with regard to race.

However, this center still marks the cultural hinterlands, still puts in relation discrepant points far (Bombay) and near (Bromley). Consequently, both are defined by not being absolute center: Karim notes the youth of Kensington are so far ahead of those in the suburbs with regard to style that "We could have been from Bombay. We'd never catch up" (Kureishi 1990: 128; see also 71). The center produces gaps that collapse space and time, differentials leaving both Bombay and Bromley spatially and temporally separated from the heart of things. However, this metaphoric suggestion is dependent on initial difference—Bombay is not Bromley, but both might be compared in relation to the centrality of London proper. Moreover, this gap of relative provinciality evokes colonization and race in Bromley's temporal lag with regard to Kensington (Fabian 1983: 32). Again, this figuration depends on an initial difference, one never erased: Charlie and Karim are English, not from Bombay.

Such a comparison indirectly highlights not only Karim's racial distinctiveness (his father was from South Asia but he hails from Orpington) but even more his situation within key suburban spaces: Karim is on the Bromley side of the ledger. Karim's suburban situation, the fact of his Englishness (and not just Britishness), is all the more striking as Kureishi himself is convinced that "England is primarily a suburban country and English values are suburban values" (Kureishi 1992: 163). Karim's presence in England is not the portentous advent of a migrant arriving but something quotidian and settled (in a word, suburban). Karim's position within the ideological heartland, in the purported center of England, marks the incorporation of difference within those key places and values: English spaces now encompass skin tones and cultural markers once deemed wholly other.

However, this establishment is not simply a proclamation of settling down; Karim's restlessness, his ongoing reliance on the hospitality of others, betrays unstable roots. Indeed, an additional element is added to the tension of margin and center, one picked up in Karim's loathing of suburbia, one situating provincialism within greater London itself. In short, Karim is drawn toward London; however, this is no longer the magnetism that once overpowered future lonely Londoners but rather a frustration with the outer suburbs, an unsettledness within bedroom communities, within (one version of) the center itself. But because Karim has been within the greater conurbation all along, his quest to journey a few miles is ironic: the pilgrimage from the provinces takes only a bus ride, and yet Karim battles the same frustrations, racism, and unhappiness as in Orpington.

London still attracts those like Karim drawn to greater possibilities for work, play, and life itself; however, such journeys simultaneously mark central London as a center while undercutting its magnetism. In fact, the suburbs, positioned as lower middle class, are strangely positioned in terms of class. Referring to his father's lover, Karim notes: "Eva always called our area 'the higher depths.' It was so quiet none of us wanted to hear the sound of our own embarrassing voices" (Kureishi 1990: 74). In such suburbs, it is not poverty or deprivation that is the source of shame but rather the uniform aspirations and desires all-too-limited in their dreams: the "done up" houses, the need to show off to the neighbors (Kureishi 1990: 74–5). The aftereffects of these shared visions persist and cannot be expunged merely by shifting residence. Rita Felski notes: "the novel ... traces the tenacity and continuing power of class distinctions, as Kureishi's hero is constantly confronted with the differences between his background and that of his new friends" (Felski 2000: 38). Karim's own ambitions lead to an acting career, one where he becomes romantically entangled with his upper-class co-star Eleanor. As his interactions with her betray, even his new location and cultural achievements only accentuate the divide between the lower-middle-class suburbs and posher districts: the performance of a different manner of speech, the salting away of cultural capital can only be "a second language, consciously acquired" (Kureishi 1990: 178), an acquisition whose acquired nature lingers and remains deflatingly distinctive.

Rather than being seduced to London from afar, Karim, the "funny kind of Englishman," hails from distant Orpington (Kureishi 1990: 3). The magnetic pull of the metropolitan center stems from dissatisfaction with his suburban lot:

> In the suburbs people rarely dreamed of striking out for happiness. It was all familiarity and endurance: security and safety were the reward of dullness. ... It would be years before I could get away to the city, to London, where life was bottomless in its temptations. (Kureishi 1990: 8)

He spends the novel's first half eagerly awaiting his "escape" from the place he loathed, the locale he characterizes as a "leaving place" (Kureishi 1990: 8, 71, 101). For Karim, Orpington and the suburbs are a punitive sentence, not just in terms of provincial banality but also because of the level of materialism:

"I often wondered why [my father had] condemned his own son to a dreary suburb of London of which it was said that when people drowned they saw not their lives but their double-glazing flashing before them" (Kureishi 1990: 23). What troubles Karim is not simply the focus on worldly goods—much of "In the Suburbs" is, in fact, composed of Karim's itemizations of his clothes and his record and tea collections—but rather the mundaneness of this materialism, of the wearily pragmatic face put forward. This snug and smug domesticity characterizes the stable and stolid world Karim wishes to flee: suburban sameness means "there was never anywhere to go," a dreariness rendering the "idea of staying behind" intolerable (Kureishi 1990: 71, 72). He finds "it did me good to be reminded of how much I loathed the suburbs, and that I had to continue my journey into London and a new life, ensuring I got away from people and streets like this" (Kureishi 1990: 101). This ordinariness is historical: "no one of note" had lived in the suburbs, save H. G. Wells (Kureishi 1990: 126), a lack spurring Karim's restlessness. Like Eva and his father, he aspires to be in "place[s] going places" (Kureishi 1990: 127), associating the suburbs with immobility and stolidity; Kureishi himself remarked in an interview that "the point of the suburbs is that they don't change" (MacCabe 1999: 45). It is only in the city's heart that contexts can radically shift or alter without a change in locale, that the places are not anchored and can themselves "go places"; in the suburbs, the uniformity of middle-class lives render these spaces veritable sepulchres of complacence. After being sprung from Orpington, Karim can scarcely contemplate a return: "if the secret police ordered you to live in the suburbs for the rest of your life, what would you do? Kill yourself? Read?" (Kureishi 1990: 145). The suburbs are a punishment, a sentence meted out, one against which escape comes only through loss of life or withdrawal into oneself.

Thus, even Eva and Haroon's affair, despite its collateral damage to Karim's family, offers escape from "dull normalcy" (Kureishi 1990: 45). This drab, quotidian existence receives its monotony from various impositions: the workday schedule expectations mean "life for commuters was regulated to the minute" (Kureishi 1990: 46). Indeed, this workweek and its concomitant conformity to domestic dreams and shared experiences produce

> a cage of umbrellas and steely regularity. It was all trains and shitting sons, and the bursting of frozen pipes in January, and the lighting of coal fires at seven in the morning: the organization of love into suburban family life in a two-up-two-down semi-detached in South London. (Kureishi 1990: 26)

Love as incarnated in suburbia is overly structured, conforms to a pattern of life, time, and space, a pattern materialized largely due to its echoing with myriad other such patterns in those environs. For this reason, the relationship between Eva and Haroon promises such rich tension for Karim: on the one hand, it threatens (and enacts) the destruction of all he has known, the home and embedded life that has heretofore composed his existence; on the other hand, this very destruction of the pattern sunders the snares that have bound Karim—and thus offers an opening to another life. Consequently, Karim is magnetized by the affair, despite its sometimes absurd character (Kureishi 1990: 16). However curious, Haroon and Eva's relationship indicates an attempt to "strike out for happiness" (Kureishi 1990: 8) against a suburban milieu characterized by a striving for the same markers of attainment and success. The affair is the first crack in suburban homogeneity, a fissure opening the possibility of performing new selves. It augurs a suburbia that breeds its own rebels—not only Eva, Karim, and Charlie (Eva's son and Karim's classmate and idol), but also Haroon (Kureishi 1990: 21).

Karim unveils his own transformed self through migration, one reworking narrative assumptions of previous metropolitan multicultural novels. His move to London proper is a shift that ultimately refuses to stay put, an internal migration that will not be settled. If Selvon, Lemming, Emecheta, and MacInnes charted characters immigrating (with Rushdie ironically doing so as well), characters who stand as first generation Britons, Karim is second generation. However, his refusal to remain in Orpington (or truly to reside with his family or anywhere else) indicates another complication introduced by Karim's situation. Mireille Rosello's work on immigrants is an instructive contrast, most particularly her argument that second generations translate between first-generation parents (those who still might retain a sense of being "guests") and presumably settled "hosts." Rosello argues that second generations serve as "mediators" or "go-betweens"; they thus blur distinctions between "guest" and "host," even while their placement marks a gap and indicates that mediation is needed (Rosello 2001: 90). Consequently, this shuttling second generation occupy a no-man's land, for they are thus neither settled nor presumably visiting.

However, in *The Buddha of Suburbia,* though Karim does assist his father in navigating the city (helping him find his way and catch buses), such aid is necessitated by his father's profound lack of worldliness, not his inability to feel at home. And though Karim does move with his father to West Kensington, this move is less about translation or mediation and more about geographical aspiration, an ambition inflected with class and status. Moreover, Karim drifts away from his father, returning at novel's end as much, or more, for Eva than for any filial obligation. In leaving his father, Karim refuses to serve as mediator and disavows any sense of being positioned and settled. Indeed, the novel situates Karim from the beginning as thoroughly British (though "a funny kind of Englishman" (Kureishi 1990: 3)), a creature of quotidian and domestic suburbs, as a native and established Briton. His restlessness is not an inability to settle in a new land so much as dissatisfaction with the provincialism of the suburbs, a dis-ease stemming from a "funny kind" of settlement: at home enough to wish to move. Karim pronounces from the opening that he is "from the South London suburbs and going somewhere" (Kureishi 1990: 3). Indeed, the fact that he is directed "somewhere" positions those suburbs as nowhere, a cartography picked up by Eva's comment that only in West Kensington had they found a "place going places" (Kureishi 1990: 127).

The opportunities offered by the city proper reflect possible lines of movement. Indeed, the city is disorienting precisely as it is not composed of rigid pathways but rather fluid passages of possibility:

> Being in a place so bright, fast and brilliant made you vertiginous with possibility: it didn't necessarily help you grasp those possibilities. ... I felt directionless and lost in the crowd. I couldn't yet see how the city worked, but I began to find out ... London seemed like a house with five thousand rooms, all different; the kick was to work out how they connected, and eventually to walk through all of them. (Kureishi 1990: 126)

One can get lost in the city not just because of its vast and myriad possibilities but because there are no set patterns of movements between the different points of opportunity. The suburbs have well-worn paths in terms of putative dreams and expectations; the city in contrast offers destinations without a set trajectory. Such a topographical distinction is a far remove from Selvon's lonely Londoners and their pilgrimage to fixed places magnetically drawing in future residents the world over. In contrast, though Karim gravitates too toward central London locales, this movement is because the places themselves are unfixed, can be developed, can change their relation on a social map, not because they operate as a fixed pole or universal lodestone. The suburbs cannot shift position, not just because they are seemingly more stable places, but because they also do not appear on the same social map (being comparative "Bombays"). The suburbs then initially signify for Karim only a point of departure, a "leaving place," for it is only as the start of a journey that suburbia might be charted at all. Karim's departure from this placelessness takes him away from Orpington, from suburbia.

Karim speculates this rootlessness might stem from his genealogy: "Perhaps it is the odd mixture of continents and blood, of here and there, of belonging and not, that makes me restless and easily bored" (Kureishi 1990: 3). Karim's deracination comes not from exile or from having left home but rather from a fundamental restlessness, an inability to settle—not because he is not welcome but rather because sinking firm roots is not his nature. However, though he certainly experiences no end of racism and prejudice, his interest and alliance remains thoroughly with London, this "old city that I loved"

(Kureishi 1990: 284). Indeed, Karim is all too aware that his dissatisfaction stems from his place of origin: "Or perhaps it was being brought up in the suburbs that did it" (Kureishi 1990: 3). Indeed, the first half of the novel is his mad rush to leave his "leaving place" and the second half chronicles a certain failure ever to fully leave it behind.

In fact, the center of Karim's attraction can only be approached as with an asymptote: he can near the magnetic center but never finally reach, "never catch up," as he hails from the cultural equivalent of Bombay. The distance marked here is not that from a province, from a colony, but rather the stylistic, social, and cultural distance of the suburbs from the trendy center. It is this aesthetic gap that also acts as a temporal gulf—the suburbs (and its denizens) forever trail behind, cannot achieve a cultural simultaneity with the toney districts. The distance of a few tube zones marks a significant time lag, a belatedness that cannot be overcome. Ultimately, this sense of separation, this distinction of deficit, provides the final suburban shame: Karim notes that Eva's efforts to transcend her suburban past are doomed to fail: she wants "to scour that suburban stigma right off her body. She didn't realize it was in the blood and not on the skin; she didn't see there could be nothing more suburban than suburbanites repudiating themselves" (Kureishi 1990: 134). If true metropolitan style is marked by ease, insouciance, the suburbanite cannot eradicate the labor needed to cover the distance of those crucial few miles; indeed, attempting to suppress that distance signals it all the more.

Significantly, the suburban malaise has been acquired even by migrants. They too have partaken so deeply of surburban dreams that they have run afoul of its dangers, as seen with the friends of Karim's family: "The idea of enjoyment has passed Jeeta and Anwar by. They behaved as if they had unlimited lives: this life was of no consequence, it was merely the first of many hundreds to come in which they could relish existence" (Kureishi 1990: 51). Consequently, these suburban lives of British Muslims assume some reincarnation, an afterlife part and parcel of suburban existence more broadly. Ironically, it is Ted (Karim's uncle) who migrates from suburban alienation to a newfound Eastern-inspired spiritualism (Kureishi 1990: 48) offering freedom (101) and the opportunity to develop meaning (102) rather than accept an ill-fitting prefabricated sort. If it is true that Haroon and Anwar have begun an "internal return" to India, then this migration is a condition not bound by ethnicity or point of origin—stolid Ted can be altered just as much as Jeeta might find herself rooted in suburban values. Indeed, at novel's end, Karim makes a point of visiting the settled suburban residences of first-generation immigrants: their "unchanged" status provides "relief" by offering a contrast to his own "interesting life" (Kureishi 1990: 271). Karim thus still needs the domesticated suburbs to prove to himself how far he has moved.

This uncertain negotiation of race, one where Karim marks demographic shifts and conceptual reworkings of national identity, is extended in Karim's existence as a "funny kind of Englishman, a new breed as it were" (Kureishi 1990: 3). Being a quotidian "exotic" is precisely what the theater directors Shadwell and Pyke wish to exploit in him when they cast him in their respective plays:

> What a breed of people two hundred years of imperialism has given birth to. If the pioneers from the East India Company could see you. What puzzlement there'd be. Everyone looks at you, I'm sure, and thinks: an Indian boy, how exotic, how interesting, what stories of aunties and elephants we'll hear now from him. And you're from Orpington. ... The immigrant is the Everyman of the twentieth century. (Kureishi 1990: 141)

And yet Karim is not an immigrant but something Shadwell cannot quite accept: a native suburbanite whose complexion half-promises an intimacy with a language and land not in fact his own, insinuates a foreignness he does not actually possess. Even his "exotic" complexion and accent must be supplemented to signify the dust of India.

As these reversals suggest, the novel refuses any easy situation of authenticity. Though Karim does locate "the real thing" (Kureishi 1990: 113) in the city, it is not a question of one side or another being merely an image. The suburbs depend on maintaining a studied air of respectability: Karim relates, "My mother could never hang out the washing in the garden without combing her hair" (Kureishi 1990: 188). However, the suburbs also specialize in producing those who attempt desperately to stand out from its trackless landscape, performing roles and projecting selves to break free from uniformity: during Eva's first soiree, Karim notes of the guests, "Whoever these people were, there was a terrific amount of showing off going on—more in this room than in the whole of the rest of southern England put together" (Kureishi 1990: 12). Similarly, Karim and Charlie trade on playing identities they do not fully possess: Karim develops a character for Pyke's play based on Changez (who arrives from India for an arranged marriage with Jeeta and Anwar's daughter, Jamila) (Kureishi 1990: 186); Charlie affects a Cockney accent as he becomes a punk rock star (Kureishi 1990: 247).

These attempts to make their own distinctive way permit them to assimilate better into the city scene: John McLeod notes that "the city is above all a *theatrical* space, a locus of performance, display and spectatorship" (McLeod 2004: 135). Both suburban and central urban spaces are then inhabited as if under a proscenium. However, suburban spaces perform variations on "safety and security" while the personas performed in Kensington are far more expansive. Indeed, the difference might perhaps be seen in the distinction between Karim's parents: "Mum's ambition was to be unnoticed, to be like everyone else, whereas Dad liked to stand out like a juggler at a funeral" (Kureishi 1990: 42). Both play roles, but Karim's mother Margaret performs a thoroughgoing unobtrusiveness, a performance firmly situated in the suburbs where she remains. Haroon in contrast affects the garish, an exceptionality corresponding to the city center where Eva takes him as well as his own performance of Indianness (Ball 2004: 233). Karim's own nervy displays trade on elements of stolidity to inhabit more fully an outlandish mobility: he creates characters on stage solidly positioned by Cockney accents and migrant mannerisms to accomplish his own social climb.

Karim is certainly affected by racism, but he turns such reactions to his own partial advantage, inhabiting characters (Mowgli from *The Jungle Book*, an Indian immigrant in Pyke's play, "the rebellious student son of an Indian shopkeeper" (Kureishi 1990: 259) in a TV soap opera) that play with the very racialized expectations with which he has done battle. His restlessness is thus not wholly generated from a sense of exile or nonacceptance as were the very different peregrinations of Selvon's and MacInnes's characters. Rather, his is a psychic and cultural wandering, a desire to partake of the music, drugs, sex, fun, and culture symbolized by the capital (Kureishi 1990: 121), the sense that there are pleasures to be had that are unavailable in the suburbs. Indeed, in many ways, following his time in New York, his final return to London is instructive. Karim returns to the place he hails as "my favourite city, my playground, my home" (Kureishi 1990: 196). However, his time in London reprises his previous time there: he does not stay in any one place but again shuttles between a host of different people who have some claim on him, and continues to make a circuit of the suburban and central sites where he crashes. He seems to take a complex and mixed pleasure in his peregrinations, just as he had before:

> I liked it all, because I was lonely for the first time ... and an itinerant. ... I was not too unhappy, criss-crossing South London and the suburbs by bus, no one knowing where I was. Whenever someone ... tried to locate me, I was always somewhere else ... (Kureishi 1990: 94)

This always being somewhere else accurately conveys his rootlessness: he is by no means an alien, yet he seems not to belong squarely in any geographical, racial, class, or sexual camp. Karim maintains connections but refuses to be rooted, refuses to be situated and confined by them. Indeed, he seems dissatisfied with each: longing to keep up the connection but desirous of distance. At novel's end, he lacks a true residence but cycles through sleeping at the residences of his family and friends and the flat he has borrowed.

As Susan Brook notes, the BBC adaptation of *The Buddha of Suburbia* ends on the eve of the 1979 election with Karim assuring everyone regarding Margaret Thatcher: "'Nobody is going to vote for that cow', to which Eva responds 'Don't we live in a suburban country?'" (quoted in Brook 2005: 221). Brook writes that in the novel itself, "suburbia, rather than race, unites the imagined national community ... form[ing] a point of return as well as departure ... disrupting a simple linear structure" (Brook 2005: 221). However, in both novel and adaptation, it might be more accurate to suggest that suburbia generates its own dissidents from what Brook labels its "hedgemony," from its own apparent triumph. As the link to Thatcher helps mark, even the decade governed by her premiership brought not unification under the privet hedge but rather divisions within cities and suburbs alike.

Kureishi's next published novel, *The Black Album* (1995), illustrates this well. Indeed, *The Black Album* constitutes something of an intertext with *The Buddha of Suburbia* as it portrays glimpses of the successful careers of both Karim and Charlie: Karim Amir is now a "fashionable actor" appearing with Zulma (the trendy sister-in-law of the novel's protagonist, Shahid Hasan) in *Hello!* magazine (Kureishi 1995: 86); Charlie Hero has become a star mentioned in the same breath with the Dead and the Sex Pistols, musicians all spurring bootleg trade in the streets around Islington (Kureishi 1995: 112). For Shahid, both Karim and Charlie now represent the city center, themselves now exerting a magnetism on him as he attempts to replicate their journey into London proper from his own starting point in the Kent suburb of Sevenoaks. Though Shahid had some trepidation about the poverty and picturesque danger of the city (Kureishi 1995: 3), he, like Karim before, is thankful to be freed from his suburban situation as a "freak" because of his racial difference: "'Everywhere I went I was the only dark-skinned person. How did this make people see me?'" (Kureishi 1995: 10). As with his suburban avatars before him, Shahid's choice for the city goes beyond a desire to feel no longer racially exposed; it is more to flee the tightly circumscribed world of the suburbs: among his schoolmates, "some he had come to despise for their lack of hope. Almost all were unemployed. And their parents, usually patriotic people and proud of their Union Jack, knew nothing of their own culture. Few of them even had books in their houses—not purchased, opened books, but only gardening guides, atlases, Reader's Digests" (Kureishi 1995: 26–7).

Like Karim, Shahid gravitates toward London for it encompasses experiences not found in the suburbs: cultural, social, sexual, and pharmaceutical encounters. Shahid's discovery of the city is conducted under the tutelage of Deedee Osgood, his teacher and lover: "She knew London and would enjoy showing it to him. Wasn't she an educator?" (Kureishi 1995: 77). For this suburbanite, London is a site of seduction and pedagogy, an erotic and mind-expanding experience. He is overcome by the size and anonymity of the city, one leading him to have "never felt more invisible" in this "unreal" and "limitless" metropolis (Kureishi 1995: 5, 67). This sense of limitlessness, of not being tied to a "reality" seen and assigned by those who know him, generates for Shahid the liberty he fears will be stripped from him if he must return to the suburbs: Zulma's summons to return to Sevenoaks means "The freedom he had come to London for was being snatched from him," an end to his "escape" (Kureishi 1995: 190, 87). This liberty is generated in main through London's failure to be unified and harmonious—in short, homogeneous. Instead, it is multiple and varied, so much so that its internal divisions permit it to consort with itself: "London mingled with itself ceaselessly" (Kureishi 1995: 198). This interior multeity seems of a piece with the performances of Karim, Charlie, and Haroon, guises projected upon them or that they half inhabit, masks they identify with through performance but also diverge from. As they perform these roles, these characters are not fully them—but rather a splitting of the self, rendering them multiple. Just so, as with Karim and Charlie before, the influence of the city leads Shahid to settle on permanent instability: "There was no fixed self; surely our several selves melted and mutated daily? There had to be innumerable ways of being in the world. He would spread himself out, in his work and in love, following his curiosity" (Kureishi 1995: 274).

This limitlessness is defined by self-division, a variety marked by internal and external diversity, a habitation of self, characterized not by a fixity produced through conformity with a façade held in common with others but rather through a provisional, contingent self. Such subjectivity does not so much settle into a home as maintain a host of residences where it might dwell. Suburbia then helps *The Buddha of Suburbia* (and *The Black Album*) offer a quiet follow-up to previous postimperial metropolitan fiction: domestic spaces indicate London is truly the home of Karim's generation, but being domiciled does not mean they have necessarily settled. The suburbs signal a conflicted message. Karim (and Shahid after him) is marked as English and thus domesticated through his suburban origin. In such inclusions the suburbs thus mark a transformation of those who are counted as being at home in Britain. However, this "at homeness" also marks a change in the notion of home itself, for it is no longer an anchorage but more a base of operation, a site from which to move away.

Frustration and restlessness with the suburbs then sparks a rootlessness and mobility very different from that of previous lonely Londoners. Karim is truly at home in England but his version of home means no fixed address; indeed, central to his being at home is the only partially successful desire to leave such security and middle-class domesticity behind. This signals an internal journey from Lamming and Selvon: characters who are born English (if a "funny" sort); however, Englishness and the home are no longer the same, a change reflected in a fresh restlessness. In short, this new version of home might be viewed through Karim's own peregrinations: he has no fixed abode but rather moves confidently through the city he claims as home, finding a multitude of places to dwell. Indeed, as he himself demonstrates, perhaps being most at home is manifested through a sense that all of London provides a place of refuge: it offers shelter, but is not an anchorage.

5

Hanif Kureishi's "better philosophy": From *The Black Album* and *My Son the Fanatic* to *The Word and the Bomb*

Susan Alice Fischer

Chapter Summary: The fatwa against Salman Rushdie for allegedly blaspheming Islam in *The Satanic Verses* (1988) led Hanif Kureishi to question what would draw some young Asian Britons to extreme forms of religion—an exploration he carried out through his novel *The Black Album* (1995; also performed as a play in 2009), his film *My Son the Fanatic* (1997; originally a short story published in the same year), and his essays in *The Word and the Bomb* (2005). In the film *My Son the Fanatic*, Kureishi juxtaposes the extremes of contemporary religion and advanced capitalism to highlight what he presents as the worst of two colliding worldviews, suggesting they are both morally bankrupt. The chapter looks at Kureishi's attempt to locate productive spaces between these poles. In seeking "a better philosophy," Kureishi reclaims a central role not only for the outsider, the artist, and the intellectual in the twenty-first century, but also for the radical possibilities of love.

Keywords: *The Black Album*, *My Son the Fanatic*, *The Word and the Bomb*, fatwa, religious extremism, capitalism

Following a long opening shot of a 1980s London wasteland, ripe for the developers' plucking, during which we hear Thatcher saying "we've got a big job to do in some of those inner cities," the main action in Hanif Kureishi's second film, *Sammy and Rosie Get Laid* (1987), begins with the police erupting, without warning, into the flat of a black woman in South London, in search of a young man who flees. The woman flings a frying pan full of chips and hot grease at one of the officers. Another shoots her dead. During the ensuing revolt on the streets of London, one of the characters, Danny, is tempted to join in. Instead he asks, "But how should we fight? That's what I want to know" (Kureishi 2002[1988]: 122).

Throughout his work, Kureishi has been asking this question, and his answer, perhaps deliberately never fully formulated, is partially captured by what he has called "the carnival of culture" in his essay of that title in *The Word and the Bomb* (Kureishi 2005; also collected in Kureishi 2011). Kureishi's "carnival of culture" refers not only to sexuality, "but the whole carnival of culture which comes from human desire. Our stories, dreams, poems, drawings, enable us to experience ourselves as strange to ourselves. *It is also where we think of how we should live*" (Kureishi 2005: 100, my emphasis). The "carnival of culture" enables contradictions and complexities to be held together as we seek what one of Kureishi's characters calls "a better philosophy," rather than the overarching political or religious narratives claiming to have the only right answer (Kureishi 2002[1997]: 325).

Not only does Kureishi's "carnival of culture" allow for competing ideas to coexist, but it also presents a wide-ranging panoply of characters that claim the right to representational space without being boxed into already established ways of being. His work shows many who had, at best, been only sketchily represented before. Recognized as the author responsible for bringing Asian Britons into the public eye, as Sandhu has famously noted (Sandhu 2003: 230), Kureishi portrays them in literature and film in ways that resist "meek or subservient" stereotypes (Sandhu, quoted in Malik 2009). As Kureishi has said, "There were no representations of Pakistanis in films or novels in those days. Or not Pakistanis that I recognised" (quoted in Malik 2009). In his refusal to look for pat answers to difficult problems, Kureishi also resists the urge to create the "positive images" that many have called for. Instead, in drawing his characters' complex and messy lives, he shows Asian people as no better or worse than anyone else, and no character of any group as wholly good or thoroughly bad. His later works often focus on white characters who are shown to be equally complicated and flawed.

Kureishi's "carnival of culture" not only resists easy answers and "positive images," but also refuses to keep people and their cultures separate and "pure." When the title character of the film *My Son the Fanatic*, Farid, wishes for "purity" and claims that "in the end our cultures ... cannot be mixed," his father Parvez replies, "Everything is mingling already together, this thing and the other!" (Kureishi 2002[1997]: 313), thus seeming to presage his author's call for a "carnival of culture." By creating complex characters from a broad cross section of society in terms of ethnicity, nationality, class, gender, sexuality, and age, Kureishi shows interactions between diverse groups of people that are often erased through cultural production. In this way, his work resists what Susie Thomas (2005a) has called "literary apartheid" in her article of that title, which she describes not only as the ways that (particularly white) authors seem to write about only one group of people, but also as the ways publishers, reviewers, distributors, and, indeed, readers tend to separate writers and cultural production according to ethnicity. Kureishi echoes Thomas in the title essay of *The Word and the Bomb* when he notes that "a curious sort of literary apartheid has developed, with the latest 'post-colonial' generation exploring the racial and religious transformation of post-war Britain, while the rest leave the subject alone" (Kureishi 2005: 4; also collected in Kureishi 2011). His work deliberately breaks through such categories in search of a "better philosophy."

Indeed, by "mingling" everything together, Kureishi's work seeks another space, in which the range of ideas he values can be held together, rather than discarded in favor of one overarching narrative or ideology. Kureishi's work celebrates the "carnival of culture" by allowing the messiness of life's questions and people's behaviors to remain complex, contradictory, and, thus, often without resolution, but continuing what he calls "the arduous conversation" (Kureishi 2005: 89–93; also collected in Kureishi 2011; see also Thomas 2009). In some ways Kureishi's "carnival of culture" recalls Mikhail Bahktin's notion of the subversive potential of the carnivalesque, though in the medieval feast of carnival, which Bakhtin describes, the interlude of freedom from the hierarchy and control of daily life acts as a sort of safety valve, a letting off of steam—thus allowing for a return to the status quo that Kureishi's work does not advocate. Yet carnival is also a "feast of becoming, change, and renewal," in which the "bodily element is deeply positive" (Bakhtin 2004[1965]: 684–7). In Kureishi's work, bodily transgression subverts established power relations, provoking and unsettling the audience (Kureishi 2009: xiii; also published in Kureishi 2011; see also Fischer 2014; Ross 2006). As Kureishi says, "There's nothing like a useful provocation to start a good conversation" (Kureishi 2009: xiii).

In Kureishi's early work from the mid-1980s to the early 1990s, this conversation focuses often on race, class, and sexuality during Thatcherism, as seen in such works as *My Beautiful Laundrette* (1985), *Sammy and Rosie Get Laid* (1987), *The Buddha of Suburbia* (1990), and *London Kills Me* (1991). While these concerns remain in his work, by the mid-1990s, the conversation moves to an attempt to understand extreme forms of contemporary Islam as one response to the exclusion that Asian Britons experience in the wake of colonialism. While *My Beautiful Laundrette* had attracted the attention of some Muslims against the film because of its homosexuality (Malik 2009), and Kureishi had written about the conflict between East and West in "The Rainbow Sign" and "Bradford," both of 1986, it was not until the Rushdie affair, when Ayatollah Khomeini issued a fatwa against the author in 1989 following Penguin's publication of *The Satanic Verses* (1988), that Kureishi turned his attention more fully to questions of contemporary forms of religious extremism. Malik reports that Kureishi, already a friend of Rushdie's, had read *The Satanic Verses* in proofs, and it did not occur to him that things would escalate as they did. Indeed, he felt that just as protest against his film had "fizzled out" (quoted in Malik 2009), so too would the uproar against Rushdie's novel. Kureishi was among the writers who came out in support of Rushdie during this time.

The reaction against *The Satanic Verses* had a profound effect on Kureishi, and his artistic response to the Rushdie affair is the fruit of his attempt to figure out why some young British Muslim men find "fundamentalism" attractive and why they want to keep "pleasure at a distance" (Kureishi 2005: 53):

> It changed the direction of my writing. Unlike Salman I had never taken a real interest in Islam. I come from a Muslim family. But they were middle-class—intellectuals, journalists, writers—very anti-clerical. I was an atheist, like Salman, like many Asians of our generation were. I was interested in race, in identity, in mixture, but never in Islam. The fatwa changed all that. I started researching fundamentalism. I started visiting mosques, talking to Islamists. (quoted in Malik 2009)

Kureishi's contribution to this discussion emerges with his novel *The Black Album* (1995; also performed as a play in 2009), where the burning of an unnamed book recalls the Rushdie affair, as well as with *My Son the Fanatic* (1997), both a short story and a film, about a father trying to understand why his son is embracing an extreme form of Islam, and with a collection of essays, *The Word and the Bomb* (2005), in which the author explores both the appeal of such "fundamentalist" religion, and the role of the West in its rise. His artistic response suggests that it is, at least in part, because of their marginalization by white British society, which his earlier work illustrated, that some young Muslims are attracted to extreme forms of religion. In "The Road Exactly," an essay from 1998 about writing *My Son the Fanatic*, Kureishi references Edward Said, reminding us that "the lives of these young people includes colonialism—being made to feel inferior in your own country. And then, in Britain, racism; again, being made to feel inferior in your own country" (Kureishi 2005: 57; also collected in Kureishi 2011). The previous generations knew that coming to Britain would be "difficult," but felt "it would be worth it" because "'belonging' ... would happen eventually" (Kureishi 2005: 57). However, in many cases it simply hasn't, and for the most part, "Asians are still at the bottom of the pile" in Britain (Kureishi 2005: 57). Kureishi thus recognizes that religious certitude might offer something to hold on to because

> Enlightenment values—rationalism, tolerance, scepticism—don't get you through a dreadful night; they don't provide spiritual comfort or community or solidarity. Fundamentalist Islam could do this in a country that was supposed to be home but which could, from day to day, seem alien. (Kureishi 2005: 58)

In the title essay of *The Word and the Bomb* and in "The Arduous Conversation Will Continue," both written immediately after the 2005 London bombings, Kureishi looks at the breakdown of dialogue between East and West and points out that "Modern Western politicians believe we can murder real others in faraway places without the same thing happening to us, and without any physical or moral suffering on our part" (Kureishi 2005: 92; also collected in Kureishi 2011). On the one hand, Kureishi characterizes the British establishment's reaction to the 2005 bombings, which predictably resulted in calls for tighter border control and a return to older—and whiter and more Christian—versions of Britishness, as "a failure [to understand] 'what it is to burn with a sense of injustice and oppression'" (quoted in Waraich 2006). On the other, he is critical of all forms of extremism, which he defines as "an attempt to create purity," something that he sees in British racists and proponents of extreme Islam alike: "And you can see that mixing, you know, was terrifying, just as racists find mixing terrifying. But of course it's inevitable" (MacCabe 1999: 50). Kureishi's analysis seems particularly compelling as extremists on the other side have called for the abandonment of "multiculturalism," claiming that it has not only failed, but that it will also lead to the specter of "Eurabia" that scaremongers dangle before our eyes (Thomas 2009). In "The Carnival of Culture," Kureishi writes that "If the idea of multi-culturalism makes some people vertiginous, mono-culturalism—of whatever sort—is much worse" (Kureishi 2005: 99)—something his "carnival of culture" militates against. Kureishi's fiction, films, and essays explore how the legacy of colonialism and the ongoing exclusion of Asian youth in Britain have contributed to the development of extreme positions on both sides. Kureishi looks to a more complex solution that highlights the responsibilities of both the liberal West and extreme religion: the West must find the "moral honesty about what we have brought about" while extreme religious groups "have to purge themselves of their own intolerant and deeply authoritarian aspects," which include "body-hatred and terror of sexuality," as he states in "The Arduous Conversation Will Continue" (Kureishi 2005: 93; also collected in Kureishi 2011).

In lambasting entrenched positions and an intolerance for difference, Kureishi opts for a politics that sees the positive and negative elements of both Asian and British cultures and rejects grand narratives on the left or on the right, in extreme religion or advanced capitalism (Fischer 2014). In between the poles, he seeks "a third value and locality," which becomes a "subversive in-between space" (Thomas 2011). This "subversive in-between space" crops up in much of Kureishi's work and underlines his political stance of refusing to be caught in a dichotomous conflict between East and West or between other entrenched ideologies. Artistically and intellectually, his work locates such a space by undermining overarching political and religious narratives, by "mingling" everything together and by provoking dialogue through humor, satire, and the outrageous. Kureishi claims that "the whole carnival of culture which comes from human desire" is being left out of extreme religious discourses and must be reclaimed, and he points to Muslim scholars who are trying to open those doors, within the culture itself (Kureishi 2005: 100). Recognizing that "you can't ask people to give up their religion" even if illusory, as "these are important and profound illusions," he argues for "a robust and committed exchange of ideas ... rather than a war" (Kureishi 2005: 100). His work thus upholds the need for dialogue. He has said, "The attacks on Rushdie showed that words can be dangerous. They also showed why critical thought is more important than ever, why blasphemy and immorality and insult need protection" (quoted in Malik 2009). In refusing to align himself fully with any faction of unproductive binary positions, Kureishi attempts instead to shift the parameters of the discussion by envisaging other spaces that might be productive of "a better philosophy."

While not spelling out what this "better philosophy" is, Kureishi represents it in both *The Black Album* and *My Son the Fanatic* as existing in a space apart in which dialogue and debate may take place. Needham suggests that through these works Kureishi urges "a state of radical openness ... an openness that does not bypass or displace antagonisms, conflicts, and disagreements, but that is premised nonetheless on an engagement with different or opposing views that is not dismissive or close-minded" (Needham 2000: 127–8). This "radical openness" is represented not only by a refusal to abide by preestablished norms, but also through these works' exploration of love or connection between two characters who come from diverse backgrounds and life experiences but who can see past the social prejudices that separate them because they are curious about one another and about life. A "better philosophy" can thus be located in a "subversive in-between space," and it rests on a "radical openness" to love.

Perhaps the idea that this deceptively simple premise could generate a "better philosophy" is part of what has made some critics see Kureishi's work after the Thatcher years as less politically engaged (see Perfect 2015 in this volume for a discussion of the limitations of this view of Kureishi's work). Yet the idea of the radical possibilities of love was present in his early work as well with such characters as Omar and Johnny in *My Beautiful Laundrette*—a premise that reminds us that the personal is indeed political. Unconventional interpersonal relations and the commitment to remaining curious about the other contain a political dimension, as does the refusal to subscribe to fixed political discourses, a proposition Kureishi explores in both *The Black Album* and *My Son the Fanatic*.

In *The Black Album* (1995), Kureishi presents Shahid Hasan who finds himself torn between two opposing discourses as he comes to London from the suburbs to study and to find a sense of self and belonging. He feels rudderless both because his father has recently died and because of his destabilizing experiences in contemporary Britain. An aspiring writer, Shahid vacillates between antithetical worldviews: toward the life of intellectual and sexual inquiry—two libidinal impulses often intertwined in Kureishi's work—and the brotherhood of young Asian English men, headed up by Riaz, who come together to defend their communities from racist attacks, but who also organize against the publication of an unnamed novel clearly alluding to Rushdie's. Coming from the white suburbs where he has experienced alienation, as the title of his first short story "Paki Wog Fuck Off Home" suggests (Kureishi 1995: 72), Shahid pursues his studies in London and longs for a place where "he wouldn't be excluded; [where] he could belong" (Kureishi 1995: 16). Here he is torn in different directions, most obviously between the brotherhood of young men who advocate for Islamic purity and his white tutor and lover Deedee Osgood who encourages intellectual and sexual exploration, culture, and pleasure. Familial obligation also tugs at Shahid. His sister-in-law Zulma attempts to force him back to Sevenoaks when Shahid's brother, Chili, who is supposed to be taking care of the family travel agency, goes on a drug-induced journey of his own, from which Shahid tries to rescue him.

In this turmoil, religious purity seems one possible answer as it provides a sense of belonging that Shahid does not otherwise experience. As his new friend Chad puts it, "No more Paki. Me a Muslim" (Kureishi 1995: 128), underlining the possibility of finding a new way of conceiving of himself in a racist environment. When he visits the mosque with his new friends, Shahid experiences it as a positive space where "race and class barriers had been suspended" (Kureishi 1995: 132). This contrasts with the places he goes to with Deedee for drug and sex parties, which he also enjoys, but which take place in exclusively white environments: their first destination is a party at "the White Room," while their next stop is at a gated white mansion, which produces its own form of "desolation" in Shahid (Kureishi 1995: 59, 61, 63).

The novel's emphasis on the destructive nature of religious or political orthodoxy soon emerges. Not only does Kureishi show Riaz and his other friends as "devoid of doubt" (Kureishi 1995: 110), which ultimately troubles Shahid, but he also depicts the diehard Marxist Professor Brownlow, Deedee's soon-to-be ex-husband, as similarly dogmatic. As Riaz says to Brownlow, "You think moral superiority over the rest of mankind is a fact. You want to dominate others with your particular morality, which has—as you also well know—gone hand-in-hand with fascist imperialism" (Kureishi 1995: 98). Ultimately recognizing that certainty cannot hold him, Shahid comes to accept that "Maybe wisdom would come from what one didn't know, rather than from confidence" (Kureishi 1995: 227). *The Black Album* thus attempts to overthrow inflexible political and religious discourses.

Instead, Shahid will choose the option that allows him to continue to question and "follow ... his curiosity" (Kureishi 1995: 274). Kureishi has written that ultimately, "after flirting with extreme religion [Shahid realizes] that he'd rather affect the world as an artist than an activist" (Kureishi 2009: xiii). At the end of the novel, Shahid and Deedee will get away to a space apart in Brighton, where they first met, which represents their rejection of a paradigm based on dualistic thinking (and which prefigures the place elsewhere in the woods in *My Son the Fanatic*). Shahid's decision to stay with Deedee "Until it stops being fun" is more profound than it might at first seem (Kureishi 1995: 276). As she notes earlier, having admitted uncertainty following her involvement in "the party" and feminism, Deedee now wishes to "wait for experience and knowledge ... there existed only the present, tonight belonged to them, and she liked him" (Kureishi 1995: 116). The focus on the present and the contingent also underlines Shahid's—and Kureishi's—refusal to opt for certitude.

The novel suggests that personal relations that admit curiosity and move beyond the socially acceptable or expected not only have political implications, but also just might lead toward "a better philosophy." Kureishi has said that "the subject for me, and for any writer, is love. Love concerns people's interest in one another; what they want from one another; what they can do; and how they inspire each other" (Chambers 2011b: 232). As he puts it elsewhere, "Love is a kind of curiosity" (Kureishi 1999: 24). More broadly, it is an attempt to see the other. Thus, what Thomas refers to as the "odd couple"—here Shahid and Deedee—that appears throughout Kureishi's work (Thomas 2005b: 132) has implications that transcend the curiosity and love of two oddly matched individuals. Ultimately, Shahid

> rejects what Arundhati Roy terms the politics of "the big," the large structures and discourses demanding his allegiance and commitment. Instead, he restarts with politics of "the small," on an individual level (for which the book has been accused of being apolitical): for the first time in his life he begins provisionally to trust and to commit to something or someone, his lover Deedee. (Ghose 2007: 123)

Unconventional interpersonal relations and the commitment to remaining curious about the other are thus posited as political, as is the refusal to subscribe to fixed political discourses. Unconventional, unexpected, or unaccepted relations subvert rigid categories and reaffirm freedom of thought and existence.

Many elements from *The Black Album*—from the ideological oppositions to the search for a space apart in which a "better philosophy" and the radical possibilities of love may be explored—are again present in the film *My Son the Fanatic* (1997, dir. Udayan Prasad), where Kureishi hones in on generational conflict as he examines the attractions of an extreme form of Islam for some Asian British youth, who not only see their parents' generation lose their way in their encounter with the West, but who also feel they have no future in their country of birth. While *The Black Album* tells the story exclusively from the British-born generation's point of view, *My Son the Fanatic* centers more on the devoted father Parvez, a taxi-driver, who attempts to understand his British-born son's choice to forego the material goods and "opportunities" he has worked so hard to provide. The son, Farid, turns to the "belief" and "purity" of orthodox religion as a response to the values of extreme capitalism that promise the sorts of "freedoms" and pleasures that can be purchased and consumed, yet provide little beyond exploitation through work and marginalization. The conflicts in the film are thus not only generational, but also about religious strictures, racism, and oppressive work conditions, which leave little scope for a more fulfilling life. Farid's search for purpose ultimately also unsettles Parvez, leading him to seek some other space in which to find connection and meaning.

Having migrated from Pakistan twenty-five years earlier to the northern English city in which the film takes place, Parvez lives with his son, Farid, who is supposedly studying accountancy, and his stay-at-home wife, Minoo, with whom he has a frayed relationship. While the main focus of the film is on the father's attempt to understand his son, Parvez also gradually becomes aware of his own frustrations with life through his conversations with and growing relation to Bettina, whose real name is Sandra, a white sex worker whom he shuttles around the city and who helps him to understand his relation to his son and England. In the process, she becomes his friend and eventually his lover. The film opens at the large, upscale country house of the city's white police commissioner, Fingerhut, just as his daughter, Madeline, has become engaged to Farid. This scene efficiently sets the stage for the rest of the film, showing Parvez's eagerness for acceptance for his son and his hope that the marriage will provide this, the Fingerhut parents' intense discomfort at the prospect of connection with this Pakistani family, and Farid's embarrassment and anger at both. This humiliation and resentment foreshadow a change in Farid, who ultimately rejects this path.

Parvez has attempted to provide every opportunity to his son, but it proves not to be enough to give Farid a sense of purpose and belonging, particularly in an environment that does not accept him. As he begins to notice a change in Farid that perplexes him, Parvez is initially reluctant to talk to his son, as Bettina suggests, because he doesn't "want to be some fool interfering with his freedoms" (Kureishi 2002[1997]: 295). Farid, however, does not seek the kinds of freedoms Parvez imagines he wants. Parvez's wife, Minoo, says of Farid, "He has had many things to take in" (Kureishi 2002[1997]: 314). While she does not spell out what these "things" are, she has more insight into Farid as he gives up these "freedoms," which he comes to feel offer him nothing. Indeed, Farid recognizes that "we lack something inside" (331). Instead, Farid, who has flitted between modeling and accountancy studies, stand-ins for the principles of capitalism and consumerism that he has been encouraged to follow, seeks a sense of self and purpose in religion, something his father cannot understand. As a youth in Pakistan, Parvez rejected religion after questioning the Maulvi about "why my best friend, a Hindu, would go to Kaffir hell when he was such a good chap" (Kureishi 2002[1997]: 324). The Maulvi's angry response to this and his strict treatment of the young Parvez made him say "goodbye permanently to the next life and ... hello to—*to work*" (Kureishi 2002[1997]: 325, my emphasis).

While religion offers him nothing, Parvez has embraced the promises of capitalism. However, work provides its own frustrations, and he has not managed to progress in an economy in which he works too hard for too few rewards. He notes that early on he worked in a factory "five years double shift, seven day a week" (Kureishi 2002[1997]: 305). He claims that his main goal—besides seeing his son succeed in life—is to pay off his mortgage (Kureishi 2002[1997]: 292). The film highlights the toll work takes upon Parvez, who can be summoned at any moment and who works long hours for "nothing but abuses and little money" (Kureishi 2002[1997]: 292). As Parvez becomes more worried about the changes he sees in Farid, he says, "I thought—anything he wants he can do. ... I never before cursed the day I brought us to this country" (Kureishi 2002[1997]: 310). As his son changes, Parvez comes to question his focus on his hard work in Britain: "where has it got us, and how many of us are happy here?" (Kureishi 2002[1997]: 321).

The film's critique of capitalism and Parvez's dissatisfactions with work are highlighted when, early in the film, he begins driving a German businessman, the aptly named Schitz, who purchases both Parvez's and Bettina's services and organizes a sex party for businessmen. Schitz seems to represent not so much pleasure, always an important principle in Kureishi's work, as the worst aspects of capitalism. He throws money around as he buys and uses people, with little interest in their humanity. His interaction with Parvez is at best patronizing. Countering Parvez's claim for respect as an important value with "Respect is no substitute for pleasure" (Kureishi 2002[1997]: 307), Schitz, in fact, shows no respect for Parvez, calling him "little man" and "kick[ing] him up the arse and laugh[ing]" (Kureishi 2002[1997]: 366).

The humiliation to which Parvez is subjected is highlighted elsewhere in the film as well. When he accompanies Schitz and Bettina to a comedy club, he is allowed entrance only because Schitz "slips the bouncer some money" (Kureishi 2002[1997]: 318). During the act, which is based on "Paki, Rushdie and Muslim jokes," the spotlight falls on Parvez, "the only brown face there" (Kureishi 2002[1997]: 318). The scene highlights the sorts of humiliations that Parvez and other Asians encounter in Britain, and which drive Farid to seek other options. That Farid keenly feels the humiliation is highlighted in a conversation in which Parvez concedes to his son that he has not been embraced in England and that "not one single Englishman has invited me to his house—apart from Fingerhut, who is a top-class gentleman!" (Kureishi 2002[1997]: 334). However, Farid refuses to engage in this quest for acceptance and says, "It is useless to grovel to the whites! ... It sickens me to see you lacking pride" and "toadying to Fingerhut" (Kureishi 2002[1997]: 334, 337), thus recalling the film's opening scene. He feels that "Whatever we do here we will always be inferior. ... How many times have they beaten you?" (Kureishi 2002[1997]: 334). In seeking a new path through religion, Farid urges his father to see that "we have our own system" (Kureishi 2002[1997]: 334) and that his notion of "purity" is the way: "They say integrate, but they live in pornography and filth, and tell us how backward we are!" (Kureishi 2002[1997]: 333). As the disagreement over Farid's increased interest in religion drives a wedge between them, Parvez nonetheless accedes to his son's wish to invite a Maulvi from Pakistan to stay.

Farid's trajectory in the film is diametrically opposed to his father's as he rejects capitalism and consumer "choice" in favor of "purity" and religious "truth." In embracing religious orthodoxy, he "says goodbye" to attempting to get on in capitalist Britain by breaking up with the police chief's daughter, telling her that her "father was the only pig he'd ever wanted to eat" and quitting his accountancy studies, which he comes to see as "just capitalism and taking advantage" (Kureishi 2002[1997]: 305, 337). He and his friends fight the "corruption" they see in the West, but, as one of the older men at the mosque points out, at least "They stand up for things. We never did that" (Kureishi 2002[1997]: 328). Yet the Maulvi who comes to stay at the family home at Farid's invitation is shown to be no better than Schitz. The parallels between the two extremes they represent are also seen in the analogous tours that father and son give Schitz and the Maulvi on their rides into the city from the airport. Indeed, the Maulvi is also an exploitative hypocrite who runs up bills for the family and tries to enlist Parvez's assistance to stay in a country that he apparently despises (Kureishi 2002[1997]: 372), while Farid and his friends organize a campaign against the sex workers.

Kureishi's film illustrates how the ideological struggles of both extreme capitalism and religion—represented here by Schitz and the Maulvi—play out on women's bodies, exploiting them for their own purposes. Not only are Bettina and the other sex workers bought and sometimes beaten by their customers, but they are also violently harassed by Farid and his religious friends as they become the object of a campaign for "purity." The effects of these ideological conflicts on women are also apparent in the way that Minoo is treated at home—and we rarely see her anywhere else. Although they have fleeting moments of laughter, insufficient to repair their relationship, she spends her time looking after Parvez. When they do talk, Minoo criticizes Parvez for driving a taxi for twenty-five years and claims, "If I'd been given your freedom ... think what I would have done ... I would have studied. I would have gone everywhere. And talked ... and talked" (Kureishi 2002[1997]: 299). When Parvez asks, "Talked—who the hell to?," she replies, "Anyone. And not stood here day after day washing filthy trousers." The best Parvez can reply is, "It's easy to say" (Kureishi 2002[1997]: 299). While his words seem dismissive, they also speak to the struggle he has had to get on in Britain. Parvez's interactions with Minoo are complex. On the one hand, when, at Farid's request, the Maulvi comes to stay, Parvez is incensed to find that Minoo is now eating separately from the men, and he refuses to eat without her at the table. On the other, he fails to see that she is cleaning the shoes he has muddied and drying the trousers he has drenched during an outing in the woods with Bettina. A scene in the screenplay, cut from the film, shows him "grab[bing] her and viciously forc[ing] her onto the bed" (Kureishi 2002[1997]: 346). As she escapes from him, Minoo's forceful "Don't ever do that to me again! I will kill you" (Kureishi 2002[1997]: 347) echoes Parvez's weaker plea to Schitz: "Please, don't ever do that to me, sir!" (Kureishi 2002[1997]: 366) for "kick[ing] him up the arse"—thus highlighting the experiences of humiliation all round.

The conflict between the characters—and competing ideologies—comes to a head as Parvez sees a violent attack on the sex workers as he is driving Schitz back to the airport. With the Maulvi looking on, Farid spits in Bettina's face. Parvez wipes her cheek, and, intent on getting his son away before the police arrive, he furiously grabs Farid and shoves him into the car. In the process, he throws Schitz and his baggage out into the street, threatening him with a cricket bat and leaving him to fend for himself—an action indicating Parvez's shifting priorities with regard to all Schitz stands for. When he and Farid get home, Parvez similarly insists that the Maulvi's possessions be tossed out (Kureishi 2002[1997]: 378), signaling that his worldview has to be cast out as well. In the altercation with Farid, Parvez screams that he "won't stand for the extremity of anti-democratic and anti-Jewish rubbish! ... There is nothing of God in spitting on a woman's face! This cannot be the way for us to take!" (Kureishi 2002[1997]: 379). When Farid yells back, asking why he is "so interested in dirty whores," Parvez strikes him. Farid calls out, "You call me fanatic, dirty man, but who is the fanatic now?" (Kureishi 2002[1997]: 379, 380)—thus echoing the line with which the original short story ended (Kureishi 2010[1997]: 127).

Each member of Parvez's family finds a different way out of the conflict, and *My Son the Fanatic* ends with the dissolution of Parvez's family, at least for the time being. The scene in which Parvez hits his son results in Farid leaving home, but also in Minoo feeling that she has been made "a fool": "All this time I stayed here to serve you, and you were out, laughing with low-class people!" (Kureishi 2002[1997]: 381). Minoo too is packing up to return to Pakistan, and she begs Parvez to come with her, but he feels "There is nothing there for me" (Kureishi 2002[1997]: 382). While Parvez claims he has done nothing wrong, she counters with "Oh yes, one unforgivable thing. ... Put self before family," to which he replies "Oh God, yes. The first time! But not the last!" (Kureishi 2002[1997]: 382–3). Even so, Parvez feels he needs to remain at home to await his son, should he return: just before the last shot of Farid in the film, which shows him silently turning his back on his father and walking off with his friends, his father urges him to remember that "there are many ways of being a good man. And I will be at home" (Kureishi 2002[1997]: 382).

Parvez has thus come to recognize that he needs to reevaluate his life, and this has come about largely through his growing relationship with Bettina/Sandra. While the necessity for grueling work has shaped both Parvez's and Bettina's lives as they try to make a better future for their children, Parvez realizes what he has lost to come to Britain: "The second we stepped from the boat we never stopped working for our families here" (Kureishi 2002[1997]: 324). Now that Parvez wishes to "say hello" to life, and not just work, Sandra astutely asks, "Who can blame the young for believing in something besides money? They are puzzled why a few people have everything and the poor must sell their bodies. It is positive, in some ways. ... There is one thing you can try. *Give him a better philosophy*" in how "*we treat each other*" (Kureishi 2002[1997]: 325, my emphasis). His relationship with Sandra, which bridges two cultures, suggests this.

This "better philosophy" exists in a space apart in which there is room for difference and for the radical possibilities of love. By juxtaposing the extremes of religion, as represented by the hypocritical Maulvi, and capitalism and hedonism, as represented by the exploitative Schitz, what is presented as the worst of two cultures collides, showing that both are morally bankrupt. The other space, represented by the unlikely intercultural relationship between Parvez and Sandra, is located literally elsewhere—outside the city, in the woods, in a place that reminds him of his Pakistani "home"—and represents neither England, nor Pakistan, but something in between. Parvez and Sandra's last scene together takes place in the woods, where Parvez recognizes that he has "destroy[ed] everything" and has "never felt worse ... or better" (Kureishi 2002[1997]: 383). He has had to break through the constricting parameters of his life to begin to seek something else.

The film version ends with Parvez in his house, alone, a glass of whiskey in his hand, and Percy Mayfield's "Please send me someone to love" blaring from the record player. The lyrics of this song speak not only about individual love, but also about peace and understanding for all humanity, thus echoing the film's concerns about connection across difference and the search for a third space and "a better philosophy." With little in his personal life resolved—and perhaps that is part of the point—Parvez has thus begun to search for his "better philosophy," as he opens himself up to the curiosity of exploring his relationship with Sandra, and to a time when he and his son might be able to communicate again.

Some have criticized *The Black Album* and *My Son the Fanatic*, questioning whether, in a world that overwhelmingly portrays Muslims as "fanatics," "fundamentalists," and "terrorists," Kureishi's Muslim characters reinforce such stereotyping. Ruvani Ranasinha uses the word "muslimophobia" to describe *The Black Album* (quoted in Ghose 2007: 134). She acknowledges that Kureishi's work is politically engaged and resists dualistic responses while also arguing that the "range" of Muslim voices in his work could be more "heterogeneous" and more "nuanced" (Ranasinha 2002: 242; see also Thomas 2005b: 129). Noting that Kureishi ably sidesteps the "binary" choice of "positive images" or insulation from the "external power structures" in *The Buddha of Suburbia*, Wendy O'Shea-Meddour also claims that he fails in this in *The Black Album*, which she reads as an "overwhelmingly conservative" novel that does not "admit the possibility of heterogeneous, complex, and nuanced Muslim subjectivities" and that is "blinkered by a very rigid form of secular liberal fundamentalism," in which Islam seems to have no other attraction than as a "protection against racism" (O'Shea-Meddour 2007: 83–5, 92, 97, 98). Melanie J. Wright argues that *My Son the Fanatic* "participates in the elision of 'Islam' into 'fundamentalism' in contemporary popular Western discourse, feeding ... the 'moral panic' surrounding young Muslims in the West today" (Wright 2006: 116). Sheila Ghose (2007) explores some of the problems with what she calls the "trope" of the "fundamentalist" that she sees in both *The Black Album* and the short story "My Son the Fanatic" while giving a somewhat more nuanced appraisal of the portrayal of Kureishi's Muslim characters (see also Sara Upstone 2006, 2010).

Two points are worth remembering in this regard. First of all, Kureishi's writing is often highly satirical. Satire is most obvious in *The Black Album* with the aubergine in which the faithful believe to see a divine sign. While the devout are obviously being sent up, Kureishi saves his most caustically clever commentary for the Labour council leader, Rudder, known as "the Rubber Messiah," who seizes upon the nightshade with the complete cynicism and opportunism of the professional politician, saying, "Let's hope they curry this blue fruit. Brinjal I believe it's called. I could murder an Indian, couldn't you, lads?" (Kureishi 1995: 179–80; Fischer 2014: 292; on laughter in Kureishi's work, see also Ross 2006). While Kureishi's use of satire does not automatically cancel out the claims of stereotypical portrayals of the Muslim characters, particularly given the context of their lesser political power in Western society, it does at the very least make such an assessment complicated.

Second, much of the criticism of Kureishi's portrayal of Muslims in *The Black Album* and *My Son the Fanatic*, works that were written *before* 9/11 and 7/7, is by critics writing *after* that time. While Islamophobia certainly predates those events, it becomes much more pervasive afterward with the ensuing War on Terror. Although this does not erase the plausibility of such criticism, context is important. As noted, *The Black Album* and *My Son the Fanatic* were written in response to the Rushdie affair. While Muslims were already being stereotyped at this time, it is not the same as a world in which all Muslims suddenly find themselves scrutinized as potential "terrorists." (This altered context may also have been one of the challenges with *The Black Album*'s reprisal as a play in 2009.) Moreover, Claire Chambers reminds us that in *Something to Tell You* (2008), his first novel written after the New York and London attacks, Kureishi portrays "London as 'one of the great Muslim cities,' evident in a description of Shepherd's Bush Market, in which Morocco, the Middle East and Europe coalesce in the pursuit of commerce." She also notes that the author "explores increasing Islamophobia in a Britain where Muslims' 'fortunes and fears [rise] and [fall] according to the daily news'" (Chambers 2011a: 128–9), as can be seen in *The Word and the Bomb*.

Kureishi's essay "Sex and Secularity," written less than two months after the attacks on the World Trade Center, begins to grapple with the new reality. Asked how artists are to respond to a post-9/11 world, he replies, "I didn't know what to say; *it had to be thought about*" (Kureishi 2005: 87, my emphasis; also collected in Kureishi 2011). Still he reiterates the necessity of culture, which "opposes the domination of either materialism or puritanism" (Kureishi 2005: 87). As discussed earlier, the three essays in *The Word and the Bomb* that are written in 2005 in the wake of the London bombings—the title essay, "The Arduous Conversation Will Continue," and "The Carnival of Culture"—represent Kureishi's attempt to think about these new complexities in nuanced ways in contexts that differ from those of *The Black Album* and *My Son the Fanatic*.

Nonetheless, Kureishi's large body of fiction and film continues to provide an opening for vital political debate through the creation of a "subversive in-between space." A "better philosophy" in both *The Black Album* and *My Son the Fanatic* is represented by love or connection between two people who come from diverse backgrounds and life experiences but who can see past the social prejudices that separate them because they are curious about one another and about life. His essay "The Arduous Conversation Will Continue"—and his other essays in *The Word and the* Bomb—similarly emphasizes the necessity of such debate, arguing that "criticism on both sides is the only way to temper an inevitable legacy of bitterness, hatred and conflict" (Kureishi 2005: 93).

Perhaps Kureishi's "final" word on "how to fight" is to remind us of the necessity of refusing to align ourselves exclusively with either side and of continuing to engage in dialogue: "That is why we have literature, the theatre, newspapers—a culture, in other words" (Kureishi 2005: 92). In seeking "a better philosophy" through the radical possibilities of both love and culture, Kureishi thus reclaims a central role for the outsider, the artist, and the intellectual in the twenty-first century.

6

The parallax of aging: Hanif Kureishi's *The Body*

Jago Morrison

Chapter Summary: Kureishi's *The Body* (2002) develops a fantasy scenario in which an ailing male dramatist is given the chance to have his brain transplanted into a desirable young body. Escaping an "Oldbody" that seems to manifest every biologistic cliché of aging, his challenge is to relearn the performance of youth. On a simple level, *The Body* is an amusing iteration of the Faust narrative in which a mature protagonist who should know better makes a deal with dark forces. As the chapter will show using Slavoj Žižek's notion of the "parallax view", however, this is also a text in which Kureishi manipulates readerly perspective with extraordinary skill and radicalism, throwing the dynamics of contemporary age culture—the politics of looking, the "etiquette of touching"—into relief. Contesting commentary by critics who have seen only "creative exhaustion" in this text, the chapter will read *The Body* as a significant development in Kureishi's *oeuvre*.

Keywords: *The Body*, Hanif Kureishi, aging, Slavoj Žižek, parallax, Literary Gerontology

Hanif Kureishi's 2002 novella *The Body* is a work of fantasy, in which an aging playwright gets a second chance at youth. Its protagonist Adam, although only in his mid-sixties, personifies what gerontologists such as Margaret Morganroth Gullette would term the "decline narrative" of aging

(Gullette 2004: 36). He is tired, his knees and back hurt, and his teeth are falling out. He is becoming insular, impatient, and curmudgeonly. Professionally, Adam believes himself spent, and it is with only a little irony that he tells us "my bed is my boat across these final years" (Kureishi 2002: 3). Adam, however, is a man with another, unusual choice. At a party for London theater types, a young actor calling himself Ralph has made a startling proposal. For a large, but affordable, amount of money, Adam could have his brain transplanted into a new, healthy body of his choosing. The offer seems inauspicious, far too good to be true, but with only a little hesitation, Adam accepts, and off Kureishi takes us on a journey to the land of wish fulfillment.

In philosophical terms, as Jason Cowley (2002) points out in an early review for *The Observer*, the Cartesian model of mind/body as categorically separable entities has been an anachronism for years. As far as science is concerned, Kureishi spends little time exploring the ramifications of nerve matching and splicing, or any of the other technical barriers to brain transplant surgery. When Adam enters the transplant clinic with Ralph, his attention is less caught by the details—or even risks—of the operation he is about to undergo, than by the sight of "a withered old woman in a pink flannel night-gown being pushed in a wheelchair by an orderly" (Kureishi 2002: 37). After Adam has undergone the procedure, she appears again, when a "long-haired, model-like young woman approached, requesting a taxi. Her hip, slightly Hispanic look was so ravishing I must have audibly sighed, because she smiled" (Kureishi 2002: 37). Each of them is about to embark on a new life in which they will always be in disguise, always imposters. It is Adam's experiences as a "Newbody," his pleasures and desires, that we will be exploring. When he moves out into the world, he courts anonymity, and he is seriously put out when he is recognized by friends of Mark, the young suicide victim whose flesh he has acquired. In choosing this "neither white nor dark but lightly toasted" body with "a fine, thick penis and heavy balls" (Kureishi 2002: 25), he does not want to be encumbered by another man's history. To his new guise Leo, he gives few opinions or convictions. The undemanding, nonjudgmental manner Adam chooses for him elicits easy intimacy and confidences. In a fashionable hair salon, Adam reports:

> I enjoyed trying out my new persona on the hairdresser, making myself up. I told her I was single, had been brought up in west London and had been a philosophy and psychology student; I had worked in restaurants and bars, and now I was deciding what to do. (Kureishi 2002: 41)

Adam, invisible to the girl behind Leo's eyes, has begun his new career as a spy, or mole, and our informant. As the narrative scenario of *The Body* develops, his split or doubled view becomes the central conceit of Kureishi's text.

In Slavoj Žižek's 2004 essay "The Parallax View", later developed in the 2006 volume of the same name, the idea of parallax as a gap or division in perception is developed in a way that is useful for illuminating *The Body* and its relationship to Kureishi's previous work. In its common formulation from optics, parallax refers to the way an object appears differently when viewed from different angles. In the human face, for example, the eyes are spaced a few inches apart, and as such each eye receives a slightly different perception of objects and their relation to one another. Without that gap, or split in perception, the estimation of depth and distance becomes difficult, and three-dimensional vision itself is impossible. In Žižek's work, however, the idea of having two views of the same thing is explored in a way which, in important respects, goes beyond its sense in optics. He begins with a historical example with the emergence of the opposition pig/pork in English around a thousand years ago. "Pig," a Saxon word, refers to the farm animals that, at the time of the Norman invasion of England, were reared for the consumption of the new ruling class by indigenous farmers. "Porque", the meat enjoyed by the conquerors, comes from French. Inasmuch as these two words seem, on one level, to name the same thing and, on another level, to denote fundamentally different relations to and conceptions of it, the schism they embody points, for Žižek, to the radical potential implicit in the idea of the parallax gap (Žižek 2004: 121).

Philosophically, Žižek draws the idea of parallax from a number of different sources. In the thought of Kant, it is related to the idea of the antinomy, an irresolvable contradiction between two laws, each of which is reasonable and necessary. In classical Marxism, it relates to the idea of "unresolved antagonism" that is central to dialectical materialism. In both, the key idea Žižek is interested in is that of nonalignment. Indeed, as James Mellard writes in an essay on parallax and politics in Toni Morrison's *Paradise*, what his various deployments of the term consistently stress is the idea of a close juxtaposition of perspectives that, nevertheless, refuse to resolve into one another. As Mellard suggests, "as in the familiar visual paradox in which one may see a duck or a rabbit but not both at once" (Mellard 2010: 369), his conception points not to an opposition of positions or perspectives that might be brought together in a new (Marxian) synthesis, but rather, to an opposition for which "there is no common language, no shared ground" (Mellard 2010: 369). In the philosopher's work more generally, Mellard comments,

> For all the jokes and humor and clownishness for which in his public persona the Slovenian is known, and no doubt by which he is misunderstood, Žižek's world view is more tragic than comic. It is not unity but division and antagonism that are primordial. (Mellard 2010: 369)

In Kureishi's story, the protagonist Adam agrees to partake in an experience of duality by buying the desirable, hard body of a young suicide victim, and taking it out for a pleasure trip. Hung up in a warehouse among many others for purchasers to browse, the "facility" he chooses is offered to him, entirely unsentimentally, as a commodity. As such, even before he has "put it on," his new body exhibits precisely the Janus-faced characteristics that Žižek refers to with the notion of the parallax view. Only a handful of expert surgeons are able to perform the procedure Adam undergoes; only a few hundred of the operations have been performed. By producing "Leo" in the union of Adam's brain and Mark's body, those surgeons have imbued him with value by investing their skills and labor in him. As Žižek points out, in the economics of Adam Smith and David Ricardo, the investment of labor required to produce such a product would present, in itself, the only real measure of that commodity's value. In this perspective Leo, like a fine pork pie, can be considered as having value inasmuch as its producers, whether doctor or butcher, have lavished their time and care in creating him. When their product comes to market, however, it assumes value in a very different way. Its price, measured in money, is no longer a measure of love or care but the result of an equation between forces of supply and demand. Priced, it becomes an object of exchange whose value, far from deriving from its own particularity, becomes value precisely because of its equivalency to the value of all other products, including labor itself.

This schism of labor value/exchange value typifies the form of opposition Žižek is interested in exploring. Very often in the Marxist tradition, the "exchange value" of the commodity has been dismissed as purely abstract or illusory, while the value of a product as the fruit of human endeavor has been valorized as "real." In a reading of *Capital* itself, however, Žižek suggests that for Marx himself, this is far from the case. Indeed, as he argues from Marx's writing:

> The very tension between the processes of production and circulation is ... once again that of a parallax. Yes, value is created in the production process; however, it is created there as it were only potentially, since it is only *actualized* as value when the commodity is sold. ... It is retroactively activated, performatively enacted. (Žižek 2004: 123–4)

Only by recognizing the subtlety in Marx's thinking here, Žižek argues, can the implications of his analysis be appreciated. Far from being a banal object of consumption to be chosen or rejected at will, the commodity is a slippery and shape-shifting form with the power to enthrall and enslave. In Adam's purchase of his new self, by implication, more sorcery is implied than he is able to recognize.

In Kureishi's novella, the ambivalent and divided position of the body as a commodity, a vehicle of enjoyment, and an object of desire is explored in a number of interesting ways. In Kureishi's work as a whole, this is not an entirely new departure. Again and again in successive texts, corporeal pleasure in its different forms is overlaid with questions of power and inflected with elements of unease. Themes of self-division and masquerade are well established throughout his *oeuvre*. Indeed, as Mehmet Ali Çelicel (2009) suggests in an essay on *The Body*, the novella draws strongly on ideas of disguise, performance, and body image, including ornamentation and deformities of the body, in Kureishi's earlier writing. To give an example from *My Beautiful Laundrette* (1985), in a pivotal scene protagonist Omar stands in the office and lover Johnny peers toward him through the one-way glass that separates it from the laundrette. Here, the breakdown of barriers between the young men is visualized by the merging of their reflected and illuminated faces. In a different kind of parallax, in the film's final image, we see the two of them again in the back room, splashing each other over a sink, in a prelude to sex. We are aware that Omar's cousin Tanya, wearied by the expectations and complexities of tradition and family life, has disappeared in search of new freedoms. The power of Kureishi's ending however, is not accomplished by these affirmative representations in themselves, but also by the viewer's recognition that, behind them, lurk the entrenched, unsolved problems of racism, social exclusion, and class inequality that the film has brought into view.

In all of Kureishi's early film work, as Bart Moore-Gilbert observes, we see a conscious oscillation between modes of viewing. He quotes the author's own description of *Sammy and Rosie Get Laid* (1987) as a "mixture of realism and surrealism, seriousness and comedy, art and gratuitous sex" (Moore-Gilbert 2001: 69). In *The Buddha of Suburbia*, Kureishi's interest in the representation of ambivalence and undecidability is also clearly in evidence. Even the generic choice of the *Bildungsroman* for his first major foray into prose fiction, Moore-Gilbert argues, "is particularly significant, given that it is one which insistently presents identity as a developmental, unstable and shifting *process*, rather than a given and stable *product*" (Moore-Gilbert 2001: 127). Like *My Beautiful Laundrette*, this novel dwells a great deal on different forms and expressions of racism in postwar Britain, and like Omar, Karim himself is always partly complicit with his own othering. In an appalling dramatization of Kipling that cast members critically rename *The Jungle Bunny*, for example, we see him dubiously affecting an "authentic" Indian accent, and sporting "a loin cloth and brown make-up, so that I resembled a turd in a bikini bottom" (Kureishi 1990: 146). In a reversal that Kureishi takes care to highlight through Jamila, we are invited to see how his vanity and ambition have led him to a place where, physically and publically, he finds himself enacting the very racist, colonial mindset he purports to oppose.

On the level of bodies, genders, and sexuality, ideas of transformation and slippage are, of course, well established in Kureishi's work. In a pivotal scene of *The Black Album* (1995) highlighted by Kenneth Kaleta (1998), Shahid's lecturer Deedee playfully emasculates him, having him strip for her pleasure while she reclines clothed, before making him up as a girl using the cosmetics from her handbag: "She hummed and fussed over him, reddening his lips, darkening his eyelashes, applying blusher, pushing a pencil under his eye" (Kureishi 1995: 117). Although here, we see Shahid as "troubled" by her attentions, we are soon invited to consider the possibilities of flirtation with his new guise, as he experiments with the performance of "demure, flirtatious, teasing," while at the same time "throwing his head back, pouting, kicking his legs out, showing her his arse and cock" (Kureishi 1995: 118). Shahid's transformation here is, in one sense, much less radical than Adam's. What it clearly illustrates, however, is that the interest in ideas of bodily plasticity, splitting, and doubleness we see in *The Body* are better read as a development of established themes within Kureishi's *oeuvre* than as an entirely new departure.

For all their self-conscious play with ambivalence and mutability, however, none of Kureishi's previous texts explore the idea of the parallax view with the same concentration and intensity as this one. In *The Body*, Leo is never simply a young man thirsty for experience, but also a vehicle of wish fulfillment, the fantasy projection of an aging consciousness. In an early scene, an exchanged glance with a stranger on an escalator leads, with a boldness entirely alien to Adam himself, to a drink, a walk in the park, and an urgent sexual encounter in a hotel bedroom. The two take time out to watch a film before coupling again, but it is the spectacle they make with their entangled bodies that Kureishi has us dwell on:

> She loved my body and couldn't get enough of it. Her pleasure increased mine. She and I looked at and admired each other's bodies—bodies which did as much as two willing bodies could do, several times, before parting for ever, a perfect paradigm of impersonal love, both generous and selfish. We could imagine around each other, playing with our bodies, living in our minds. We became machines for making pornography of ourselves. (Kureishi 2002: 49)

Kureishi is, arguably, being deliberately sensational here, (successfully) courting reviewers with the provocative question that follows from Adam: "What were refinement and the intellect compared to a sublime fuck?" (Kureishi 2002: 49). The idea of Leo as the object of a pornographic gaze is, however, certainly not something that is developed only for shock value. In Kureishi's careful framing here, its effect is to split the narrative view between, on the one hand, the erotic performance of Leo and the girl and, on the other hand, an awareness of the strange position from which Adam, the narrator, invites us to observe them. What we see here is two very different sexual acts in one. It isn't just two young, vigorous bodies coupling, but also and at the same time, an old man hiding, getting off by watching them. Here, the gap or split between "eroticism" and "pornography," two terms that are themselves highly mobile, is very difficult to define. Insofar as the latter can be considered in terms of an interplay between pleasure, objectification, and *proscription*, however, we can begin to grasp something of the parallax effect Kureishi's text sets up here. On the one hand, we see Adam in simple, unabashed enjoyment of Leo's beautiful, fuckable body, and the opportunities for arousal it so effortlessly affords him. After sleeping with the young woman, he informs us, "it occurred to me that this was an excellent way to live" (Kureishi 2002: 49). On the other hand, however, Kureishi is also concerned to let us see the voyeuristic and masturbatory nature of Adam's pleasure in the spectacle of the young woman's deception. She may have consented to sex, but not with an imposter. On an ethical, legal, and every other level, this is a rape-by-fraud.

As the narrative unfolds, the nature (and politics) of the gaze we are invited to share shifts in several interesting ways. As he moves across Europe, Adam is impressed by the number of "open bodies" making themselves available all around him. In one day and night, he has sex with half a dozen. In Switzerland, he meets a group of twenty-somethings making a film "about feckless young people like themselves" (Kureishi 2002: 56–7). With characteristic rapidity, we see him insinuate himself into the group, quickly overriding their plans and commandeering their cameras. Imaged through his eyes rather than their own, the young people are rendered incomprehensible, speaking straight to the camera but with their voices muted, drowned out by a music soundtrack. While Adam finds the youngsters' own dialogue "banal" and "everyday," he is touched and moved by the transformation he himself engenders. Stripped of identity and agency, their "unreachable, silent, moving mouths ... not being attended to" (Kureishi 2002: 59) strongly reflect themes within his own performance as Leo.

A kind of parallax, it could be argued, is always potentially implicit in the aged gaze, as the subject views things from the vantage point of the present and, at the same time, through the eyes of his or her younger self. Within the framework of Kureishi's narrative, however, this idea is developed in radical and disturbing ways. Many times in the novella, where Leo is shown hedonistically immersed in "the pornographic circus of rough sex" (Kureishi 2002: 58), the gaze we are shown is that of an aging interloper, observing the young and their pleasures as if through a pervert's spy cam. Elsewhere, this dynamic is reversed, as Kureishi uses Leo's youth to focalize aging and its fleshly manifestations. In Rome, he forms a relationship with an aging literary biographer, and we are spared nothing of the repulsion he experiences at the latter's physical attentions:

> At dinner, this British hack said he wanted me to be his assistant, which I did agree to try, while insisting, as I'd learned I had to, that I would not be his lover. He claimed that all he wanted was to lick my ears. ... I closed my eyes and let his old tongue enjoy me. It was as pleasant as having a snail crawl across your eyeball. (Kureishi 2002: 53)

Entirely self-consciously, here, Adam plays Leo as boy to this aging queen, allowing him(self) to be exhibited as a trophy, used as a plaything. In one of the few critical essays on *The Body*, Annette Bühler-Dietrich contends that Adam's presumption from the beginning of his body holiday is that "youth, not experience [is] the guarantor for a successful participation in life" (Bühler-Dietrich 2006: 172). As we see here, however, an interesting doubleness is in play. When he is given the opportunity to reenter the world of the young and to replay youthfulness itself, the way he chooses to act that part is in the role of a pretty cipher. "I begged to be turned into meat" (Kureishi 2002: 58), he tells us on another occasion. While Adam, in his original guise, is imagined without ambivalence as "the life I had made, the sum total of my achievement made flesh" (Kureishi 2002: 62), the life he pursues in Leo is nothing so much as a masturbatory fantasy.

During a sojourn in Vienna, he is paid for sex by an old American heiress. Now explicitly prostituting himself, he goes about the work of inciting and sustaining her desire with a professionalism that pushes toward parody, "limbering up, bathing, meditating, a proud professor of satisfaction" (Kureishi 2002: 55). Again, the gaze we are offered is interestingly divided. After sex, he waits by the bed until she is safely asleep, checking "to assess her temperature, her hand in mine" (Kureishi 2002: 55) like a geriatric nurse. When he leaves, she is shown as a barren and bereft image of aging-as-decline, "her eyes ... on my back; she did not know where her next love would come from, if at all" (Kureishi 2002: 56). Using and allowing himself to be used, flaunting himself and lying concealed, we hear from Kureishi's protagonist that "I loved this multiplicity of lives" (Kureishi 2002: 56). In Greece, working as a menial at a spiritual center, he experiments with celibacy. Once again, however, Adam's pleasure depends upon positioning Leo as the object of an older, desiring gaze:

> It had been years since I had danced, and now, since I didn't need much sleep, I danced every night in one or other of the town's discos, with women from the Centre. Most of them were older than forty, some were over fifty. They knew the chances of their being loved, caressed, wanted, was diminishing, even as their passion increased, in the sun. I danced with

them, but I didn't touch them. If I'd been a "real" kid, I probably would have gone to bed, or to the beach, with several of them. I was their pornography, a cunt teaser. (Kureishi 2002: 78)

Directly echoing the scenes in Rome with the aging queen, where Adam (from his position of concealment) freely submits Leo to the role of "bauble, or pornography, to be shown off to friends" (Kureishi 2002: 54), here again Kureishi keeps the dynamics of objectification and exploitation interestingly double faced.

The fact that Leo is, for Adam, a conscious accession adds a supplementary dimension to all of his encounters. At the center, a young woman responding to his easy-going, nonjudgmental imposture confesses, painfully, that she is a virgin, has never had an orgasm, and believes herself frigid. When she asks him to touch her, a moment of intense connection seems to develop. Taking a notebook and pen, Leo begins an inventory of her body, attending especially to its points of tenderness:

I found a purplish bruise, recent, on her side where, perhaps, she had knocked into a table. On her knees there were three little childhood scars. I ran my fingers along the still-livid scar where, I guessed, she'd had her gall-bladder removed. She had five painted toenails, all chipped, and five, on the other foot, unpainted: I guess she must have got bored. ... There were random and quite deep scratch-marks on one arm (left), which I had noticed before but hadn't attended to. They appeared to have been done with an insufficiently sharp object—a penknife, say, rather than a razor-blade ... (Kureishi 2002: 83)

Leo's careful accounting of all Alicia's intimate vulnerabilities seems on one level, if not the consummation she had requested, certainly an act of love. "No one's ever done a nicer thing for me," she responds, as he shares the fruits of his labor, including collected samples. "I kept the dead insects, the leaf, a couple of pubic hairs, an example of the dirt, a smear of blood and vaginal mucus, and a record of the words" (Kureishi 2002: 83–4). Here, Kureishi shows us the difficult, conflicted nature of the girl's desire, while also keeping us aware of her companion's duplicitous, split gaze. Through one eye we see Leo's labor on Alicia's body as the most intimate friendship offering he can make. Through the other eye, peering at the harmed flesh and between the legs of this fragile, exploitable young woman, we become witness through Adam's eyes to an extreme act of fraudulence and voyeurism that, once again, feels tantamount to a rape.

This dualism, in which the possibility of innocence, spontaneity, and connection rubs shoulders with a jaded, masturbatory gaze, is something that

Kureishi pursues boldly and interestingly throughout *The Body*. Through all of his intimate interactions, Adam's imposture means that Leo can never be party to what, in *Violence: Six Sideways Reflections*, Žižek calls "intersubjectivity proper; the encounter with an Other" (Žižek 2008: 26–7). Like the participants of the masturbate-a-thon Žižek discusses in that book, who attempt to find collectivity in the "egotism of their stupid pleasure" (Žižek 2008: 26), all of Adam/Leo's attempts to take pleasure without consequence are foreclosed by the solipsism and dislocation that were their progenitors. At the Center, his unassuming yet narcissistic presence is ruinous of the peace and equilibrium that its female guests have gone there to seek. His casual, feigned-innocent seduction of its charismatic leader is a raw use of Leo's power. Later, at a party on a pleasure boat, we see this clearly as she is reduced to begging for his body, while he ambivalently examines "the folds and creases of her old neck and full arms, the excess flesh of her living body ... her mottled hands" and ponders the question, "who wants a lot of Oldbodies hanging about in the world? They're ugly and expensive to maintain. Soon, they'll be irrelevant" (Kureishi 2002: 103).

Just as he keeps us continually aware that the power of Leo's beauty is a pure imposture, however, Kureishi also ensures that Adam is the butt of his own joke. Back in London, we find him in a bar, lying in wait for an encounter with his wife. When the perfect opportunity presents itself—across the street, the wheel of her shopping cart has come off, providing an entrée for capable male assistance—he seizes the chance to make a connection. In what he deceptively characterizes as "my good deed for the week, perhaps for the century" (Kureishi 2002:114), he carries the cart back to their house and accepts her invitation to come in. On this occasion, however, Leo's seductive openness elicits reactions that disallow Adam from taking the complacent, voyeuristic enjoyment he prefers. Almost immediately, he is confronted with a shocking image of his own mortality, as his wife Margot describes her absent husband:

> I said, "Can I ask what anniversary it is?"
> "Not my wedding anniversary," she said, "but the anniversary of the day I met my husband. He's away on business at the moment, the fool."
> "Why fool?"
> "His breathing was painful. He couldn't walk far. I could see it in his face, but I don't think he knew how ill he had become. Before he started out on his jaunt across the continent, I had decided we should enjoy the time we had left together." (Kureishi 2002:115)

Throughout the novella, it is Adam's relationship to his own aging that we have been circling, his sense of his failing powers, and the opportunities Leo can provide him for deferral. Now Kureishi begins to stage a confrontation with his ultimate expendability, as Leo puts on some music and, almost effortlessly, commences the business of moving with, dancing with, and kissing Margot. "If I was surprised by the seducibility of my wife," Adam says, "I was also shocked by how forgettable, or how disposable, I seemed to be" (Kureishi 2002:118).

Adam's masquerade has, in one sense, been entirely rumbled here, but it is on the pleasure boat that Kureishi chooses to set the novella's key conflagration. As we have seen, throughout his "holiday" Adam has consistently treated Leo's body as a plaything or costume that can be taken off when its amusement value has dissipated. When Matte, a rich playboy, offers to buy it off him for a substantial sum, however, he is forced to look on it in a different way, and our viewpoint as readers is shifted again. A successful, moneyed white man, he has acquired this "lightly toasted" body for nothing but selfish enjoyment, without seriously considering the implications. In acquiring Leo, however, he has not merely purchased an object of desire, but become one. A chase ensues, ending where it must, at the old warehouse where the transplant clinic was hidden. No familiar Oldbody awaits Adam for the reverse transplant, but only a box big enough to dispose of his old brain. Adam's only remaining play is to threaten to destroy what his pursuers desire, and doused in petrol, he threatens to torch himself in a last, successful bid to escape:

> I was carrying my credit cards, but I realized there was nowhere I could go now; not back to my wife, to my hotel, or to stay with friends. I wouldn't be safe until Matte's brother died, or Matte turned his attention elsewhere. Even then there could be other criminals pursuing me. It was as though I were wearing the *Mona Lisa*.
> I was a stranger on the earth, a nobody with nothing, belonging nowhere, a body alone, condemned to begin again, in the nightmare of eternal life. (Kureishi 2002: 126)

Adam is not nothing at all, in fact, but a highly prized commodity. In a neat circular motion, Kureishi has taken the writer with his vanity and careless consumerism, and turned him into the image of his own desire. To return to Žižek, *The Body* concludes by offering a quintessential instance of the parallax view. For Matte, the value of Leo's body is seen entirely in terms of the investment of specialized labor it embodies. "Bodies have to be adapted," he tells Adam. "The 'mark' on the head tells you that's been achieved. The body you are in now isn't valuable in itself, but the work that's been done on it is" (Kureishi 2002: 98). Like the succession of Marxists that Žižek critiques, he sees only the value of the made product. For Žižek, however, and for Marx in his reading, every commodity is two things in one. It is both a product invested in by its makers and a pure token of supply and demand. Until sold, that is, formally constituted as valuable in an act of monetary exchange, the value of any product to its producer is nothing more than only potential. At the moment of sale, both dimensions of value are realized at the same time: the producer's effort is repaid, and the commodity has found its selling price. In this Žižekian analysis, the rare labor that has been invested in Leo's body, its singularity, evidenced by its hallmark, is precisely what makes it infinitely tradable.

Throughout, Adam has treated the body in the same way that he enjoys his sexy laptop and the other tools of his trade—as a pleasurable object to be used, shown off, and ultimately disposed of. However greedily he consumes, he has believed that there will be a route back to the real, human contact, aging, pain, death. He does not anticipate that, with the loss of his old body, this one might come to represent a more immediate and vital need—the final use value of allowing him to stay alive. Accepting the gift of youth, he has made a Faustian pact, without looking too carefully at its terms and conditions. In the same turnabout that finally forces him to confront the real value of the flesh that keeps him living, he has also become the ultimate, must-have commodity, destined to be relentlessly hunted by forces of pure demand.

In one sense, *The Body* attempts no more than a playful iteration of the Faust/Dorian Gray story in which a protagonist who should know better makes a deal with dark forces. By some critics, it has been treated as little more than that. According to Benjamin Kunkel's review for *The New York Times* in 2004, this is a text capable of showing us little except its author's own "creative exhaustion" (5). Both in its own right and considered within Kureishi's *oeuvre* as a whole, however, I would argue that *The Body* is a much more provocative and interesting text than such responses allow. Like much of his writing, it plays strikingly with questions of pleasure, power, youth, and maturity, exploring the increasingly hegemonic culture of disciplining of the body through more or less violent enhancements. If Karim in *The Buddha of Suburbia* is willing to sculpt, exoticize, and commodify himself for sex, experience, and opportunity, Adam's narrative takes that theme to a new extreme, with its privileged white protagonist who buys a pretty brown body for the pleasures it can afford him. As I have tried to suggest through the notion of the parallax view, moreover, one of the most important features of *The Body* as a development in Kureishi's writing is the innovative way in which it splits and plays with the narrative gaze. Unlike Omar in *My Beautiful Laundrette*, Shahid in *The Black Album*, or Karim in *The Buddha of Suburbia*, Adam is an imposter in his desirable young body, a spy among the young people he plays with. His gaze, and ours, is always mobile, never unitary. Read through Slavoj Žižek, moreover, one of the most interesting aspects of Kureishi's play with perspective here is the conscious refusal to let his self-doubling narrative resolve into a reassuring synthesis. While he may begin with the picaresque, setting a young man off on a journey of discovery, he resolutely resists the compensatory conventions of that form, where some kind of maturity and stability of perspective should be the protagonist's reward. Instead, *The Body*'s protagonist moves in the opposite direction, from maturity and (relative) balance toward the spectacle of an exile, a "nobody with nothing" (Kureishi 2002: 126), fleeing for his life. By and through its intricate reversals and inversions, this is a text that significantly extends and complicates the engagement with aging masculinity that we see in many of Kureishi's writings, from *My Son the Fanatic* (1997) to *Gabriel's Gift* (2001). In so doing, it introduces a new dimension to his ongoing exploration of what (to adapt Adrienne Rich) might be described as our culture of compulsory youth.

7

The other Kureishi: A psychoanalytic reading of *Something to Tell You*

Geoff Boucher

Chapter Summary: "The other Kureishi" challenges the critical consensus that after *The Black Album* (1995) Kureishi's fiction lost its public, political character, shifting its focus toward private interiority and existential questions. Interpreting *Something to Tell You* (2008) through a mode of psychoanalytical reading, this essay proposes that, although its apparent focus is on the personal secrets and romantic idiosyncrasies of its characters, the novel uses this lens to pose very large questions concerning the human condition. Reading in light of the figure of the psychoanalyst as literary protagonist and cultural hero makes it possible to grasp the novel as presenting a fictionalized case study whose ambition is to convince the reader of the experiential validity of psychoanalysis. In conclusion, the novel's reflections on "civilization and its discontents" are positioned in terms of a meditation on the relation between society and intimacy, politics and the personal.

Keywords: *Something to Tell You*, Freud, Lacan, religion, romance

In *Something to Tell You* (2008), Hanif Kureishi presents explicitly something that has long been implicit in his work, namely, the psychoanalyst as cultural hero. For the novel's protagonist, Jamal Khan, psychoanalysis is a modern philosophy of life before it is a form of therapy, and it is certainly not a technique of psychological readjustment to conventional expectations. Specifically, it is a modern form of the ancient philosophy of Epicureanism, a philosophy that held that human beings are natural animals driven by pleasure and pain toward transient secular quests for instant happiness and religious expressions of anxiety and guilt, respectively. For the Epicurean, the aim of the good life is to transcend these fleeting pleasures and unnecessary anxieties in order to attain tranquillity, which, translated into psychoanalytic terms, implies an art of living that embraces the life force and rejects the death drive. More pointedly, psychoanalysis seems to be an alternative set of ideals, not to mainstream secular culture, which lacks any, but to religious fundamentalism, which appears in the novel as the only serious challenge to the value-freefall of consumer capitalism. Psychoanalysis is therefore positioned by Jamal as a cultural force less because it undoes repression than because it provides for identification in ways that promote realistic kinds of human happiness. What, then, is at stake in the idea of the analyst as cultural hero, providing the Epicurean wisdom that both secular and religious perspectives lack?

For the critical consensus, the answer to this question is as devastating as it is obvious: a retreat from postcolonial politics and the critique of the racial discontents of multicultural Britain. "After *The Buddha of Suburbia* and *The Black Album*, Kureishi's fiction seems to lose some of its public, political character," Bradley Buchanan notes, summarizing critical reception of his recent work. It seems that "the message of his later fiction is clear—family and sexual problems erode life's pleasures" (Buchanan 2007: 69). Indeed, he continues, "reactions to Kureishi's work have grown increasingly evaluative (and largely hostile) as he has moved decisively away from the racially specific, international issues that are a central feature in postcolonial writing" (Buchanan 2007: 147).

Given that the reception of Kureishi's work has been dominated by the categories of postcolonial criticism, it is perhaps not surprising that the perception of a turn from the public to the private and from the political to the personal generates antagonistic responses. At a minimum, critics express concern that Kureishi's interest in the peculiarities of individuals amounts to a naturalization of the liberal conception of the private person. Ruvani Ranasinha, for instance, confidently asserts that Kureishi's later works do "not engage with the possibility of a rethinking of liberal ideology" (Ranasinha 2002: 83). At a maximum, a focus on the individual, supposedly in worrying abstraction from sociopolitical determinants of identity, is thought to imply a highly conservative turn, from a progressive opposition to political inequalities to their endorsement. For Bart Moore-Gilbert, for example, the agenda of *Intimacy* is nothing less than "a reassertion of traditional forms of patriarchal masculinity" (Moore-Gilbert 2001: 173–4).

Certainly, *Something to Tell You* seems to position the author in a quasi-confessional mode, dealing with the intimate "secrets of desire" rather than the problems of social identity. But the accusation that the book ignores political questions altogether in order to focus exclusively on personal issues seems obdurate, even perverse. For this apparently highly personal narrative is overtly lent a sociopolitical context within a dense network of historical references, including multicultural England, the London bombings, and the War on Terror. Indeed, the novel insistently alludes to Kureishi's other work, particularly *The Buddha of Suburbia* (1990) and *The Black Album* (1995), rereading it in light of the figure of the analyst as literary protagonist and cultural detective.

Very few critics have taken seriously Kureishi's own claim that after *Love in a Blue Time* (1997), his aim has been to express "what it is like to be a human being" (quoted in Ranasinha 2002: 102). Yet as one of this critical minority, Susie Thomas, has argued, "it is not the case that there was a sudden break from social themes to the self" (Thomas 2005: 164). On the one hand, Kureishi "has always experimented with autobiographical fiction," and on the other hand, "from the very beginning, Kureishi has highlighted the ways in which the personal is political" (Thomas 2005: 165).

I want to propose that although *Something to Tell You* focuses on the personal secrets and romantic idiosyncrasies of its characters, the novel poses very large questions concerning the human condition, through the lens of Freudian psychoanalysis. Framed in particular by Freud's reflections on widespread discontent with modern society in *Civilization and Its Discontents* (1930), the novel connects its characters' disordered love lives and problems with guilt to wider issues. These include the aggression motivating radical politics, the way in which group belonging implies projections of hostility onto the excluded, and the dialectics of masochistic self-punishment and resentment of the other's pleasure that happens in religious fundamentalism. But all of these things are positioned by the novel as consequences of the way that contemporary Western consumer culture deals with what is, at least from the Freudian perspective that Jamal adopts, the fundamental problem of human existence, the resolution of the Oedipus Complex. For Freud, and therefore for the novel's protagonist and narrator, that notorious maturational complex, involving the young boy's replacement of his parricidal intentions and incestuous desires with an identification with the father figure and substitution of an extrafamilial love object for the mother, is really the crux of human social development. Because the resolution of the Oedipus Complex depends on repression of erotic instincts with the assistance of the force of aggressive energies that become focused in the superego, social progress, and guilt-inducing moral self-punishment, most visible in the history of religious ideas, are dangerously entwined (Freud 1924: 114, 127, 142). The novel, in other words, raises anew Freud's "fateful question for the human species": whether there are any viable cultural alternatives to the increasing aggressivity of the superego that seems to accompany civilizational advance (Freud 1924: 145). It does so, however, through a representation of the way in which psychoanalysis itself provides a cultural solution to the pressures of an otherwise intolerable guilt that is part and parcel of the "civilizational discontent" at the heart of the modern world.

This interpretation depends on reading the narrative as centrally concerned with psychoanalytic ideas, rather than just contingently about a character who happens to be an analyst. I argue that the narrator, the psychoanalyst Jamal Khan, speaks at once as analysand and analyst, presenting us with what is both Jamal's own case history and a fragmented discourse in which he presents an Oedipal drama in a disguised form. Indeed, Jamal says that he is writing a work that presents psychoanalysis through concrete images, rather than theoretical descriptions, and he adds that analysands always present aspects of themselves by speaking about others. The implication is that the idea of a repressed wish to murder the father is concretized through a literal event that haunts Jamal's existence, while his Oedipal relation to his parents is projected onto the constellation of characters he encounters. Drawing upon Lacan's efforts to clarify the dynamics of the Freudian Oedipus Complex, I show that this interpretive perspective can illuminate the father figures in Jamal's life, throwing light on the solution to Oedipal guilt that Jamal embraces. In closing, I open up the reflections on culture that the novel proposes, and, in particular, its concerns with the unconscious motivations that inflect collective identities and political allegiances.

Modernist transposition

Something to Tell You concerns the haunting power of past events in the life of its main character, told in the potentially confusing form of the juxtaposition of multiple plotlines and different temporalities. The protagonist-narrator, Jamal Khan, is a middle-aged psychoanalyst of no particular school whose love life is in the usual disarray of contemporary marriages. As the narrative opens, he has been eighteen months separated from his wife, Josephine, and in the following twelve months, he ricochets off his long-lost love, Ajita, former girlfriend, Karen Pearl, and favorite prostitute, The Goddess, not entirely sure what love can mean for him anymore. Despite his analytic training, Jamal is the normal sort of incompetent mess as an (ex)husband, whose former wife's two new boyfriends evoke jealousy and bouts of introspection. Similarly, Jamal is the standard sort of humiliated late modern father, whose precociously alienated twelve-year-old son scornfully refers to him as "Mr Cunty Cunt."

"What's wrong with that?" Jamal exclaims absurdly. "The *Mister* shows respect" (Kureishi 2008: 17–8).

But if Jamal's professional, familial, and marital situation is fairly routine, the thing in his life that makes it such a confusion is rather unusual. Like everybody, Jamal "sail[s] with a corpse in the cargo" (Kureishi 2008: 7), but unlike most, his is literal. "I live every day with a murder," he says at the start. "A real one. Killer, me" (Kureishi 2008: 16). About three decades before the novel begins, Jamal has committed a crime of passion. In the narrated past, Jamal recalls the summer of love with Ajita leading up to her father's death—which Jamal insists is a "murder"—and its sequel in her leaving him "forever" (romantically). Having discovered that Ajita was being systematically raped by her father, Jamal had planned to scare the father off with the help of shadowy acquaintances Wolf and Valentin, but brandishing a knife during the mock robbery that they stage, Jamal triggers the father's heart attack. This flashback narrative is tied in to the present of Jamal's disordered love life, as both its explanatory ground and the thing that returns amidst his second year of separation from Josephine.

Psychoanalysis has made Jamal urbane and unconventional, so that, narrating the story in the first person, he maintains a façade of tranquillity. But the turbulent events in his emotional life and his acute anxiety when, in the present tense of the narrative, Ajita's brother Mustaq questions him about events and then Wolf returns to blackmail him, give the lie to this surface calm. As he admits, "The murdered man wouldn't let me go that easily. He clung to me, his fingernails in my flesh. I would wake up staring at the flickering fright of his doomed eyes. The past rode on my back like a devil …" (Kureishi 2008: 71). It rips Jamal's life apart until he finds a way to come to terms with the guilt through psychotherapy. But ultimately, Jamal can only lay the past to rest through confessing the truth to Ajita, which involves his recollecting the surprising circumstances of this traumatic event and coming to terms with the ways in which it shaped his subsequent life.

This is a year of reunions with former lovers. In particular, because Jamal has insisted on keeping Ajita's father's watch and wearing it, when he accidentally meets Ajita's brother Mustaq once again, he arouses the curiosity of Mustaq and, following a reunion with Ajita brokered by Mustaq, the suspicions of Ajita. This narrative thread connects with the return of Jamal's former partner-in-crime, Wolf, who after the death of the other partner-in-crime, Valentin, has returned to blackmail Jamal—but as it happens, also takes up romantically with Ajita. Wolf's death from a heart attack is the catalyst for a cascade of disclosures, so that Jamal eventually confesses to Ajita his role in things—whereupon she replies that she "wished [father] dead a million times" (Kureishi 2008: 360) and should not have let Jamal intervene. Ajita embraces Islam and then turns from religion to psychoanalysis, and it seems to help a bit. This is a kind of forgiveness, and its reconciliatory tone ties in with Jamal's own tentative speculations that he might try once again with Josephine, as well as the modest optimism of the other plotline's conclusion.

In that thread, the initially passionate relationship between Jamal's sister Miriam and his best friend Henry curves downward from love to sex, toward boredom. Miriam insists, absurdly, that they marry; Henry has problems of his own with his ex-wife Valerie, son Sam, and hysterical daughter Lisa. But in truth, Henry and Miriam's relationship is like a marriage anyway because they share in the relationship Miriam's sidekick, taxi-driver, lowlife, and guitarist, Bushie Perkins, as something like a son. That leaves only Lisa, whose problems are solved by Jamal with the assistance of poetry and fellatio.

There are several indications in the narrative that this is about psychoanalysis. Jamal's role as an analyst means that he can pose the questions of the torments of the human soul in a typical psychoanalytic dialectic, according to which the things that seem most marginal and aberrant turn out to be most central and normal. For starters, Jamal's role as an analyst means that he poses the specific problem of the narrative as a paradox that is fully intelligible only within the psychoanalytic field: how does one manage to "kill a dead father" without intolerable guilt (Kureishi 2008: 7)? From Jamal's psychoanalytic perspective, this guilt is fundamentally connected to our ambivalent relation to our first loves and role models, our parents. But he connects this Oedipal question to a broader problematic of how the fact that "pleasure is at the center of the human situation" relates to the fate of contemporary individuals (Kureishi 2008: 51). This is a question that Jamal returns to several times in the novel, ultimately in the context of a meditation on Freud's *Civilization and Its Discontents*, which implies an answer framed in terms of how a whole way of life comes to terms with the superego.

We learn very little of Jamal's work, however, beyond the fact that he does it and has written several popular books that present case studies in a literary form, with titles like *Six Characters in Search of a Cure*. We discover during the story, though, that Jamal is writing a book about Ajita as a young woman that turns into a book about guilt—in other words, the narrative and Jamal's book are probably the same. The implication of this is that the narrative announces itself as a case history that is presented through modernist narration. It is important that the multiple plotlines have the feeling of a textual collage, of the sort of juxtaposition of fragments characteristic of modernism, because one effect of this is to transpose the interpretive dilemma of the protagonist—how meaning forms around desire—on to the reader.

In the technical terms of narratology, *Something to Tell You* might be described as a first-person, consonant psycho-narration (Cohn 1978: 153–60), which means that there is almost nothing in Jamal's reports of the diegetic world that clashes with his subjective perceptions of that world. Jamal at one stage says of his analysands that "even when they are speaking the truth they are lying, and when they speak of someone else they are speaking of themselves" (Kureishi 2008: 57). Jamal himself does no differently. The narrator uses the minor characters as projective screens for the protagonist's fantasies: we should not take at face value that when Jamal talks of another character, it is only this character that he means to refer to. Furthermore, the telling of the tale by Jamal means that the sequence of events—their connections and relations—are significant as indications of what Jamal thinks about these events. They have the force, in other words, of free associations in the sometimes-confusing juxtapositions of the multiple plotlines. Jamal tells us that doing psychoanalysis is like "trying to decode *The Waste Land*" (Kureishi 2008: 191); we might equally say that decoding a fragmented narrative is like doing psychoanalysis.

Probably the best way to understand the novel is to suppose that what the figure of Jamal makes possible is not a *description of what happens* in psychoanalysis, but a *representation of what it feels like*. Kureishi provides us with a point of identification that allows us vividly, if vicariously, to experience the idea of the murder of a father, the notion of a shocking sexual satisfaction, and the guilt that follows in the wake of these events. An excellent illustration of this strategy of literalization is when Ajita, after her first analytic session, says that being psychoanalyzed is like being stirred inside by a giant spoon. Jamal's graphic and visceral representation of the results of his first session, which is something like the objective correlative of Ajita's report, lets the reader get the point:

> I began: hallucinations, panic attacks, inexplicable furies, frantic passions and dreams. It seemed only a minute before he said we had to finish. When I was outside, standing in the street knowing I would return in a couple of days, waves of terror tore through me, my body disassembled, exploding. To prevent myself collapsing, I had to hold onto a lamppost. I began to defecate uncontrollably. Shit ran down my legs and into my shoes. I began to weep; then I vomited—vomiting the past. My shirt was covered in sick. My insides were on the outside; everyone could see me. It wasn't pretty and I had ruined my suit, but something had started. I came to love my analyst more than my father. He gave me more; he saved my life; he made and remade me. (Kureishi 2008: 67)

The story of Jamal's "crime of passion," the suspense and anxiety that the reader vicariously experiences in identification with Jamal, and the release that comes with speaking about this, is what it is like to be freed from guilt after letting it disfigure the whole of one's adult life. The point of the narrative, then, is that by the end of the novel, the reader might understand the answer that the text proposes to its riddle of the hidden link between guilt and pleasure.

The unconscious drama

Against the background of the suspicion that we are being presented with a case history in a literary form, in which the characters might be used as projective screens for the protagonist's unconscious conflicts, one structural feature of the narrative stands out. That is that the novel works through triangular sets of relationships, which establish a stark contrast between past events and present time. First, there is Jamal's relationship to his former wife and girlfriends, including Ajita in the present time of the narration. Secondly, there is Jamal's sister Miriam Khan and his friend Henry Richardson's affair, also in the narrative present, but which I shall neglect for reasons of space. Finally, there is the narrated past, about Ajita and Jamal's romance and how it led up to her father's death about thirty years ago.

The first striking thing about Jamal's past is that it contains Wolf and Valentin, who can be seen as quasi-allegorical characters. Both are from central Europe (Germany, Bulgaria), not as a geographical place but a mysterious "other scene," and the key feature to them is their apparent inseparability and contrasting characteristics—they represent a binary opposition. Wolf is a menacing figure of sudden anger and smoldering resentment, who is associated with violent intensity and the factor of guilt. Represented as a steel spring of great destructive force (Kureishi 2008: 277), he is asexual and aggressive: completely indifferent to the "fuck-stained sheets" of the strip bar he lives in, he is characterized by a "look of ... psychotic... violen[ce]" (Kureishi 2008: 279, 255). In contrast, Valentin is a self-wounded Cupid, who delves into existentialist philosophy and the literature of the absurd in quest of an art of living that might enable him to exist with the longing that desire implies. He is elegant and attractive, and "women, rich and poor, old and young ... wanted to sleep with him" (Kureishi 2008: 292). The pair suggest that the wolf of aggression—or the death drive—and the valentine of romance—or the erotic instincts—are twinned in Jamal's past.

As has already been discussed, Freud proposes that the history of individuals' increasing discontentment with civilization is best grasped as a struggle between the life-giving instinct of desire, or Eros, and the deathly force of aggression, or Thanatos. He proposes that the basic coordinate for this strife between psychological drives is the renunciation of instinctual satisfactions that accompanies civilizational advance, which leads to a secular history of increasing repression. Eros and Thanatos, the life and death drives, are also the coordinates of Jamal's "momentous question of the fate of culture," but this is mediated by his navigation of the Oedipus Complex. We learn little about Jamal's mother and father directly. Jamal's reason for becoming a psychoanalyst, he protests, is a real murder, not a fantasy of incest and parricide. Or is it? The catalyst for the narrative is that "my work [as an analyst] began with a murder—today is the anniversary ... followed by my first love, Ajita, going away forever" (Kureishi 2008: 3). Explaining this, Jamal goes back to the corpse in the cargo idea, but repeats it in association to a new thought—Ajita: "She was my first love, but I was not hers" (Kureishi 2008: 33). His first, and it should be said, practically only love: "You never loved me", says Karen. "You've been in love with Ajita all this time. You can't accept she's gone" (Kureishi 2008: 197).

Reinforcing the impression that the narrated past contains unconscious content, the second striking thing about it is that the death of Ajita's father retains its full psychological impact, although it is apparently completely cut off from present time by a seeming lack of consequences. We might well say that the past event that determines Jamal's present existence is atemporal, by contrast with present events, which have the psychological property that their significance fades with time. Furthermore, the London of Jamal and Ajita's past love is a libidinally enhanced green world strongly contrasted with the harshly realistic mercantile city of the present, suggesting that the "story-within-a-story" of Ajita and Jamal functions as a screen onto which Jamal can project the "other scene" of the unconscious.

The truth is that Ajita is constantly, even insistently, associated with Jamal's mother by three things. First, in the mental geography of Jamal's past, Ajita is located right next to his mother. Jamal introduces Ajita's family home by explaining its significance in terms of an apparent digression on his childhood ideal of masculinity, which makes it easy to miss how Jamal "liked [Ajita's] house and wanted to be there, not only because of her" but also because it reminds him of the shop his maternal grandparents gave "to Mum" (Kureishi 2008: 39). In other words, Ajita occupies the place of Mother. Second, Ajita's representation of femininity is the same as Mother's. Jamal's mother feels intellectually "low-wattage" and hails from a materialistic culture, involving "over-dressed, perfumed [...] ladies" (Kureishi 2008: 46, 40). Even when she acquires a love of modernist art, Mother's femininity is articulated in terms of high heels and lipstick. Similarly, what is sexually attractive about Ajita is that she wears "expensive clothes with jewellery, handbags and high heels. She might have been Indian, but she dressed like an Italian girl, sprinkled with gold" (40); she "was no wild girl, hippy or mod" but appreciates money and struggles with metaphysics (Kureishi 2008: 40). In her representation of femininity, in short, Ajita is the same sort of woman that Mother was. Finally, Ajita is in the place of Mother qua sexual partner. But unlike the standard post-Oedipal topic of the substitution of another woman for the lost maternal love, Ajita takes on—at least in Jamal's recollections—the aura of that lost love itself. Ajita is Jamal's first and only true love, whom he cannot accept he has lost (Kureishi 2008: 197). "She'd told me she loved me," Jamal reports, "but, in the end, she didn't want me" because in between them falls the shadow of the father of Ajita (who is, shockingly, her lover). Importantly, at one point in the narration, Ajita's desertion of Jamal for a "married man" is immediately associated by Jamal with leaving his mother (Kureishi 2008: 60). Even more significantly, Jamal associates Ajita with a crime of passion that involves not just parricide but also excessive sexuality, an absolute pleasure gained through a criminal transgression. This decisively positions Ajita—in Jamal's recollections—as a maternal figure within the Oedipal triangle.

Killing the father

If this is a plausible interpretation so far, then the clear implication is that the death of Ajita's father has for Jamal the psychological significance of murdering his own father, thus completing the Oedipal tableau. And there is every reason to believe that this is the case, for the major characteristic of Ajita's father is that he is the rapist of the woman who stands in for Jamal's mother. But it's a curious rape, because after Ajita confesses her terrible secret that "sometimes, after midnight, my father comes into my room and makes love to me" (Kureishi 2008: 116), she immediately adds that "there's no force" (Kureishi 2008: 118). This dreadful scene makes Jamal want "to masturbate, to rid [him]self of the image" of the father's "large penis" penetrating Ajita (Kureishi 2008: 119). In Jamal's chain of associations, the father's large penis is linked to limitless enjoyment, the excess of pleasure that is connected to absolute transgression. The figure of the paternal ogre is recognizable from Freud's case studies as the Oedipal rival of the castration threat. Like the father of the primal horde, who Freud thought recurred psychologically in every infant's life, this father is a terrible figure whose phallic endowment makes possible an abominable satisfaction.

For Jamal, the image of the paternal seduction of Ajita has the force of a primal scene of parental copulation. The fantasy scene of him entering her door echoes in Jamal's mind (Kureishi 2008: 116–19). Jamal's response is to claim Ajita from her "infidelity" to Jamal by being the man for her, which involves brandishing a knife at the paternal rapist. The scene of the murder of Ajita's father closes with "the dead man's words echoing in my ears: 'What do you want of me?'" (Kureishi 2008: 75). Jamal indicates his answer to this pretty clearly by depositing the knife with his own mother. But the deposit—the fantasy of incest and parricide—fails: the father remains a ghost in Jamal's life.

There are, however, two more fathers in Jamal's past, and the best way to understand this is to suppose that Jamal (or more plausibly, Kureishi) has done his psychoanalytic homework. Freud's conception of the resolution of the Oedipus Complex involves the infant's shifting from an incestuous and parricidal wish to its repression, through identification with a paternal ideal and adoption of a substitute love object (modeled on some aspect of the parent of the opposite sex) (e.g., "New Introductory Lectures on Psycho-Analysis", Freud 1933: 80). The genesis of the superego, then, involves the repression of the "paternal rapist" of Oedipal rivalry and its replacement with an image of the rational father of the social ideal. Freud's point, however, is that the parricidal wish is *repressed*, not *eliminated*, so that the vanishing afterimage of the dead (i.e., murdered) father is crucial to the establishment of the pacifying moral ideal. The superego forms when the ambivalent relation to the paternal imago is introjected as an identification; thus it fuses love for the father with aggression turned inward against the individual's own ego, in punishment for the hidden desire to murder the bearer of the ideal.

In *Seminar IV*, Lacan (1994) reworks this typology by introducing a distinction between three different aspects or roles of the father in the Oedipal drama. The Lacanian distinction between the three registers, the Imaginary, the Symbolic, and the Real, is probably familiar. The Imaginary is the register of mirror images, the ego, and social ideals. The Symbolic is the register of the sociocultural network of norms transmitted through language in which the social ideals float. The Real is the register of the erotic and aggressive drives that underlies our relation to language and culture. In the context of the role of the father in the Oedipal crisis, Lacan proposes to use these three registers to differentiate between the Real father of the primal scene and Oedipal rivalry, on the one hand, and the Imaginary father of the paternal imago that resolves the Oedipal crisis through identification with an ideal (Lacan 1994: 59–75, 215–30). According to Lacan, between these two intervenes the Symbolic father, Freud's vanishing, dead father of post-Oedipal guilt. The Symbolic father, the father of cultural norms and moral rules, in other words, is the key to the resolution of the Oedipus Complex and is quite different from the Real father of transgressive enjoyment, and from the Imaginary ideal that succeeds the resolution of the Oedipus Complex.

Now, Jamal's father is an idealized figure possessing phallic intellectual attributes. Even father's prostitutes are "amazing beauties with brains" (Kureishi 2008: 45). But he is not a representative of the paternal law: "Dad rarely gave us instructions or prohibitions" (Kureishi 2008: 48). Father is a figure of "independence, authority and integrity" (Kureishi 2008: 142), whose opinion of Jamal is that he has turned out a "bloody fool" (Kureishi 2008: 49) and a "bum," who is "fucking useless lazy stupid" (Kureishi 2008: 145). But, significantly, the paternal library is an ideal of cultivation through education rather than a repository of words, because, in a marvelous image, father's books are all unopened and worm-eaten.

So far there is still one father missing from Jamal's familial constellation as outlined so far—the dead, Symbolic father. Instead, what we have had is the Real father with no name and the ideal father with no library. We could even say that Jamal's inability to love is the correlate of his disturbed relation to what Lacan calls the Symbolic Order—the sociocultural network of norms and ideals articulated in language that the Symbolic father introduces the child to.

For Jamal, the role of the Symbolic father is performed by his first psychoanalyst, Tahir Hussein. Jamal falls in love with Hussein and testifies that he loves him more than he loved his own father (Kureishi 2008: 69). It is Hussein who opens up the world of universal culture to Jamal Khan—"Proust, Marx, Emerson, Keats, Dostoyevsky, Whitman and Blake" (Kureishi 2008: 69). Indeed, psychoanalysis, via the books *with* contents that Jamal borrows from Hussein, is a passport to the world of secular culture:

> He said that analysis was part of literary culture, but that literature was bigger than psychoanalysis, and swallowed it as a whale devoured a minnow. What great artist hadn't been aware of the unconscious, which was not discovered by Freud but only mapped by him? (Kureishi 2008: 69)

As a consequence, Jamal's life contains the library of which his ideal father's dust jackets are merely the titles.

It is this symbolic identification with the figure of the analyst as replacement paternal name that makes possible Jamal's adoption of a social ideal, that of the analyst as cultural hero. For Jamal, psychoanalysis is not a clinical technique and body of knowledge. Rather, it is an art of living deeply respondent to the ultimate questions of life and death, love and hate, God and humanity. When, as a student, Ajita discusses with Jamal the question of philosophy, she speaks words that keep "returning to me over and over, the devil's whisper": "Isn't it about the wisdom of living, and about what is right and wrong?" (Kureishi 2008: 51). Jamal only encounters a discourse that can provide an art of living when he enters analysis.

Civilization and its discontents

In this reading, then, the novel has a double brief for psychoanalysis. Although the novel indicates some implications of this in relation to the problematics of race and radical politics, I want to focus finally on Islam as the main competitor to psychoanalysis in the narrative, and the most important collective allegiance whose motivational basis is interrogated by the novel.

On the one hand, psychoanalysis is a way of understanding the hidden connection between pleasure and guilt, and the paradoxical link between values and aggression, that freights individual and collective life with problems. Kureishi's novels have always explored the complexity of sociologically defined material interests, such as class, race, and gender, through characters who are highly individuated, often by means of underlying motivations and hidden desires best grasped through psychoanalysis. That is to say, Kureishi's interest in Freud and Lacan is reflected in his development of characters who exhibit considerable psychological depth, so that the social conditions of identity formation are only the most superficial determinations of their represented personality structures. Indeed, these characters' relation to forms of social identity is labile, but often characterized by a yearning for collective belonging that is mediated by their own response to parental ideals. One way to understand this is to suppose that, with Kureishi, we have probably always been on the terrain of Freud's meditations on group psychology, according to which the social component of individual identity partly depends on identification with those group ideals that are personified by leader figures (Freud 1921: 100, 116). This is particularly the case where lack of ego maturity leads individuals to supplement their own self-identity with group-based identifications that buttress an insufficiently worked through relation to parental authority, that is, a lack of resolution of the Oedipus Complex. From the Freudian perspective, individuals act upon material interests, the sociological conditions of social identity, in ways consistent with the social and political values that they hold, and these are determined by persons' relationships to authority figures and the ideals that they represent. Identifications, then, especially those with parental authority and group ideals, intervene between social locations and individual agency. Consistent with this view of how socialization affects personality, Kureishi appears to be most interested in characters whose conflicted unconscious desires, located in unresolved relations to authority figures, lead them to have highly idiosyncratic responses to the nexus of interests and ideals in the social field. Simply stated, his characters are anything but cookie-cutter placemarkers for social issues, pressed out of the templates of class, race, and gender.

The potential for unconscious motivations to play out in the transition from material interests to political values is reflected in many of the characters in *The Black Album*. *Something to Tell You* is also overshadowed by the emergence of religion as a new fault line in British society, which, although it runs parallel to race, has the potential to generate new political allegiances that mobilize hidden resources of anxiety and aggression. The novel postulates that Islamic identification is a defensive response to the truly irrational aggression of the invasion of Iraq and the War on Terror. Ajita's search for a social identity through collective belonging is a response to social suffering, that is, to the way that racial discrimination annuls class privilege and then becomes rearticulated as religious affiliation. Nonetheless, in formulating this particular reaction, as opposed to any other, Ajita compromises between her need for a positive assertion of collective belonging and her unconscious desire for self-punishment. Stricken individuals, such as Ajita, supplement their own problematic self-identity through forms of identification that turn aggression inward as well as outward.

On the other hand, psychoanalysis is represented as a path of wisdom, perhaps even a way of life, with the potential to alter dramatically individuals' relationships to both sexuality and culture. As the novel makes explicit toward the end, Jamal's way of posing the question of how one can kill a dead father without incurring intolerable guilt stands within the matrix of Freud's *Civilization and Its Discontents*. In this bleak text, the balance seems to tip toward Thanatos, as the renunciation of sexual pleasure is not counter-balanced by an equal renunciation of aggressive outlets, despite highly formal civility. This is because aggression finds an outlet in the hypertrophy of the superego, as that "pure culture of the death instinct" necessary to enforce growing repression, within an increasingly unhappy civilization (Freud 1930: 53).

What is perhaps less well known is that in posing the momentous question of the fate of civilization—life or death—as a question of the superego, Freud engages in a major revision of his theory of religion. In *The Future of an Illusion*, Freud famously claimed that religious belief was the continuation of an "infantile prototype," arising from narcissistic investment of the Ego Ideal with an aggressive infantile wish for complete protection from a hostile world (Freud 1927–31: 17). But in *Civilization and Its Discontents*, Freud enlarges on the speculations of *Totem and Taboo* (1913–14) and *Moses and Monotheism* (1937–39): religion arises through guilt, as the fantasy of parricide followed by identification with the paternal ideal involves guilt about the dead father (Freud 1930: 100; 133–4; 141, n. 1). Religion is an ally of the civilizational process, but only because it invests the superego with extended punitive powers by placing the pressure of guilt beyond rational scrutiny. Religion is in league with death, deeply hostile to life. The only alternative to an increasingly neurotic and anxious society is to lessen somehow the pressure of the superego through a return to the erotic wellsprings of human existence.

Certainly, it is significant that the two characters who get involved with religion are Wolf—that bearer of the death drive, who finds God in jail (Kureishi 2008: 256)—and Ajita in the present of Jamal's story. Ajita is still angry that she could not kill her father. But we might suspect that this is a projection of guilt for having wanted to, because her sexuality has become connected with aggression turned inward, in the form of masochism. Ajita's turn to Islam, including the burqa, is linked to the sadistic sexuality she enjoys and the hidden guilt she suffers. Her central response to Islamophobia in British society is self-imposed isolation, in a lonely gesture that begins in solidarity and ends in paranoia. Wolf's return in the lives of both Ajita and Jamal is a form of self-punishment that is ended only by their turn from religion to psychoanalysis.

For Jamal, psychoanalysis seems to represent an art of living that embraces the life force—a modern Epicureanism. He approvingly quotes Schopenhauer to the effect that "sexual passion is the most perfect manifestation of the will to live" (Kureishi 2008: 73), suggesting that psychoanalysis releases the individual from the deathly grip of ascetic ideals. To be precise, psychoanalysis represents an alternative set of ideals—not to Western culture, which seems to lack them, but to religious fundamentalism. This happens, the novel proposes, under conditions where the Symbolic father is *in general* absent, that is, because of the decline of symbolic authority since the 1960s. The implication is that an entire generation lacks the symbolic resources for a satisfactory resolution of their Oedipal problems, something that can only reinforce a sense of *anomie* and the desire for group belonging.

Freud's tentative solution at the end of *Civilization and Its Discontents*, by contrast, was not psychoanalysis, but sublimation. According to Freud in that work, as well as his *New Introductory Lectures* (1933) from about the same time, there is a significant difference between identification with authority (involving idealization with repression) and sublimation in art and culture (involving idealization without repression). Both involve a desexualization of the erotic drives, but in identification this is accomplished by repression of the drive object (that is, of the idea of the object of satisfaction), whereas in sublimation this is achieved by an inhibition of the aim and an alteration of the object of the drive. Art and culture, then, allow a sustained, partial satisfaction of the sexual drives (art is shameless, as Adorno says), whereas identification with authority involves preventing that satisfaction. And if religion is a primary form of desexualization through idealization, it has to be said that identification with the analyst as a replacement Symbolic father is another (Adorno and Horkheimer 2002 [1947]: 111). Jamal has *converted* to psychoanalysis just as Ajita converts to Islam (and back). Perhaps, in the end, then, it is Henry who has the last word on the civilizational politics of the novel: "'Against death and authoritarianism, there is only one thing,' he said once. 'Love?' I suggested. 'Culture …' he said" (Kureishi 2008: 55).

Acknowledgments: This article is a substantially modified version of a paper originally published in conference proceedings as "The Other Kureishi," in Nurten Birlek, ed., *Hanif Kureishi and His Work* (Ankara: METU Press in association with the British Institute: 17–32).

8

The Last Word on Hanif Kureishi

Susie Thomas

Chapter Summary: This chapter rereads Hanif Kureishi's fiction in the light of his most recent novel, *The Last Word* (2014), in order to analyze how his preoccupation with the role of the writer in society and the use of storytelling in the creation of identity has developed. I argue that there has been a conspicuous absence in Kureishi criticism: a failure to analyze his words and sentences in terms of style as well as content. The tendency to focus on content attests to the fact that his work speaks about urgent matters: racism, new British identities, family, sexuality, and the West's complicity in the rise of Islamism. However, since Kureishi is not a simple realist whose particular use of words can be taken for granted, an analysis of his style is overdue. This chapter identifies the most distinctive feature of Kureishi's fictional prose— his self-subverting sentences, in which the end disrupts the beginning—and contrasts this with the more direct prose of his essays. It links these self-subverting sentences with the trope of disguise in his fiction, the dubious reliability of his narrators and the metafictional elements of his earlier novels.

Keywords: Style, self-subverting sentences, metafiction, disguise, writer-as-Great-Man, male/female hierarchy

"The best words and good sentences, mattered" (Kureishi 2014: 37). This claim occurs in Hanif Kureishi's new novel *The Last Word* (2014), though its precise provenance within the fiction is unclear because the novel's third-person narrative uses free indirect discourse that sometimes blurs the attribution of particular utterances to a specific character or narrator. But the claim can serve to highlight a conspicuous absence in Kureishi criticism: a failure to analyze his words and sentences in terms of style as well as content. Sukhdev Sandhu has stated that "Kureishi is not a prose writer of any distinction" and, judging by the silence on the subject of his sentences, the critical consensus seems to be that he is important mainly for *what* he says (Sandhu 2000). The almost exclusive focus of Kureishi critics on content attests to the fact that his work speaks about urgent matters: racism, new British identities, family, sexuality, and the West's complicity in the rise of Islamism. Although content and style are inseparable, in practice most academics tend to treat his style as an optional accessory and to regard him as a simple realist whose particular use of words can be taken for granted. However, an analysis of Kureishi's prose is overdue and reading his fiction through the lens of his most recent novel, *The Last Word*, reveals that storytelling—whose stories count and how they are told—has always been a central preoccupation. This chapter identifies the most distinctive feature of Kureishi's fictional prose—his self-subverting sentences, in which the end disrupts the beginning—and contrasts this with the more direct prose of his essays. It links these self-subverting sentences with the trope of disguise in his fiction, the dubious reliability of his narrators, and the metafictional elements of his earlier novels. The chapter concludes with an analysis of how the celebration of the power of the pen in *The Last Word* is subverted by its own ironic treatment of the writer-as-Great-Man, an irony that also challenges the male/female hierarchy it ostensibly asserts.

Unlike more obviously experimental contemporary fiction, Kureishi's novels are not self-conscious. They tend to have linear structures. As Bart Moore-Gilbert notes, "Prolepsis and analepsis are extremely rare in comparison with Rushdie's work" (Moore-Gilbert 2012: 109). Although critics have discussed *The Buddha of Suburbia* (1990) and *The Black Album* (1995) as *Bildungsromane*, strikingly little attention has been paid to narrative voice (for a summary of the critical discussion of *The Buddha of Suburbia* as a *Bildungsroman*, see Thomas 2005: 86–8). The exception is Sukhdev Sandhu who has praised Kureishi's "voice" as talismanic for young Asians: "We had previously been mocked for our deference and timidity. Kureishi's language was a revelation. It was neither meek nor subservient. It wasn't fake posh. Instead, it was playful and casually knowing" (Sandhu 2000). But Sandhu is more interested in Asian cool than explaining how a novelist's language can be both "a revelation" and lack "any distinction." This silence about style is in complete contrast to the critical commentary that the work of Martin Amis, Ian McEwan, Salman Rushdie, and Jeanette Winterson has generated, which tends to focus in a variety of ways on style. The fatwa changed everything for Rushdie, but, until 1989, magical realism vied with postcolonialism for the attention of academics.

While Kureishi receives considerable academic attention, it is mainly for those works with a sociological significance or for those that can serve as an illustration of Homi Bhabha's theory of cultural hybridity. Interestingly, Karim in *The Buddha of Suburbia* was at first hailed as "the herald of hybridity" (Schoene 1998), but more recent studies argue that Kureishi invites "a reassessment of cultural hybridity as an ideal" (Su 2011: 84). Meanwhile, a new crop of readings on suburbia advance wildly different theses: Susan Brook's lively and provocative essay suggests that it is "a camp and queer space" in which the emphasis on public display "provides Karim with strategies to reshape himself" in London and New York (Brook 2005: 218). In contrast, Kuchta (2010) argues that although Karim "eludes racial essentialism," he can never escape being suburban because it is "in the blood and not on the skin" (Kureishi 1990: 34); moreover this suburban stability is what saves him "from creating a free-floating identity" (Kuchta 2010: 209). The capacity of this novel to generate so many different interpretations makes it, in Frank Kermode's influential definition, a classic (1983[1975]: 140). Nonetheless, it is surprising that the source of this rich ambiguity—the prose—remains unexplored. Kureishi's most recent novel, *The Last Word*, nudges us in the right direction.

Prose style, and the connection between aesthetics and politics, is a central preoccupation in *The Last Word*. The novel begins with Harry Johnson, an upper-class young Englishman, hoping to launch his career by writing the biography of "the distinguished writer, Indian-born Mamoon Azam, a novelist, essayist and playwright" whom Harry had admired since he was "a teenage book fiend" for whom writers were "gods, heroes, rock stars" (Kureishi 2014: 2). Harry's editor Rob explains that writing a biography of a living writer has advantages (you can get answers from the horse's mouth) and disadvantages; the latter tend to dominate in *The Last Word* since one of Mamoon's few remaining pleasures is making sensitive people cry. As the young biographer moves in with Mamoon and his wife Liana, he becomes involved in a terrifying Oedipal triangle: the old man wants to thrash Harry at tennis, as well as literature, while stealing Harry's girlfriend. Meanwhile, Liana wants Harry to seduce her while he turns her husband into a best-selling "brand" with a glossy biography (Kureishi 2014: 29). In the course of his research, Harry reads Mamoon's first wife's diaries ("the miseries") and flies to America to interview the cruelly discarded mistress: he learns "that a writer is loved by strangers and hated by his family," usually for very good reasons (Kureishi 2014: 92).

Metafictionally, *The Last Word* is about a controversial figure in British literature. Like V. S. Naipaul, Mamoon has written family novels set in the colonies, extended essays on Empire, and critiques of Islamism. Mamoon is a writer from "the third world" whom conservative critics can enjoy: down on Muslims and more than ready to identify with tweedy Englishmen. But, perhaps surprisingly, the bogeyman of lefty postcolonialists emerges as the hero of *The Last Word*, or almost. The reader's sympathy with Mamoon fluctuates throughout the novel in a way that makes it difficult to judge him or come to conclusions. This radical uncertainty, which is a distinctive feature of Kureishi's fictional aesthetic, is manifest at the level of the sentence:

> For most of his adult life, Mamoon was his own kind of radical, going to some trouble to mock and invert political correctness, rebelling against the fashionable contrarians of his day, hippies, feminists, anti-racists, revolutionaries, anyone decent, kind or on the side of equality or diversity. (Kureishi 2014: 34)

As so often in Kureishi, the reader is likely to be nodding in approval at the beginning of this sentence and to be thoroughly discombobulated by the end. It embodies, in miniature, the novel's ambivalence about both of its major themes: the relationship between the writer and the man, and between ideology and literature. Does being a great novelist entitle anyone to behave badly? Is the best writing on the side of equality, and how do we evaluate literature that is misogynistic or racist? At first, the sentence seems to laud Mamoon for being "his own kind of radical" rather than being the timid adherent of what Orwell called "smelly little orthodoxies" (Orwell 2000[1939]: 78). The point at which the sentence turns from approbation to condemnation will probably depend on the politics of the reader: some may balk at Mamoon's subversion of political correctness, while for others the stumbling block will be his mockery of feminism and antiracism. Most readers will have decisively turned against Mamoon once he turns against anyone "decent and kind." Although apparently simple, the Mamoon sentence asks important questions about literature while wittily (or evasively, depending on the reader) skirting the need to provide answers. It demonstrates a distinctive feature of Kureishi's style, which could be described as the apparently artless turn from certainty to doubt.

The incipit of *The Buddha of Suburbia* provides a brilliant example of this turn: "My name is Karim Amir and I am an Englishman born and bred, almost" (Kureishi 1990: 3). In 1990 this sentence effected something of a sea-change in the culture and politics of national identity as two apparent opposites (Indian name and English breeding) were casually connected with a simple conjunction. It ushered in a host of hybrid coming-of-age novels from Zadie Smith's *White Teeth* (2000) to Robin Yassin-Kassab's *The Road to Damascus* (2008). But the sentence contains a further twist, as the adverb "almost," strategically placed as the last word, subverts the apparently reassuring self-identification of the previous clause. The meaning of this "almost" is the major preoccupation of the novel. The opening might recall another self-naming narrator, Philip Pirrup, in *Great Expectations,* who "called [him]self Pip, and came to be called Pip" (Dickens 1861). Dickens's narrator has to locate himself in terms of class while Kureishi's narrator has both class and race to contend with. As Karim doesn't quite say: "Fuck you Charles Dickens. Something's changed" (Kureishi 1990: 63). Dickens employs chiasmus while Kureishi deploys the comma but the apparently naïve openings of both novels launch the reader on epic journeys.

The apparent artlessness of Kureishi's style connects to a major trope in his novels: disguise. Just as the conventions of realism disguise the radical ambiguity of his use of language, so the characters in his novels hide behind masks. Karim constantly disguises how he feels ("So the more eager I was the less eager I seemed" (Kureishi 1990: 6)) and alters his appearance. It seems as if everyone is dressing up in *The Buddha of Suburbia*, but whether it is Haroon sneaking out of the house with a raincoat over his pajamas, Shahid cross-dressing in *The Black Album*, Adam's reincarnation in *The Body* (2002), or Ajita adopting the burqa in *Something to Tell You* (2008), the work of self-fashioning is never done. Karim's sense of certainty that all will be well once he gets out of Bromley provides the hinge between the two parts of the novel: "The Suburbs" and "The City." In a sentence that appears to be about the suburban boy's breathless anticipation of London's counter-cultural cornucopia, Kureishi disguises Karim's painful sense of exposure:

> There were kids dressed in velvet cloaks who lived free lives; there were thousands of black people everywhere, so I wouldn't feel exposed; there were bookshops with racks of magazines printed without capital letters or the bourgeois disturbance of full stops; there were shops selling all the records you could desire; there were parties where girls and boys you didn't know took you upstairs and fucked you; there were all the drugs you could use. (Kureishi 1990: 121)

As so often in Kureishi's work, the subversive clause ("so I wouldn't feel exposed") is cloaked in a hip veneer of sex and drugs and rock 'n' roll. Once Karim gets to "The City," he is faced with a dizzying set of possibilities but also humiliations disguised as opportunity (e.g., when he is smeared in brown make-up to play Mowgli). The "velvet cloak" sentence suggests that it is because Kureishi's fiction employs the realist conventions of the bourgeois novel that critics have been misled into dismissing his style as unimportant.

If uncertainty is embodied at the level of the sentence, ambiguity is deepened by Kureishi's use of point of view. The peril of ignoring focalization emerges clearly in the contradictions in Wendy O'Shea-Meddour's 2008 article, "The Politics of Imagining the Other in Hanif Kureishi's *The Buddha of Suburbia*." She argues that critics have neglected the portrayal of "racial violence" because of Karim's "disinterest" [sic], mistakenly taking their cue from him when he says: "Everything was going wrong, but I didn't want to hear about it" (Kureishi 1990: 171). As O'Shea-Meddour rightly says, "The narrator's position is not the one to follow" here (O'Shea-Meddour 2008: 48). She goes on to look at the neglected significance of Anwar's embrace of "fundamentalism" as a response to racism. Commenting on Karim's lack of sympathy with Muslim men, O'Shea-Meddour observes: "In the narrator's worldview, Islam means patriarchal authority and the suppression of women. It also means absolute certainty" (O'Shea-Meddour 2008: 49). But on this occasion Karim apparently speaks for the author: "For those familiar with Kureishi's work, this is a warning sign" (O'Shea-Meddour 2008: 50; for a different interpretation of what Islam means in Kureishi's work see Thomas 2009). The unexamined contradictions in O'Shea Meddour's argument demonstrate that Kureishi's narrators cannot be taken for granted. We need to ask when we should trust them, if ever.

Kureishi's four major novels—*The Buddha of Suburbia*, *The Black Album*, *Something to Tell You,* and *The Last Word*—employ first- or third-person narrators of varying degrees of unreliability to explore the possibilities and limitations of writing the self and society. There is, however, a political and aesthetic distinction between the essays and the fiction. Kureishi's political purpose is evident in his essays, which aim to nudge society into a particular direction and to be clear "like a window pane" stylistically. But his novels are more like stained glass: richly colored and sometimes opaque. Kureishi employs a different, and distinctive, aesthetic for each genre, which becomes clear if we contrast the narrative voice of two key texts.

"The Rainbow Sign" and *The Buddha of Suburbia* originate in an autobiographical wound made explicit in the essay: "I reckoned that at least once every day since I was five years old I had been racially abused" (Kureishi 2002[1986]: 29). Kureishi goes on to explain that this experience is what made him want to be a writer:

> The pain of that period in my life, in the mid-1960s, is with me still. And when I originally wrote this piece I put it in the third person: Hanif saw this ... , because of the difficulty of directly addressing myself to what I felt then. (Kureishi 2002[1986]: 53)

Writing was a way of refusing to be defined by other people's hatred (53). Moreover, in "The Rainbow Sign" Kureishi makes it clear that this wound is not just his own: "A society that is racist ... is reduced and degraded" and cannot lay claim to being either "humane" or "democratic" (Kureishi 2002[1986]: 49, 56). So for Kureishi the personal led directly to the political and historical. The essay is unequivocal about what needs to be done: it is "the white British" who will have to change (Kureishi 2002[1986]: 55). Stylistically, it is direct, although this is found out through indirection (using "me as Hanif" as a means to short-circuit shame). In contrast, Kureishi's distinctive fictional aesthetic emerges in the "mask" he adopted to write *The Buddha of Suburbia*. Unlike Jamila, who has "a PhD in physical retribution," Karim practically thanks people when they spit at him (Kureishi 1990: 53). He doesn't know what "black" (as a political definition) means or why he is ashamed of his Indian ancestry. He is so self-hating and unaware that when he takes Changez to a Millwall football match, he forces him to "wear a bobble-hat over his face in case the lads saw he was a Paki and imagined I was one too" (Kureishi 1990: 98). Karim is a narrator in hiding from the truths the author of "The Rainbow Sign" knows all too well.

It is unclear why there has been so little critical commentary on Karim's naïve narration and the difference that the use of the first and third person makes in *The Buddha of Suburbia* and *The Black Album*. Or why so few critics have asked whether Jamal, the narrator of *Something to Tell You*, is really so much older and wiser than Karim that we can trust him to be a reliable guide to either his own emotions or the world around him. One critic who has questioned this is Geoff Boucher whose analysis of the figure of the psychoanalyst as cultural hero in *Something to Tell You* provides the key insight that we cannot take the narrator's words at face value, any more than Jamal can take the words of his analysands for granted. Boucher's reading of *Something to Tell You* is alive to the narrator's evasions and projections, while never falling into the trap of psychoanalyzing its author (see Chapter 7 of this volume).

Kureishi's manipulation of point of view in *The Last Word* takes a surprising turn. As in *The Black Album*, he employs a third-person narrative that is limited to the protagonist but, unlike Shahid, Harry is an Englishman to the manor born. Mamoon's resemblance to Naipaul has given rise to the speculation that Harry is based on Naipaul's biographer, Patrick French, but a more interesting question is whether Harry is the hero of *The Last Word* (in the way that Shahid is the hero of his novel) or whether that role belongs to Mamoon. Harry both admires and despises Mamoon, but Harry himself is a morally ambiguous character: the reader's sympathies are likely to be divided to the very end. Indeed, the novel is a war of stories.

In *The Last Word*, Mamoon's wife Liana thinks that the privileged Harry cannot understand what it was like for a lonely immigrant such as Mamoon to try to make his way in literary London in the 1950s: "He showed people his stories and they literally said to him 'Why would you think that anyone could be interested in these bloody Indians?'" (Kureishi 2014: 56). Mamoon, like Naipaul's Ralph Singh in *The Mimic Men* (1967), was the subaltern whose story didn't count until he made it count with his novels. Harry reveres Mamoon because "for a time he did an essential thing, bringing the new into culture, speaking from where no one had spoken" (Kureishi 2014: 151). But in the course of his research Harry comes to suspect that Mamoon's story was told at the expense of his first wife Peggy and his mistress Marion.

In *The Last Word*, the pen is an instrument of revenge against injustice and a form of self-justification. With the exception of Alice, all the characters are trying to have the last word. Marion, the woman who gave up everything to be with Mamoon only to be abandoned by him, is writing a memoir in which she dishes the dirt about his sexual perversions and cruelty. The prize-winning author disparages Marion's version of events as a "balloon of unbound fantasies" without showing any awareness that she is now the subaltern who is determined to ensure that she is not written out of the record (Kureishi 2014: 165). Mamoon refuses to read his first wife's diaries and considers Ted Hughes did the right thing with Sylvia's: "push them in the oven after the woman's head" (Kureishi 2014: 149).

The battle of the books becomes farcical when Liana insists on setting up her stall next to the Great Man so that she can "pen" a self-help book about a feisty middle-aged woman bagging her genius. Meanwhile, and unknown to Harry, Mamoon is writing a novel that contains a portrait of a young man who bears a remarkable, if unflattering, resemblance to his biographer.

In Kureishi's work, writers tend to be heroes and, at the same time, exploiters, forgers, and thieves. Karim enters Changez "by the back door" to create the role of Tariq despite promising that he won't (Kureishi 1990: 185); Shahid undertakes to type up Riaz's poetry but rewrites the devotional verse as erotica, while Jamal rips off Ajita's story for one of his case histories. In *The Last Word*, Harry forces Alice to trick Mamoon into a confession of his sexual misdemeanors, which she records on her phone. He is horrified to discover that "his desire for the truth had made him a criminal" (Kureishi 2014: 195). Paradoxically, Kureishi seems to want to extol the act of writing as central to civilization while discrediting the writer as a seedy chancer.

With a biographer and a novelist at the core, clearly *The Last Word* is about literature. But the earlier novels are also metafictional because they are centrally concerned with reading and writing as a means to shape coherent narratives, even if the self and the past they construct are always labile. In *The Buddha of Suburbia*, everyone is reading as if for life: Changez ditches Conan Doyle (the classic that he got for his dowry) and takes up Harold Robbins, which leads him to a relationship with Shinko, the prostitute Jamila decides is exploiting him. Eva tells Karim that Kerouac is "just typing" and threatens to test him on the second-hand copy of *Candide* that she thrusts into his hand: her reading lists "unfold[ed] the world" for him (Kureishi 1990: 87). Jamila reads Angela Davis on the recommendation of Miss Cutmore before complaining that Miss Cutmore is trying to colonize her. Eleanor keeps a stack of Jean Rhys by her bed to cheer herself up; Haroon's transformation from civil servant into buddha of suburbia can be traced back to the books on Eastern mysticism he bought in Cecil Court. Even Charlie is educated by New York women who shower him with South American novels.

Reading leads to writing and in *The Buddha of Suburbia,* storytelling is at a premium. Jamila demands stories of sexual humiliation: "the worse the better, ... mucky and semen-stained" (Kureishi 1990: 54). O'Shea Meddour even suggests that Jamila's "editorial demands structure the narrative" (O'Shea Meddour 2008: 35). This is an entertaining possibility, but not one that is borne out by a close reading of the text. Karim is eager to satisfy Jamila with "spot-on stories ... like drinks for the thirsty" so long as they don't concern his own embarrassments and failures. He is still too keen to impress her for that: "I told her nothing about Great Danes and me" (Kureishi 1990: 54). Since Karim's experience of sexual humiliation is essential to the narrative, Jamila cannot be the shaper of the tale. In fact, Jamila is in thrall to Changez's stories: he "told her tales of run-away wives, too-small dowries, adultery among the rich of Bombay (which took many evenings) and, most delicious, political corruption" (Kureishi 1990: 98). Like Scheherazade, he spins these tales out and keeps Jamila waiting for the next installment of his "wild soap opera" (Kureishi 1990: 98). He is not the gum-chewing fool that Karim takes him for: Changez knows that his tales of India, the mother country Jamila has never known, are his (only) strong suit and mean that his wife will take him with her when she moves to the commune.

The war of stories continues when Shadwell, the director of *The Jungle Book*, who has cast Karim for "authenticity," wants his Mowgli to tell him "stories of aunties and elephants" (Kureishi 1990: 141; see also Stein 2004:108–42). But Karim is a disappointment; he can't speak Urdu and he hasn't been to India. When Karim meets Eleanor, the upper-class actress with whom he falls in love, he thinks that her stories are more important than his: "Where I could have been telling Eleanor about the time I got fucked by Hairy Back's Great Dane, it was her stories that had primacy, her stories that connected to a whole established world" (Kureishi 1990: 178). Dominic Head, one of the few critics to examine the novel's "narrative procedures," points out that "this is a crucial moment of self-reflexiveness that invites the reader's objection" because the Hairy Back episode is of central importance (Head 2002: 221). Moreover, the most significant event in Eleanor's life, the suicide of her black lover Gene, "is a story she finds too painful to tell" (Head 2002: 221). At the point where Karim decides to break from Eleanor, Gene's story becomes part of his own: "We became part of England and yet proudly stood outside it" (quoted in Head 2002: 221). Moreover, it is when Karim develops the role of Tariq for Pyke's play that he begins to "locate" himself in England by creating his own "Indian past" (Kureishi 1990: 213). It is through the appropriation of others' stories, and the gradual conviction that his own story does count, that Karim becomes the narrator who writes the novel we have just read.

The Black Album continues Kureishi's exploration of fiction as a means to create identity. It is a book of mourning, haunted by the father's ghost, but it is also Shahid's attempt to tell the story that his mother could not bear to hear. When she reads the teenager's fictionalized version of being racially abused, "Paki Wog Fuck Off Home," she asks: "Who would want to read this? People don't want this hate in their lives" (Kureishi 1995: 72–3). (Hanif Kureishi's first unpublished novel was called "Run Hard Black Man.") In the novel the mother shuts down the conversation with her son because "what she knew was too much for her," as Kureishi's own mother had done (Kureishi 1995: 73; for more on Kureishi's mother see Thomas 2013: 209). The central conflict in *The Black Album* turns on which books, if any, should be held sacred and extends the debate about the canon that began in *The Buddha of Suburbia* with Jamila and Karim rejecting "that 'old, dull, white stuff'" (Kureishi 1990: 95). Deedee, the lecturer at Shahid's rundown North London college has constructed a syllabus to suit her multicultural urban students, but Shahid soon resents the idea that Prince was "more him" than Turgenyev and embarks on the "migraine reads" (Kureishi 1995: 135). The unnamed intertext is by another father figure of postcolonial British literature, Salman Rushdie, and borrowing a technique from *The Satanic Verses*, Shahid finds his voice when he rewrites Riaz's Islamic poetry. It is when Riaz and his followers decide to burn the blasphemous book that Shahid takes sides definitively: literature is sacred and he cannot understand how others could "confine themselves to one system or creed" (Kureishi 1995: 274). The problem with *The Black Album* is that, ultimately, it is unequivocal about books and too certain about the value of uncertainty.

Kureishi's preoccupation with the metafictional is equally central to *Something to Tell You*. It is only when Jamal discovers that the books in his father's library are unread and worm-eaten that the father is exposed as a fraud, and Jamal's life is transformed when his new father figure, the psychoanalyst Tahir Hussein (who bears a distinct resemblance to Winnicott's disciple, Massud Khan) recommends "Proust, Marx, Emerson, Keats, Dostoyevsky, Whitman and Blake" and the major works of psychoanalysis (Kureishi 2008: 96). Jamal goes on to write popular case histories with titles like *Six Characters in Search of a Cure* that recall the essay collections of psychoanalysts Adam Phillips (*On Kissing, Tickling and Being Bored*) and Darian Leader (*Why Do Women Write More Letters than They Send?*). Like Karim at the end of *The Buddha of Suburbia*, Jamal goes on to write the novel we have just read. Also like that novel, the first-person narrator of *Something to Tell You* begins in the present tense: "Secrets are my currency: I deal in them for a living. The secrets of desire, of what people really want, and of what they fear the most" (3). But whereas the teenaged Karim can't see the point in searching "the inner room," the archeology of the psyche is the essence of *Something to*

Tell You. And if we substitute "stories" for "secrets," so that the incipit reads "stories are my currency: I deal in them for a living," then we can see how Kureishi here resolves the age-old rivalry between the psychoanalyst and the novelist since his narrator is both (for more on this see Appignanesi 2008).

At the end of *Something to Tell You,* psychoanalysis bats the question of "what people really want" and "what they fear the most" back to literature as Harry picks up the baton from Jamal. *The Last Word* begins with Harry's awareness "that not a moment passed when someone wasn't telling a story. And, if his luck held for the rest of the day, Harry was about to be employed to tell the story of the man he was going to visit" (Kureishi 2014: 1).

For the characters in *The Buddha of Suburbia* and *The Black Album* books are guides to life; reading provides them with primers for living. But, increasingly in Kureishi's work, characters have to write themselves out of a hole and although Jamal, and Harry and Mamoon in *The Last Word*, each have published titles to their name, they are still frightened of failing "the great test" (Kureishi 2014: 129). As he witnesses Mamoon's childish tantrums, Harry wonders whether this author of great books has any wisdom to offer. In an exchange with Rob, Harry accuses the editor of overidealizing artists and insists that "there are more interesting and useful people." Rob replies categorically: "That is blasphemy" (Kureishi 2014: 221). And it is not a heresy that Harry maintains for long; however narcissistic and unscrupulous he may be, the writer is a cultural hero to Harry, which is a convenient philosophy for him personally.

Harry and Mamoon have read the same books: indeed, they seem obsessed with the twentieth century English first eleven. They both revere Evelyn Waugh, E. M. Forster, George Orwell, and Graham Greene. Mamoon pretends to disagree (in order to test Harry) but can't help admitting that he does admire Forster and Orwell even though he denigrates them as "the poof" and "the puritan," respectively (Kureishi 2014: 77). In one of Harry and Mamoon's more genial sparring sessions, it emerges that the old man is worried about posterity and the prospect of becoming another of the forgotten ones:

> "Consider them, Bertrand Russell, A. J. Ayer, D. H. Lawrence, Aldous Huxley, Anthony Powell, Anthony Burgess, William Golding, Henry Green, Graham Greene—"
>
> "No, not *that* Greene. No—*never.*"
>
> "Good, plucky of you. But otherwise—unread, unreadable, discarded, departed, a mountain of words washed into the sea and not coming back. Popeye the Sailor Man has more cultural longevity." (Kureishi 2014: 135)

Rob, the editor in *The Last Word,* believes that "the writer should be the very devil, a disturber of dreams and wrecker of fatuous utopias, the bringer-in of reality, and the rival of God in his wish to make worlds" (Kureishi 2014: 5). But how seriously are we meant to take the literary manifesto of a drunken, amoral, borderline psychotic? The relation between the man and the writer is one of the central questions in *The Last Word*.

In the 1950s, the New Critics "broke with the Great Man theory of literature, insisting that the author's intentions in writing, even if they could be recovered, were of no relevance to the interpretation of his or her text" (Eagleton 1983: 48). Despite the waves of "theory" that followed, the need to maintain the separation between the writer and the work has to some extent remained a critical orthodoxy. Barthes declared the death of the author in 1968 and, although psychoanalytic literary criticism brought him back to life, he was more often a neurotic than a Great Man. If *Something to Tell You* invites the reader to psychoanalyze the narrator by paying attention to his silences, projections, and ambivalences, *The Last Word* licenses us to become literary biographers. In Kureishi's first exploration of literary biography, *My Ear at His Heart* (2004), he confesses that he reads his father's unpublished novels as disguised autobiography even though he (Hanif Kureishi) would object to his own novels being raided for clues into his psyche (see Thomas 2009). But in one bold sweep, *The Last Word* seems to abolish the separation between the author and the text: "the life and the writing make one continuous book" (Kureishi 2014: 205).

However, having opened the biographical floodgates, *The Last Word* itself is fearful of the deluge. As a disillusioned Harry ponders the lives of his literary heroes, he concludes that literature is a "killing field":

> Who can think of Larkin now without considering his fondness for the buttocks of schoolgirls and paranoid hatred of blacks—"I can hear fat Caribbean germs pattering after me in the underground ..." Or Eric Gill's copulations with more or less every member of his family, including the dog? Proust had rats tortured, and donated his family furniture to brothels; Dickens walled up his wife and kept her from her children; Lillian Hellman lied. While Sartre lived with his mother, Simone de Beauvoir pimped babes for him; he envied Camus, before trashing him. John Cheever loitered in toilets, nostrils aflare, before returning to his wife. P. G. Wodehouse made broadcasts for the Nazis; Mailer stabbed his second wife. Two of Ted Hughes's lovers had killed themselves. And as for Styron, Salinger, Saroyan ... no decent person had ever picked up a pen. Jack Nicholson in *The Shining* had the right approximation of a writer. (Kureishi 2014: 36–7)

Although Rob encourages Harry to skewer Mamoon, because muckraking sells, the maverick editor regards the contemporary vogue for literary biography as a form of envy:

That's where the public like their artists—exposed, trousers down, arse up, doing a long stretch among serial killers, and shitting in front of strangers. That'll teach 'em to think their talent makes them better than mediocre no-brain tax-paying wage slaves like us. (Kureishi 2014: 8)

The Last Word itself tries to steer a path between exposing the author, trousers down, for the reader's amusement and licensing novelists to be "cunts" because "literature [is] the leg-opener" and they can get away with it (Kureishi 2014: 166). Harry is part hagiographer and part tabloid hack as he tries to find the relationship between the all too human author and the sublime text.

Jamal, the Freudian narrator of *Something to Tell You* would not be surprised by Harry's discovery that Mamoon's writing, which went through the doldrums in his middle period, livened up considerably when he became a sexual sadist (Kureishi 2014: 195). Harry knows that the Marion material is dynamite and even Mamoon, while denying the specifics, admits that "'the intellect and the libido have to be linked, otherwise there's no life in the work'" (Kureishi 2014: 197). But if we return to Harry's survey of literature's killing field, it is striking that nearly all the writers on his list of greats are men. Kureishi does his best for gender parity by pointing out that Lillian Hellman lied and Simone de Beauvoir pimped, but, overwhelmingly, the amoral, borderline psychotics are male, and the ones who suffered for the art were the wives and mistresses, who acted as unpaid secretaries and editors or muses. It may be, as Rob suggests, that the public want writers to live more intensely so that they can report back from the wild side to us who read in the safety of our sitting rooms. But a comparable list of women writers whose lives have been mythologized would produce only a depressing roll call of victims (Jean Rhys), suicides (Plath, Woolf), and pussycats (Austen, Brontes, Eliot). Jean Rhys is the only female writer that Mamoon unequivocally admires. He calls her the Goddess of his "lonely mongrel alcoholic wanderings" (Kureishi 2014: 77). But Mamoon, typically, disguises his identification with Rhys in a joke about her on her back: "She's the only female writer in English you'd want to sleep with. Otherwise it's just Brontes, Eliot, Woolf, Murdoch! Can you imagine cunnilingus with any of them?" (Kureishi 2014: 77). Is there any point in feminist readers taking umbrage at this? In its way, it is a fitting tribute to Rhys who wrote so lyrically about sexual healing as well as humiliation.

Mamoon's ambivalent attitude to women writers mirrors the ambivalent representation of women in *The Last Word*. If, as I have argued elsewhere, the female characters in *The Buddha of Suburbia* are invariably stronger and more dynamic than the males, the opposite seems at first to be the case in *The Last Word* (Thomas 2005: 78–9). Harry's fiancée, Alice, is beautiful and kind but so addicted to shopping in Bond Street that Harry has to save her from the bailiffs. His working-class squeeze in the country, Julia, is much more savvy and resourceful than Alice but still apparently dependent on Harry to take her to London. She knows her place: sucking cock or looking after the kiddies. Once Alice is pregnant with twins, Julia does indeed move in with the young couple as nanny (and bit on the side). At the end of the novel, after Harry has left Alice, he moves in with Lotte, Rob's beautiful editorial assistant, whom he had previously seduced and left in therapy. The women in Mamoon's life are even more abject: his first wife Peggy remained faithful and adoring, despite his visits to prostitutes; she even begged for a page of manuscript to edit on her deathbed. Marion, his mistress and (second) amanuensis, gave up her children to be with him and, even though Mamoon abandons her, still wants him back. Liana, the second wife, is "a man's woman" (Kureishi 2014: 95). Like her predecessors, she is utterly devoted to the Great Man in the study, even though she is not allowed to venture into the sanctum, and he is consumed by what the poet Seidel calls the "hunger for younger." Mamoon, recalling Victor Hugo's funeral, thinks that a great artist should leave behind a trail of weeping women, but the reader may also suspect that his country retreat, Prospects House, sounds rather like the cottage in Goldilocks: Marion is too hot, Peggy is too cold, and Liana is just right for him, at first. As all children find out eventually, "just right" doesn't exist and Mamoon soon starts to weary of Liana's demands. As he works on his biography, *Among Strangers*, Harry vows that the women's voices will be heard and their contribution to Mamoon's work will be recognized: he would bring "them all back to life" (Kureishi 2014: 282).

At first glance, then, Kureishi would seem to be peddling an old-fashioned view of women as objects of desire, who exist only in relation to the men on whom they depend completely. But the male/female binaries in *The Last Word* prove to be at least partly self-subverting, in a manner analogous to the self-subverting sentences that constitute the most distinctive feature of Kureishi's fictional prose. The female characters may be assigned fairly traditional roles, but they have a lot of power: Liana can call Mamoon to account by forcing him to choose between "'food or mood'" (Kureishi 2014: 214). Without Peggy to open the door to literary London for him, Mamoon would have remained a lost immigrant; it was her faith in him that kept him going until he received official recognition. Harry's father's psychiatric certainties about life are undermined by the fact that he could never control his wife's sexuality, nor could he save her from suicide. Once he has finished *Among Strangers*, Harry resolves to write a book about mothers: he is haunted by a vision of her shoes and the memory of surprising her in adultery traumatizes him. Harry thinks he can take Alice for granted but she has a whole other life with Mamoon of which he is completely ignorant and which he refuses to read about when offered the chance, just as Mamoon refused to read Peggy's diaries and Marion's memoir. It is as if the women's written words are too powerful for the male characters to countenance. The fiercest rivalry between Mamoon and Harry revolves around women, with both males competing for who can be top dog: when they are not discussing Eng. Lit., Harry is boasting about his prowess with women (five in one day) while Mamoon sits slyly stroking the cat on his lap. Mamoon tries to steal Alice from Harry by listening to her and then putting her in his novel, while Harry could seduce Liana by writing a glossy book about her husband, if he wanted. Whether the female characters are ever capable of escaping the writers' attempts to ensnare them with words remains open. Marion's decision to write her own book about her relationship with Mamoon seems like a step in the right direction. But whether this is published or pushed into the oven we never find out.

Just as *The Last Word* is torn between the desire to confine women to the role of silent muse or nurturer and the determination to allow the women's voices to be heard, so the novel ends with two contradictory images of the writer-as-Great-Man. The last time that Harry sees Mamoon is at an awards ceremony: Liana wheels him in and the assembled literati spontaneously rise to their feet to pay homage to his achievement: "There wasn't a decent bookshop in the world that didn't carry this man's work, nor a serious reader who had not heard his name" (Kureishi 2014: 285). But this public recognition is juxtaposed with the news that Marion has made her long-delayed journey to Prospects House to help a distraught Liana, and the housekeeper Ruth, nurse Mamoon: "Poor Mamoon on his deathbed, thought Harry, surrounded by women he hated" (Kureishi 2014: 286). Mamoon's moribund condition suggests that Harry's title *Among Strangers* has another connotation: the women remain other to the very end. Moreover, the latent aggression of the disciple's desire to see the master surrounded by enemies is disguised as pathos: "Poor Mamoon," thought Harry. But Kureishi's penchant for whiplash transitions, whether marked by commas or full stops, manifests itself in the next sentence, which undermines the certainty of the one that precedes it, and unites the biographer with his subject: "No better way to go: that's how he would have liked it" (Kureishi 2014: 286).

Orwell may have been a puritan but in "Why I Write," he accorded "aesthetic enthusiasm" equal billing with historical impulse, political purpose, and sheer egoism (Orwell 2000[1946]: 3). With the exception of Zadie Smith, it does seem to be the fate of many writers from minority backgrounds to find that questions of style are overlooked by critics and their novels are valued primarily as voices from the margins. But Kureishi's novels are too good, and too complex aesthetically, to be reduced to sociological rubble.

In his essay "The Arduous Conversation Will Continue" Kureishi argues, "If communities are not to be corrupted by the government, the only patriotism possible is one that refuses the banality of either side" (Kureishi 2005: 92). This might seem like a political stance that condemns one to the liberal position of sitting on the fence and doing nothing. Instead, what Kureishi's radical uncertainty, both at the level of the sentence and in the use of point of view, means is that no one is allowed *The Last Word*, not even its author. This is "why we have literature, the theatre, newspapers—a culture, in other words" (Kureishi 2005: 92). Maybe "the other words" don't make a difference, but we can only hope.

Interview

"A very serious business": Hanif Kureishi in conversation with Susan Alice Fischer

This is an edited version, based on Nicholas David Lavery's transcription, of a public conversation between Hanif Kureishi, Susan Alice Fischer and the audience that took place at the end of the 'In Analysis: The Work of Hanif Kureishi' conference held at Roehampton University in London on February 25, 2012.

SAF: My first question regards something that struck me when I was reading your work, and that is the way you write about children because there are very few writers who write about younger children in a way that's actually interesting, and not just as appendages to grown-ups or as perhaps having symbolic value. I was wondering if you could talk about that.

HK: I liked having kids. It just seemed to me that you didn't have to go anywhere to be a writer; there was always a relief that you didn't have to go very far. You could just stay at home, and if there were kids in the kitchen, then you write about them and the experience of being a parent and how it ruined your life, how they charmed you, and how you hated them, and how they hated you. You're right, you don't read about them much, certainly in the older books and the nineteenth-century novel.

Writers write about what they see around them. I've got twins, and they were in the bathroom the other day with their shirts off shaving their bodies, all over, in the mirror. It was a fantastic image to see. I walked in and they said, "We're not gay." And I said, "No." I asked why they were doing this and they said, "We'll be more aerodynamic." I said, "Oh, that's good, isn't it, that'll come in handy when you're windsurfing." It was just a great scene, you know, and I thought, I've got to use that. I can't resist putting that somewhere. So it's really to do with that—you see something or somebody says something or something occurs to you. I'm sure artists, painters, and filmmakers all say, "I've got to put that in somewhere, it's striking to me so it might be striking to other people." I was talking earlier about whether you write what you want or you try to think about what the audience wants. In the end, you can just do your best work and hope people might like it. It's like having people over for dinner—you don't guess that people might like chops. So it's to do with that, really. You are your own first reader in a sense.

SAF: I was also thinking about how a lot of your work focuses on the inner life of children. I just read in *The New York Times* that wonderful article you did on "The Art of Distraction," looking at how children are boxed into a hyper-focused way of being today that doesn't allow them the kind of creative freedom they need to develop.

HK: Lots of people went crazy about that. They said, "Our children have been on Ritalin since they were four and they're really well," and it really disturbed me. I could see the children were difficult for the parents, and the parents then didn't know what to do and drugged the kids. We often as parents wished our kids were more drugged; a better solution would be to drug yourself, rather than the kids.

    I was interested in the fact that my life has been a series of distractions. I went to the Royal Court and someone said, "Would you go and work somewhere else?" And then I went there and someone said, "Will you write a film?" And I thought, I'll write a film. My life is still like that—a series of distractions. I'm supposed to be writing a novel, and I always wonder if I'll get back the original thing. But in the end, you have to follow your passion; you trust your passion and think, I'm interested in that today. You just find a little bit of life—life is so often so dead. When you're making a film, there'll be a frame, a scene or a moment between the actors that is genuinely alive, and that's what you look for, a bit of libido here and there. And with the kids you want them to have that. You know, one of my sons is dyslexic, and he won't read, but he reads football magazines. So he's not that dyslexic. And he'll really want to know what Wayne Rooney is thinking tonight. I can tell you that Wayne Rooney is not thinking a great deal tonight, but that there's a bit of libido, a bit of action there, a bit of life there—and it's that really that you look for. As a writer, I think, that's a really good idea; that would be good for a story I'm writing at the moment—life is alive.

SAF: I also was interested in the way in which you talk about teachers and teaching in your work. Your work has many people who are teacher figures and some who are actual teachers. And you're a teacher as well—so tell me about teaching.

HK: My kids will have a tennis lesson, then a piano lesson, then a football lesson, then this lesson, then that lesson. You're driving around all the time, and I've thought, it's really generous that these grown-ups are teaching these kids this stuff and it's a very good thing to do—the best thing in the world you could be doing. If you know anything, it's your duty to pass it on to other people. If I've learned anything about writing, I've learned it from editors, film directors, theater directors, and other people too. And it's my duty to do this, if I know anything, to pass it on to other people.

I teach writing. I don't know if I'm a teacher—I'm a reader. So I'll read their stuff and I'll say, "I'm on page three, I don't know what's going on, I can't work it out; either I'm stupid, or it's not clear what's going on. And if it's not clear to me, it won't be clear to everybody else, and the book goes dead there." So that's my job as a teacher. To say, "Here I've got to know that."

People want to write books. Everybody here has written a novel. Nobody in this room does not have a novel in them. But you're also helping people to speak. Most of my students are middle-aged, they're not eighteen, but they want to work out something about their lives, about who they are and where they're going, and they mostly want to try and understand their parents, the tragedy of their parents. And whatever level they are, it's your duty to help them speak, to find words for spirit. I don't think it's my job to turn people into successful novelists, but to say, "It seems to me in this piece you're trying to say *that*, and you should say *this* more." And they go and do that, and you've achieved something.

I've learned a lot from other people as a writer, particularly from directors. If a director has to shoot a scene that you've written, they've got to concentrate very hard on what's going on in the scene: "I can shoot that, but I can't shoot that, I don't know why you've said that." And you've got to say, "That's in there because of that." Writing for the theater or writing movies is a very practical business, and it's very stark. You've really got to justify everything you're doing. And that's teaching.

SAF: Speaking of films, in *Sammy and Rosie Get Laid*, at one point Danny says to Rafi, "How do we fight, that's what I want to know"—that is, how do we react to violence, and also how do we react generally to Thatcherism? To what extent is art transformative and revolutionary? In a recent interview you talked about the subversive work that emerged during those years. Could you talk about what makes your work "subversive?"

HK: I no longer talk about Thatcherism. I only talk about Streepism now. I consider the country in which I lived to have been run by Meryl Streep, and not Mrs Thatcher. And a good thing too, it seems to me. I'm looking forward to Meryl Streep coming back into power actually.

I'll give you an example of culture as being subversive actually. Last week I was in Karachi. I went to see someone I know who teaches there. And I asked her what it was like, and she said, "You were very brave the other day when you gave your speech, because you talked about Rushdie. You cannot teach Salman Rushdie in Karachi." There's a hole. If someone goes to a shop in Karachi and says, "Have you got *Midnight's Children*?" the guy in the shop says, "Are you mad? If I sold *Midnight's Children,* my shop would be burnt down and I'd go out of business." So what you see in Karachi is the erasure of a writer, of a writer's name. The unconscious of Islam that Rushdie speaks, all the doubts that Muslims have about themselves and how they live and what they believe, etc.—you're not allowed to say that. And so, you say, Salman Rushdie, just a writer? People go crazy. What he represents is some truth that cannot be spoken. So suddenly you see that speaking, literature, reading, books, and freedom is a very serious business. It might not be that serious in South Kensington, but it's certainly serious in Pakistan, in Libya, or particularly in Muslim countries at the moment, for instance.

I think that the fatwa in '89 represented a turning point for writers like me in terms of the seriousness of what we were doing. We were writing books, everybody was writing books, you could say whatever you wanted—and then suddenly there's this writer and he's saying things that can't be said, that are prohibited and for which he could be killed. And that was the big turning point for me in terms of the seriousness of what I was doing and how difficult it might be. Another person I know in Karachi is a journalist and I said, "Why have you stopped writing?" and he said, "Because I don't want to be killed." And I thought, well that's a good reason to stop writing; I wouldn't speak either. And then you realize in Karachi that it's monocultural, that there's nothing going on, nothing that can be said, people are petrified. There's no revolution, it's just dead, dead in the sense of this terror going on all the time. And there are writers there, but they're very careful. So you see what culture might mean, and maybe think about it in that context. And when you speak, people get annoyed and might want to kill you.

So it's always serious, being authentic, speaking the truth is a really big deal. And it's dangerous, and it has to be. You wonder what you're doing as a writer and why culture matters. You just have to go to a place where it's very dangerous to get a sense of what it represents—the world you represent against the world of death.

SAF: And yet, the way that you often speak is through humor. Can you tell me a little bit about the way in which you use humor in your writing and whether it has a subversive effect?

HK: Well, dictators don't like jokes. Jokes are dangerous. I try to write funny stuff or amusing stuff or witty stuff or tell jokes because that cheers me up. But I also think that a good joke is very dangerous and that people in Pakistan were making jokes in the 80s, and last week when I was there, all the time, and that's how people tell the truth. Jokes are not just jokes, they're paradoxes; the clock has stopped, they said in Karachi, or, we're living in two centuries at the same time. They find ways of speaking that show that reality. The world is very, very funny; it's also terrible. If it's only terrible or if it's only funny, the world is pointless. The world only has any sense because both of those things are running alongside each other. You laugh as you die. It always seemed to me that it was that that all the good writers have, that all the good writers are comic writers actually—apart from Tolstoy.

SAF: Watching *Sammy and Rosie* I was astonished by how prescient the film was about London and its redevelopment, but also by how different London looks twenty-five years later. I was wondering about how your relationship to London has changed over the years and also what relationship you see between the London of that period and of today?

HK: Well, London's got much, much richer—it's really rich now—and much poorer. It's also much more mixed. But I like writing about the contemporary; I want to write about what I saw last week. I don't understand it when writers write about the 50s. I get a real sense of what I saw yesterday, and I want to capture it, and *Sammy and Rosie* was an attempt to do that. I write about London because I write about stuff that happens nearby to me, that's all. I don't think, I'll go and research London and write about London. I don't think, I'll go to Pakistan and research what's happening to Pakistan. I'll go to Pakistan and someone will say something, and I'll put it in a story and that'll be that. Research for me is just living. I don't even know if I'm interested in London— I'm much more interested in what happens between people.

There's a new story that I started writing three days ago. I've got certain characters that are really good and what happens between them makes some sort of activity, some sort of action, some sort of drama. It's that. But then I was in Karachi, and I came back to England, and then I went to Paris, and I was walking around Paris thinking, what's the difference between Karachi and Paris, layers and layers of culture, most of it dead, and this other place where people are walking around with rifles. And then I want to write about these two things together and *bang*, in between them makes the story. I think that's how it happens. It's that sort of innocence—it's the innocence of the dream. When you have a dream you don't know the meaning, and then you find out and you're horrified. It's still like that when you're making a film—you've got to be innocent in a way. Five years later, or soon afterwards, you're seeing your unconscious stripped bare, but at the time it's got to be innocent.

SAF: Speaking of which, we've called this conference "In Analysis." Somebody earlier today used the phrase "psychoanalysis as a cultural force," and I was wondering if you could talk about the role of analysis in your work or your interest in it.

HK: Well, it's just a space, it's a room in which two people go in and one them speaks interminably and the other nods, and then you write them a check. But in that space you find and say things that you didn't know that you might find and say before. It's an amazing idea. Not only that, it will make the person who was saying it feel better, and it will also make them feel much, much worse. That seems an amazing, incredible invention to me, and also very strange, that we are made up of what we can't say. And I'm interested in whether philosophy, psychology, psychoanalysis, and culture are all mixed up. What do you want to know about psychoanalysis and my view of it?

SAF: I suppose among the things we were talking of during the conference was about the way in which in *Something to Tell You*, the character is an analyst—

HK: Well, he's listening to people. I don't know what to say about that—I don't do that, as a teacher it's slightly different. Being a teacher isn't like being an analyst, you really have to teach them—you really have to tell them stuff. You have to say, "If you do that, you'll be a right fuck-up." If you're an analyst you can't say that. I've got a student, she was embarking on an idea, and I thought, if you do this you'll waste three years of your life, should I say this to you? So I said so, and she said, "I want to do this anyway," and I said, "Well that's fine, I don't have to worry about you."

So it's much more instrumental in that sense, which is a relief to me actually. Rather than seeing the other person plunging into their own decisions, you can actually make decisions for them, I guess, or you can warn people; it's much more explicit. But you are doing a similar thing in a sense: you are trying to get people to say things, to say more things. How do you get them to say more things, that's all you want. You want to say something—inspires is the right and the wrong word—that makes them go away from the lesson and do more work and they feel excited, and they think, "Yes, I've learnt something, and I want to say more." That's what you're trying to do when you're teaching. To make them see something about their own life.

SAF: Your work has been translated into thirty-six languages. Do you have any sense of what it is about your work that speaks to people of vastly different experiences and backgrounds?

HK: No, the very fact that this morning you were all here talking about me as I was in my study in my pajamas tapping away, as I do, writing something while listening to The Who—writing something that I thought was really good or would be good when I finally got it. I can only think about what I'm doing now and try to make it as good as I can and believe, "This'll be all right." And I believe that people will like it, but I can't be sure. I mean, I'm not Andrew Lloyd Webber. So I don't know for certain, this'll be a good idea, I can only guess, but I really want to do this. So it's just the urgency of the desire to say something really that I have, and the hope that somebody might be interested.

SF: In the introduction to your *Collected Essays*, there's a passage in which you talk about being interviewed and about the uneasy relationship between interviewer and interviewee. So I'm just wondering, is there a question that you wish an interviewer would ask you, or that an interviewer *should* ask you?

HK: You get some very funny questions, I have to say. You get some very banal questions about where do you get your ideas from. The banal questions are the most interesting in a way because they're like Zen, aren't they? If somebody asks you a stupid question long enough, you really have to flip into a sort of super-consciousness of what can I possibly say. But they do ask you some weird questions. Like, "Did Peter O'Toole love you?" The best one was, "Do you have to see the actresses naked before you cast them?" I said, "The actresses have to see me naked." It's amazing what people want to know, but it's mostly to do with writing because they want to do it and they want to know how you do it. What is it they really want to know? I mean if you said, "It was really difficult and it took years," it'd be really depressing, but on the other hand they want to be inspired.

Writing does transform your life in some ways actually, and it really does make it better. Being a writer or living a creative life is really the best way in my view in which anybody could live, and if I had anything to say to my children, I would say do that. So that would be good thing to say to people.

Questions from the audience

Q: We have on display at the conference a couple of manuscript pages from the early drafts of *The Buddha of Suburbia*, and I couldn't help but noticing that the proposed early title was "Streets of My Heart." What were the other titles, and why did it end up as it did?

HK: Well, I wrote a short story called "The Buddha of Suburbia," which was published I think in the *LRB*. I finished the rest of the book and then went into a huge panic about the title at the end, two days before we had to choose. So it had always been called "Streets of the Heart," and then Robert McCrum at Faber said, "Just call it 'Buddha of Suburbia.'" I remember having a big panic about it, as I thought, it's not really about the father, it's about the son. He just said, "Look, it's just the best title, that's all." Why's *The Catcher in the Rye* called that? It's just the title. It sounds all right. And in the end, that's what I thought—we've got to have a title that people remember. But if you see the manuscript, I also didn't write the first page either at the beginning, "My name is Karim Amir" and all that, until the day before it went to press. It starts with "One day everything changed, my father came home" and all that stuff. I just went off and wrote it. So it's very chaotic writing a book—it's amazing that we got away with it. It could have gone the other way and been called "Streets of the Heart" and not had that opening, and I wouldn't be here now.

Q: I was thinking about how at the end of *Something to Tell You*, Jamal starts to think with Freud about the destiny of civilization and in particular starts to think about questions of aggression, of dealing with guilt, of the way in which contemporary culture doesn't seem to provide the resources for individuals to deal with the guilt that they have. What do you think psychoanalytic ideas have to do with the breakdown of paternal authority and the difficulties that individuals have in resolving their unconscious conflicts because of the lack of anything to kick against, to resist and rebel against?

HK: Being in Pakistan two weeks ago made me think a lot about what we call civilization, by which I mean people speaking, thinking, making a living in ways that are creative and more or less not destructive, because I felt that being in Karachi I was in a country that had become very destructive and was really *Thanatos*, and was really death, this culture of death. It was really violent, you were afraid, there were guns, there had been a lot of danger, there were people being kidnapped. And then I came back, and I thought that everything we have is quite fragile. It seems to be here forever, this room, the university. It seems eternal, but actually if you were in Syria tonight you would see that it's violent and dangerous, and we're hanging on by our fingernails to make it.

And in a way, under various forms of, let's say, authoritarianism, certainly radical Islam, it's the rule of the father, obedience: the father wants this, the father wants that. It's the rule, and there's a real terror of breaking the rule. But if you break that rule, you enter the realm, as you put it earlier quite rightly, of guilt. You're on your own if you leave the father behind—it's this zone where there are no rules, where you are, as it were, your own agent; and it's much worse, it's more frightening, and you really have to stand up against the sadistic father, which is maybe communism, maybe fascism, maybe radical Islam, various forms of authoritarianism. And it's very difficult and very dangerous to do that. We should think about how hard it is to keep things going and how valuable they are, and how fragile they are. I was thinking about that.

Writing a book seems to me to be plucking something out of the jaws of real violence and oppression that human beings are capable of, and I've become much more aware of that as I've got older. I mean, I grew up in rather a safe time in the 50s and 60s with the welfare state, health, education, rather benign Labour administrations, and so on. The world has become much harsher and more violent and more dangerous, and with more people excluded. And you see people in Pakistan and you think, they just want to get out; if you gave everybody in this country a visa, they would run to the airport. They've made such a hell of it, and it's really a lot of effort to destroy something so much and to have no hope. So I have become more Freudian, and I really think the forces of death on the earth are very powerful—very, very powerful and very difficult to resist, and that there is a strong urge toward death. It's not something I'd much thought about before. Somebody said about Freud that only the absurdities are true, and it's the more far out stuff that I'm more and more impressed by as I get older, and particularly that idea of the desire and the urge toward death and destructiveness.

Q: Your writings about relationships are very provocative in their view of promiscuity and commitment. How much of your idea of writing—which are for me and many scholars very ethical writings—is about love and the experience of intimacy?

HK: I guess it is provocative. It didn't seem like that at the time—I mean, when I wrote *My Beautiful Laundrette* and I had two boys kissing, and one of them was a gay Pakistani and the other one was a skinhead. Looking back at the twentieth century and the history of gay people, and the oppression of gay people, you can see suddenly that to make a film about this is provocative. But it was safe back then to say it; the way had been cleared by other people. You thought, nobody could have said this before, nobody could say that this man could kiss this man. So although it's provocative, it's usually quite safe. There are things that have to be said.

Q: There is also the idea of not absolute commitment and not absolute promiscuity in *Something to Tell You*. There's some form of commitment, but actually they are seeking pleasure elsewhere.

HK: What's my relationship to commitment? Well, you're committed to someone until you don't like them anymore. What else is there? And then when you don't like them anymore, you find somebody else to be committed to. That seems to me to be some version of authenticity. As Lacan says, we're divided creatures—on the one hand, there is safety; on the other hand, there is pleasure; you have a duty to other people and you have a duty to yourself. These are real tears, real difficulties, you know, it's not easy to decide; you may betray somebody else, but you may actually be betraying yourself more. So all the time you're making difficult decisions about who you are and how you should live. There isn't a safe place in that sense—there is no position you could take. In that sense, life really is existential. And a writer would just show that. I mean, I'm only saying that I'm not doing it, I'm just showing it. What's my view of it? I don't think my view of it is important, I'm just telling a story. I'm not saying you should do anything. I'm not a recommender. I'll leave that to David Cameron.

Q: I have a question about promiscuity of form, I suppose. In a way, asking you how you choose a form is as banal as asking you how you get ideas. What is it about the writing process where you get to a stage when you think, this is a film script or this is novel or this is a short story?

HK: It's partly about time. I think, if I do a story, I can finish this in two weeks and that's a relief. I don't have to labor over this for years, there's enough material in this for two weeks for me to concentrate on and really worry about this and these people and what they're doing. But if I write a novel, it's going to take me two years and then I'll spend another year doing publicity. So it's partly practical, what I want to do, and it's partly about the nature of the idea. Or if I want to write something today about Ritalin, I'll write it next week and publish it the week after, and it'll be done.

I mean, my work, you may think about it theoretically, but actually what I think about most of the time is money. I'm thinking, how am I going to pay for my kids to go to school. It's a practical job, and it's an art. Most writers, unless they're very rich, and most of them aren't, are thinking about that, so with the creative writing students you've got to say, "Look, you've got to make a living out of this." What's good about writing is that it's an art, and I'm existing, as it were, within capitalism, so it's a real job and that's what makes it interesting. It's being in the commercial world that makes it interesting for me. The highest form of criticism I've always felt for me is a check. If someone hands over a check, there's no equivocation in that.

Q: When you were working at the Royal Court you actually had the chance to work with Samuel Beckett, one of his plays was on in production there, and I was wondering if you remembered anything about the nature of the conversations and also about your relationship to Beckett's work more generally.

HK: I was a very big fan of him and his work. He was very nice, and he would sit there and he wouldn't say anything and drink his Guinness, and people would come over and talk to him. I would never ask him any questions of any serious nature. He was interested in women, and he liked cricket, and he would ask how it was going—and that was that really. I remember David Hare coming in, and he held up his kids and said, "Look at that man, he's a genius." I was very impressed by that; I thought, this man's a genius, I'm just going to sit here and look at him. I'd never met anyone who had any culture or worked in culture or was committed, that was enough for me. I learned a lot at the Royal Court. The seriousness—actually the hatred was very high, of writers they didn't like and places like the RSC.

Q: Your writing started off being received as postcolonial ethnic narratives, whereas I see you now as a British contemporary writer. There's always a theme of relationships. I was wondering, when you write the characters, is it the relationships that come first? Also where do you see yourself, and what are your thoughts on representing women?

HK: After one of my first plays, a journalist wrote, "the Anglo-Pakistani writer," and I was really shocked, because I'd never thought of myself as being Anglo or as being Pakistani, and I thought, they've just got this completely wrong. And then somebody said to me, "Oh, there'll be a lot of this."

When people describe you from the outside it's like being called Paki or an immigrant; other people's descriptions of you can be so reductive, and you have to have your own description and fight for your own words. So when I see the word "postcolonial," I always reach for my machine gun. But it's the relationship between the book, the story, and the reader, that's where it happens, the alchemy. Something happens between me and P. G. Wodehouse; Wodehouse is alive, I make him alive. And that matters to me, and the other stuff is less important—so I don't really mind, I don't think about it.

As for the representations of women, or children, older people, this, that, or the other, when I started at the Royal Court they talked about the representation of Asian people, so that you'd have to show them being particularly nice, as though anybody in literature was nice. As though, you know, "Anna Karenina, what a nice woman." "I'd have that Raskolnikov round for dinner any night." It's really beside the point; these are characters and it's their extremity that's interesting. People can really get the wrong end of the stick if they think literature is about representation.

Q: When you were starting out did you feel that burden on you?

HK: People tried to lay it on me. They said, "Look, there are no Pakistanis in English writing, if you're going to do one, why does he have to be gay, why can't he just be normal?" And you think, yes, why can't he just be normal, but you think, I really need him in this story to be gay and to kiss Daniel Day-Lewis. And I thought, I need to resist this—it's more fun to write about him if he's kissing Daniel Day-Lewis than it is to write about him as a nice, clean-cut boy. Martin Amis doesn't worry about the representation of white men, or if people will think Martin's really got it down on white men. You have to betray people; you have to really let them down in terms of representation.

Q: When you read *The Satanic Verses*, did it affect your work? And how did it affect you personally?

HK: I was very emboldened by Rushdie himself. He gave a reading with Calvino at Riverside in 1982, and I spoke to him for the first time, and then we became friends. His family and my family both live in Karachi. And he introduced me to Angela Carter. I spent time with him, and I thought, fuck, this bloke is really fucking smart, and he was impressive and that was where the influence was really earlier on, before *My Beautiful Laundrette*. I thought at the time, he's an Indian writer and I'm a British writer. Bromley's my Bombay. The fatwa had a profound effect on me, and indeed on anybody.

Q: I'd like to ask about questions of class in your writing, as we haven't talked a lot about it so far. In a way you seem more occupied with psychoanalysis, which you could argue is grounded in a particular economic and social context, Vienna at the turn of the century, but has produced a totalizing narrative. It seems like a lot of your early work does come out of a particular lower-middle-class environment.

HK: It does. I mean, I come from a lower-middle-class, white-skinhead background, with an immigrant father, and I've spent most of my life down there amongst people who were minor civil servants, manual laborers, factory workers, and I have written about that. But my father was also an upper-middle-class Indian. It was odd, because my father never thought for a moment that I couldn't get on in England. He never thought, you'll only go that far and then it'll stop. He knew there was a lot of racism, prejudice, people who thought Indians were inferior, but he still thought you could get through. It's an extraordinary thought to have actually.

I never felt excluded because of my class, although my mother would go, "Well, they're posh," and I'd always think, so what. I was aware that we were very inhibited. If you talked about Beethoven in Bromley, people thought you were an absolute cunt, that you were really pulling a fast one on them, that you were patronizing them. It took me ages to, as it were, stop pretending to be not clever, because people hated you for that. It's like what we were saying earlier, that you can say things people will be embarrassed by, so what do you do, do you shut up or do you get out?

Q: Pop culture features very heavily in *The Black Album*, particularly through the figures of Madonna and Prince. Who would be the equivalent figures to a student like Shahid today, and do you think that pop culture could still hold that level of influence?

HK: It wouldn't be for me to say. My kids like Eminem. Most black hip-hop street urban culture is made for white-middle-class boys in private school. That's who they'd be interested in. I don't like that, and I'm not supposed to like it.

Q: Do you personally feel it holds the same amount of power as it did when you wrote *The Buddha of Suburbia* and *The Black Album*?

HK: No, I don't think that, because then culture was such a liberation. It was so narrow then, you couldn't get access to anything, and when you heard a record by Jimi Hendrix, it was like a blast from another world—whereas my kids can just type anything into the Internet and hear it then and there. I don't think my kids could get that, could feel, "Oh my god, there is something else in the world, somebody else alive somewhere else." Vietnam, civil rights, black power: Jimi Hendrix would represent that to me. It wasn't just a kid listening to a pop record—it was a whole record of another world. I don't know what would liberate them now; it depends where in the world you are.

Q: How does it feel to walk into a room where people have been talking about you all day?

HK: I was very flattered, and I was very moved, and I thought that I hadn't been wasting my life, and I thought that what I'd been doing had some meaning and some value, and I'd communicated something to other people that was worth saying—and I wished my kids had been here to see that that man in his pajamas wasn't just an idiot. And I thought, on the other hand, I hope it doesn't put me off. I don't want to hang around here because it would make me self-conscious. It might make me think of myself in the third person or make me admire myself. What I'm doing when I'm writing is just trying to write. I'm not even there; there's my unconscious and then there's the words, and there's no other person. It's pure, it's there, that's what I want to do, and I don't want any interference in the radio signals, as it were. So that's what makes me nervous. I'm quite anonymous; I'm watching the kids, the family, the street, the cafés, Karachi. I'm not there. Once they're looking at you, you're fucked. I remember thinking after the fatwa: when he walks in the room, everybody looks at him. To slide in, that's your job—not to think I'm a writer, but to get the story. So I'm flattered, but that might not be good for me. Thank you everybody, for being here and taking part in this, and for reading my books.

Interview

"An extraordinary encounter": Stephen Frears in conversation with Susan Alice Fischer and Deanna Kamiel

This is an edited version of an interview that took place via Skype between Stephen Frears, Susan Alice Fischer, Deanna Kamiel, and the audience during the "In Analysis: The Work of Hanif Kureishi" conference held at Roehampton University in London on February 25, 2012.

Fischer: I'd like to welcome Stephen Frears, and thank you so much for joining us. As you know, Stephen Frears is the director of *My Beautiful Laundrette*, *Sammy and Rosie Get Laid*, as well as of films that he did with writers other than Hanif Kureishi, such as *Dirty Pretty Things*, *Prick Up Your Ears*, *The Queen,* and, of course, many more. I'd like to start by asking what attracted you in the first place to Hanif Kureishi's work and to collaborating with him?

Frears: I'm not sure that collaborating is the right word. He got the script of *My Beautiful Laundrette* to me in quite fortuitous circumstances, and I read it and said, "This is brilliant. We should do this now." I don't know if collaborating describes that. It was very, very good and very original, and it made sense of a lot of the world. I really admired what he'd written.

Fischer: Can you go into a little more detail about what you felt—given the times in the 1980s—that it was making sense of from your perspective?

Frears: Well, as a satire on Thatcherite economics, it was very funny and very relevant. Very witty and very sophisticated—absolutely not what I was expecting. It just burst on me.

Fischer: I certainly remember seeing it at the time in the 1980s and it did just burst upon the audience as well. Deanna Kamiel just did a paper on precisely that idea of seeing something for the first time, in a way that made us aware of things that either we weren't aware of before or made us see things in a new way. As you worked on the screenplay, was there collaboration with Hanif Kureishi? Was he involved in the process itself?

Frears: He was very involved. But what you call a collaboration was really my education. I was in my forties, and he had to explain the history of immigration—I was taught by Hanif and the actors.

Fischer: Was he also involved in the actual cinematic aspect of it? Or did you feel that the way it was written lent itself in particular to a visual presentation? What was that process like?

Frears: I don't remember him being involved in what you would call the visual process, though I don't particularly remember any conversations about that. His writing was so lively and the people so interesting—that was at the center of what we were doing.

Fischer: Most of us here are literary scholars and have less of a cinematic background, so I'm going to ask Deanna Kamiel, who is a documentarian and teaches at the New School in New York, to talk more about the cinematic aspect of adapting from script to film.

Kamiel: There are several marvelous scenes in *My Beautiful Laundrette* where many things happen within the scene, but they happen in one shot. For instance, the kiss—they walk, they kiss—at the same time, continuing the shot, the gang of lads start banging on the dustbins. Also that fantastic first walk when Omar leaves the car after sighting Johnny and walks over in a sense, or crosses over, to find him. That all happens in one shot. How did the idea of the one shot come to you?

Frears: Well—it just seemed a good idea. [Laughter] That sounds to me like good filmmaking—a lot of things going on at the same time. It was instinctive. Afterwards I realized that the shots did have a powerful symbolism, that it was actually Omar, the Pakistani boy, traveling from his own family, his own world, into the world of Daniel Day-Lewis. When I thought about it, it did express many of the things that were in the film, but it was never planned.

Kamiel: It *still* seems a good idea. The colors of My Beautiful Laundrette seem to be blues and pinks and orange-gold—was there a certain aesthetic or thought process about that?

Frears: The aesthetic process was that the cameraman thought it would be a good idea. [Laughter] It was very soon after Punk—we were so obviously making a youthful film, so it came from that. Why it's so good is that there's a lot of interesting stuff—I suppose you would call it sociology, what was being said in society about race in Britain, politics in Britain—and it came out in this outrageous language. Hanif said to me quite recently that he'd been rather nervous—he talked about it as a sort of Restoration Comedy. It was written in a high style, rather like Bernard Shaw's plays. I found that a source of endless delight. I'm probably more drawn to the outrageousness of the literary side than to the sociology. It was clearly the contrast between these two elements that made the film interesting and provocative. And that's very unusual—not the normal sober treatment of the subject. Because the writing was so fiercely intelligent, that didn't really matter.

Fischer: I just watched Sammy and Rosie Get Laid again in preparation for the conference—I hadn't seen it since it first came out, and I was struck by a number of things—about how relevant in some ways it still was, but also about how much London seemed to have changed since then. And I thought the movie really captured that change wonderfully with the bulldozers coming in and so on. Can you talk a little about, first of all, where it was filmed—was it filmed on location and where specifically—and then about how you see the lasting relevance of these films?

Frears: It was filmed on location, but I moved its location. It was originally set in Brixton and I moved it to the Harrow Road by the flyover. I didn't know how to make a film in Brixton—it seemed rather forbidding and inaccessible. I don't remember a long conversation about it but it was moved and certainly moved in my head.

About the relevance of it: its origin was Hanif's uncle—a man who loved England and cricket and all those things—who came to England and discovered himself in the middle of a riot. It came from the contrast between his romantic view of England as the cradle of democracy and the real world in which kids were rioting. I guess it's relevant—

Fischer: I mean given that there were recently riots in London last year—

Frears: I can see that. It's sad—

Fischer: Yes, that not as much has changed as one would have hoped—

Frears: In many ways the economic conditions now are worse.

Audience member: Did you foresee that Daniel Day-Lewis would become as big a star as he has? His performance in *My Beautiful Laundrette* is just amazing. Could you talk about working with him toward the beginning of his career?

Frears: We were very innocent in those days—it never crossed any of our minds that Dan would become the huge star that he became. Dan I knew slightly and knew he was a very, very good actor. When we cast him, I said to Hanif that I thought it would shift the balance of the script in some quite striking way to have that powerful an actor playing that part. But Dan was great, very good. We certainly didn't anticipate what was going to happen. We made the film in a state of almost complete innocence. It was paid for by British television and there was no obligation to do anything other than make a good film. Everything happened fortuitously.

Fischer: Is there anything that we overlooked to ask you about your collaboration with Hanif Kureishi and the legacy of the films that perhaps you'd like to address?

Frears: It was an extraordinary encounter with someone who was to become one of the most interesting writers in Britain. I remember reading years later that he was the first Asian novelist born in England, and I can see that that made his perspective very, very original, very interesting. I just bumped into him one night and backed his talent, thought what he was saying was interesting and lively.

Fischer: So you just happened to run into him and that's how you got started on the project?

Frears: No, he brought me the script—I liked the frivolousness of how we ran into each other. There was never much serious analysis. What you should look at are the plays that he'd been writing before that. The first time we ever showed the *Laundrette*, everyone was very enthusiastic but there was a group of rather grumpy looking people; I said, "Who are they?" and Hanif said,

"They are the ones who were in the plays." The plays are more sober, more serious. He always gave the impression that when he wrote the *Laundrette*, he was fed up with writing about race seriously and that he wrote the film as a joke—as a sort of black comedy. The themes were the same; he'd written before about corner shops and things like that. He was really trying to write about his own predicament—he went to a comprehensive and had this white friend who one day came in with his head shaved—it was as simple as that. If you look at the plays that he wrote just before *Laundrette*, you can see the frustration inside him which brought the same subject out as a series of jokes. I was standing somewhere at the right moment. I was lucky.

Fischer: All of us were lucky—these two films had such a transformative power on all of us who saw them at that time and continue to do so.

Frears: It's peculiar that, because it was only some years later that English people like me started to understand how complex the subject was. I didn't know anything—I was just a white English man. Now we all know too much about race relations. I thought the script was just *Hamlet*, about a boy rebelling against his father. Nowadays there would be much more self-censoring, and that would be a great pity.

Fischer: Yes, it would. I want to thank you for joining us and giving us a different perspective on Hanif Kureishi's work. Thank you for your generosity.

Frears: All right—give him my love.

References

Works cited by contributors

Introduction, Susan Alice Fischer

Works by Hanif Kureishi

Kureishi, H. (1992[1981]), *Outskirts and Other Plays*. London: Faber and Faber.
—(1985), *My Beautiful Laundrette*. Dir. Stephen Frears. Channel Four Films.
—(1987), *Sammy and Rosie Get Laid*. Dir. Stephen Frears. Channel Four Films.
—(1990), *The Buddha of Suburbia*. London: Faber and Faber.
—(1995), *The Black Album*. London: Faber and Faber.
—(1997), *My Son the Fanatic*. Dir. Udayan Prasad. Arts Council of England.
—(1998), *Intimacy*. London: Faber and Faber.
—(1999), *Sleep with Me*. London: Faber and Faber.
—(2001), *Gabriel's Gift*. London: Faber and Faber.
—(2002), *The Body and Seven Stories*. London: Faber and Faber.
—(2003), *The Mother*. Dir. Roger Michell. BBC Films.
—(2004a), *My Ear at His Heart: Reading My Father*. London: Faber and Faber.
—(2004b), *When Night Begins*. London: Faber and Faber.
—(2005), *The Word and the Bomb*. London: Faber and Faber.
—(2006), *Venus*. Dir. Roger Michell. Miramax.
—(2008), *Something to Tell You*. London: Faber and Faber.
—(2009), *The Black Album: Adapted for the Stage*. London: Faber and Faber.
—(2010[1987]), "With Your Tongue Down My Throat," *Collected Stories*. London: Faber and Faber, pp. 60–103.
—(2010[1995]), "We're Not Jews," *Collected Stories*. London: Faber and Faber, pp. 41–50.
—(2010[1997]), "The Tale of the Turd," *Collected Stories*. London: Faber and Faber, pp. 128–33.
—(2010[1999a]), "Four Blue Chairs," *Collected Stories*. London: Faber and Faber, pp. 245–52.
—(2010[1999b]), "The Penis," *Collected Stories*. London: Faber and Faber, pp. 358–66.
—(2010[2002]), "Hullabaloo in the Tree," *Collected Stories*. London: Faber and Faber, pp. 485–93.
—(2010[2006]), "Weddings and Beheadings," *Collected Stories*. London: Faber and Faber, pp. 611–13.

—(2012), "The Art of Distraction," *The New York Times*. February 18, http://www.nytimes.com/2012/02/19/opinion/sunday/the-art-of-distraction.html?pagewanted=all&_r=0 [accessed October 14, 2014].
—(2013), *Le Week-End*. Dir. Roger Michell. Film Four.
—(2014), *The Last Word*. London: Faber and Faber.

Secondary reading

Thomas, S. (2005), *Hanif Kureishi: A Reader's Guide to Essential Criticism*. New York: Palgrave Macmillan.

Chapter 1: The enigma of abandonment: Rethinking Hanif Kureishi's importance for multiculturalism, Michael Perfect

Works by Hanif Kureishi

Kureishi, H. (1985), *My Beautiful Launderette*. Dir. Stephen Frears. Channel Four Films.
—(1988), *"Sammy and Rosie Get Laid": The Script and The Diary*. London: Faber and Faber.
—(1990), *The Buddha of Suburbia*. London: Faber and Faber.
—(1991), *London Kills Me*. London: Faber and Faber.
—(1995), *The Black Album*. London: Faber and Faber.
—(1997), *My Son the Fanatic*. Dir. Udayan Prasad. Arts Council of England.
—(1998), *Intimacy*. London: Faber and Faber.
—(2001), *Gabriel's Gift*. London: Faber and Faber.
—(2002a), *The Body and Seven Stories*. London: Faber and Faber.
—(2002b), "Some Time with Stephen: A Diary," in *Dreaming and Scheming: Reflections of Writing and Politics*. London: Faber and Faber and Faber, pp. 127–99.
—(2003a), *The Mother*. London: Faber and Faber.
—(2003b), "Loose Tongues and Liberty," *The Guardian*. June 7, http://www.theguardian.com/books/2003/jun/07/hayfestival2003.hayfestival [accessed October 11, 2014].
—(2004), *My Ear at His Heart: Reading My Father*. London: Faber and Faber.
—(2006), *Venus*. Dir. Roger Michell. Miramax.
—(2008), *Something To Tell You*. London: Faber and Faber.
—(2009), *The Black Album: Adapted for the Stage*. London: Faber and Faber.
—(2013), *Le Week-End*. Dir. Roger Michell. Film Four.
—(2014), *The Last Word*. London: Faber and Faber.

Secondary reading

Degabriele, M. (1999), "Prince of Darkness Meets Priestess of Porn: Sexual and Political Identities in Hanif Kureishi's *The Black Album*," *Intersections: Gender, History, and Culture in the Asian Context*, 2, 29–40.

Holmes, F. M. (2001), "The Postcolonial Subject Divided between East and West: Kureishi's *The Black Album* as an Intertext of Rushdie's *The Satanic Verses*," *Papers on Language and Literature*, 37 (3), 296–314.

Huggan, G. (2001), *The Postcolonial Exotic: Marketing the Margins*. London: Routledge.

Kaleta, K. C. (1998), *Hanif Kureishi: Postcolonial Storyteller*. Austin: University of Texas Press.

Kumar, A. and Kureishi, H. (2001), "A Bang and a Whimper: A Conversation with Hanif Kureishi," *Transition: An International Review*, 10 (4), 114–31.

Malik, K. (1998), "Hanif Kureishi *Intimacy*," *Independent on Sunday*. May 3, http://www.kenanmalik.com/reviews/kureishi.html [accessed October 11, 2014].

Mars-Jones, A. (2008), "True Tales from the Couch," (Review of *Something to Tell You*), *The Observer*. February 23, http://www.guardian.co.uk/books/2008/feb/24/fiction.hanifkureishi [accessed October 11, 2014].

Monteith, S., Newman, J. and Wheeler, P. (eds) (2004), *Contemporary British and Irish Fiction: An Introduction Through Interviews*. London: Arnold.

Moore-Gilbert, B. (2001), *Hanif Kureishi*. Manchester: Manchester University Press.

Rushdie, S. (1988), *The Satanic Verses*. New York: Viking Press.

Stein, M. (2004), *Black British Literature: Novels of Transformation*. Columbus: Ohio State University Press.

Wachinger, T. (2003), *Posing In-Between: Postcolonial Englishness and the Commodification of Hybridity*. Frankfurt: Peter Lang.

Chapter 2: "I believe my eyes": The transformative cinema of Hanif Kureishi, Deanna Kamiel

Works by Hanif Kureishi

Kureishi, H. (1985), *My Beautiful Laundrette*. Dir. Stephen Frears. Channel Four Films.

—(1988), "England Bloody England," *The Guardian*. January 15, 19.

—(1995), *The Black Album*. New York: Scribner. Print.

—(2002[1985]), "My Beautiful Laundrette," in *Collected Screenplays*, vol. 1. London: Faber and Faber, pp. 1–90.

—(2006a), *Venus*. Dir. Roger Michell. Miramax.

—(2006b), *Venus*. London: Faber and Faber.

—(2011[1986]), "The Rainbow Sign," in *Collected Essays*. London: Faber and Faber, pp. 3–34.
—(2011[2006]), "Mad Old Men: The Writing of *Venus*," in *Collected Essays*. London: Faber and Faber, pp. 259–69.
—(2011[2009]), "Newness in the World," in *Collected Essays*. London: Faber and Faber, pp. 112–19.

Secondary reading

Andrew, D. (1985), "Cinema and Culture," *Humanities*, 6 (4), 24–5, http://www.csulb.edu/~jvancamp/361_r3.html [accessed October 11, 2014].
—(1995[1947]), *Mists of Regret: Culture and Sensibility in Classic French Film*. Princeton: Princeton University Press.
Bazin, A. (2005[1967]), "The Ontology of the Photographic Image," in *What is Cinema? Vol. 1*. Berkeley: University of California Press, pp. 9–16.
—(2008), "Every Film Is A Social Documentary," *Film Comment*, November–December, 40.
Benjamin, W. (2008), "The Work of Art: Second Version," in M. W. Jennings, B. Doherty and T. Y. Levin (eds), *The Work of Art in The Age of Its Technological Reproducibility, and Other Writings on Media*. Cambridge, MA: Harvard University Press, pp. 19–55.
Brunsdon, C. (2007), *London in Cinema: The Cinematic City Since 1945*. London: British Film Institute.
Friedman, L. and Stewart, S. (1994), "Keeping His Own Voice: An Interview with Stephen Frears," in W. W. Dixon (ed.), *Reviewing British Cinema 1900–1992*. Albany: State University of New York Press, pp. 221–40.
Geraghty, C. (2005), *My Beautiful Laundrette*. London: I. B. Tauris.
Henriques, J. (1987), "Realism and The New Language," in K. Mercer (ed.), *Black Film British Cinema*. London: ICA Documents, p. 19.
Higson, A. (ed.) (1996), "Space, Place, Spectacle," in *Dissolving Views*. London: Cassell, pp. 133–56.
Hill, J. (1999), *British Cinema in the 1980s*. Oxford: Clarendon Press.
Kamiel, D. (1980), *Godard*. Interview with Jean-Luc Godard. PBS. Twin Cities Public Television, St. Paul-Minneapolis.
MacCabe, C. (1999), "Hanif Kureishi on London," *Critical Quarterly*, 41 (3), 37–56.
Said, E. (2004), "Thoughts On Late Style," *London Review of Books*, 26 (15) (5 August), 3.
Sandhu, S. (2003), *London Calling: How Black and Asian Writers Imagined a City*. London: HarperCollins.
Sontag, S. (1961), *Against Interpretation and Other Essays*. New York: Farrar, Straus, Giroux.
Stone, N. (1988), "Through A Glass Darkly," *The Sunday Times*. January 10, C1–2.
Tanizaki, J. (1965), *Diary of a Mad Old Man*. New York: Knopf.
Wachtel, E. (2006), "Interview with Hanif Kureishi," *The Arts Today*. CBC Radio One, September 11.
Williams, R. (1983), "Problems of the Coming Period," *New Left Review*, 140 (July–August), 7–18.

Chapter 3: Culture and anarchy in Thatcher's London: Hanif Kureishi's *Sammy and Rosie Get Laid*, Peter Hitchcock

Works by Hanif Kureishi

Kureishi, H. (1985), *My Beautiful Laundrette*. Dir. Stephen Frears. Channel Four Films.
—(1986), *My Beautiful Laundrette and The Rainbow Sign*. London: Faber and Faber.
—(1987), *Sammy and Rosie Get Laid*. Dir. Stephen Frears. Channel Four Films.
—(1988), *Sammy and Rosie Get Laid*. New York: Penguin.
—(1990), *The Buddha of Suburbia*. London: Faber and Faber.
—(1991), *London Kills Me*. Dir. Hanif Kureishi. Channel Four Films.
—(1995), *The Black Album*. London: Faber and Faber.
—(2003), "Loose Tongues and Liberty," *The Guardian*. June 7, http://www.theguardian.com/books/2003/jun/07/hayfestival2003.hayfestival [accessed October 4, 2014].

Secondary reading

Arnold, M. (1971[1869]), *Culture and Anarchy*. New York: Bobbs Merrill.
Bhabha, H. (1990), "DissemiNation: Time, Narrative, and the Margins of the Modern Nation," in *Nation and Narration*. London: Routledge, pp. 291–322.
Eagleton, T. (1976), *Criticism and Ideology*. London: Verso.
Eliot, T. S. (1922), *The Waste Land*. New York: Horace Liveright.
Hall, S. (1988), *The Hard Road to Renewal*. London: Verso.
Handsworth Songs (1986). Dir. John Akomfrah. Black Audio Collective.
Kaleta, K. C. (1998), *Hanif Kureishi: Postcolonial Storyteller*. Austin: University of Texas Press.
Moore-Gilbert, B. (2001), *Hanif Kureishi*. Manchester: Manchester University Press.
Rushdie, S. (1988), *The Satanic Verses*. London: Penguin.
Rutherford, J. (ed.) (1990), *Identity: Community, Culture, Difference*. London: Lawrence and Wishart.
Sandhu, S. (2003), *London Calling: How Black and Asian Writers Imagined a City*. New York: HarperCollins.
Solomos, J. (1988), *Black Youth, Racism and the State*. Cambridge: Cambridge University Press.
Walters, M. (1990), "Kureishi's England," *London Review of Books*, 12 (7), (5 April), 16–17.
Yeats, W. B. (1986[1888]), "Letter, August 25, 1888, to writer Katharine Tynan (later Hinkson)," in J. Kelly (ed.), *Collected Letters of W. B. Yeats, vol. 1*. London: Oxford University Press, p. 43.

Chapter 4: "The suburbs that did it": Hanif Kureishi's *The Buddha of Suburbia* and metropolitan multicultural fiction, Ryan Trimm

Works by Hanif Kureishi

Kureishi, H. (1990), *The Buddha of Suburbia*. London: Faber and Faber.
—(1992), *London Kills Me: Three Screenplays and Four Essays*. New York: Penguin. Print.
—(1995), *The Black Album*. New York: Scribner.

Secondary reading

Ball, J. C. (1996), "The Semi-Detached Metropolis: Hanif Kureishi's London," *ARIEL: A Review of International English Literature*, 27 (4), 7–27.
—(2004), *Imagining London: Postcolonial Fiction and the Transnational Metropolis*. Toronto: University of Toronto Press.
Brook, S. (2005), "Hedgemony? Suburban Space in *The Buddha of Suburbia*," in N. Bentley (ed.), *British Fiction of the 1990s*. New York: Routledge, pp. 209–25.
Dennis, N. (1955), *Cards of Identity*. London: Weidenfeld & Nicolson.
Eliot, G. (1874), *Middlemarch*. Edinburgh: William Blackwood & Sons.
Emecheta, B. (1974), *Second Class Citizen*. New York: George Braziller.
Fabian, J. (1983), *Time and the Other: How Anthropology Makes Its Object*. New York: Columbia University Press.
Felski, R. (2000), "Nothing to Declare: Identity, Shame, and the Lower Middle Class," *PMLA*, 115 (1), 33–45.
Forster, E. M. (1998[1910]), *Howards End*. New York: W. W. Norton.
Hartley, L. P. (1953), *The Go-Between*. London: Heinemann.
Ishiguro, K. (1989), *The Remains of the Day*. Boston: Faber and Faber.
Lamming, G. (1955[1954]), *The Emigrants*. New York: McGraw-Hill.
MacCabe, C. (1999), "Hanif Kureishi on London," *Critical Quarterly*, 41 (3), 37–56.
MacInnes, C. (2007[1957]), *The London Novels: City of Spades, Absolute Beginners, and Mr Love and Justice*. London: Allison & Busby.
McLeod, J. (2004), *Postcolonial London: Rewriting the Metropolis*. New York: Routledge.
Naipaul, V. S. (1967), *The Mimic Men*. New York: Macmillan.
O'Reilly, N. (2009), "Embracing Suburbia: Breaking Tradition and Accepting the Self in Hanif Kureishi's *The Buddha of Suburbia*," *Literary London: Interdisciplinary Studies in the Representation of London* 7 (2), http://www.literarylondon.org/london-journal/september2009/index.html [accessed October 11, 2014].

Procter, J. (2006), "New Ethnicities, the Novel, and the Burdens of Representation," in J. F. English (ed.), *A Concise Companion to Contemporary British Fiction*. Malden, MA: Blackwell, 2006, pp. 101–20.
Rosello, M. (2001), *Postcolonial Hospitality: The Immigrant as Guest*. Stanford: Stanford University Press.
Rushdie, S. (1988), *The Satanic Verses*. New York: Picador.
Selvon, S. (1956), *The Lonely Londoners*. New York: Longman.
Stein, M. (2004), *Black British Literature: Novels of Transformation*. Columbus: Ohio State University Press.
Thomas, S. (2005), *Hanif Kureishi: A Reader's Guide to Essential Criticism*. New York: Palgrave Macmillan.
Thompson, M. (2005), "'Happy Multicultural Land?' The Implications of an 'Excess of Belonging' in Zadie Smith's *White Teeth*," in K. Sesay (ed.), *Write Black, Write British: From Post Colonial to Black British*. London: Hansib, pp. 122–40.
Waugh, E. (1945), *Brideshead Revisited: The Sacred & Profane Memoires of Captain Charles Ryder*. London: Chapman and Hall.
Williams, R. (1973), *The Country and the City*. New York: Oxford University Press.

Chapter 5: Hanif Kureishi's "better philosophy": From *The Black Album* and *My Son the Fanatic* to *The Word and the Bomb*, Susan Alice Fischer

Works by Hanif Kureishi

Kureishi, H. (1985), *My Beautiful Laundrette*. Dir. Stephen Frears. Channel Four Films.
—(1987), *Sammy and Rosie Get Laid*. Dir. Stephen Frears. Channel Four Films.
—(1990), *The Buddha of Suburbia*. London: Faber and Faber.
—(1991), *London Kills Me*. Dir. Hanif Kureishi. Channel Four Films.
—(1995), *The Black Album*. London: Faber and Faber.
—(1997), *My Son the Fanatic*. Dir. Udayan Prasad. Arts Council of England.
—(1999), *Sleep with Me*. London: Faber and Faber.
—(2002[1988]), "Sammy and Rosie Get Laid," in *Collected Screenplays*, vol. 1. London: Faber and Faber, pp. 91–76.
—(2002[1997]), "My Son the Fanatic," in *Collected Screenplays*, vol. 1. London: Faber and Faber, pp. 279–385.
—(2005), *The Word and the Bomb*. London: Faber and Faber.
—(2009), "Newness in the World: An Introduction to The Black Album–The Play," in *The Black Album: Adapted for the Stage by the Author*. London: Faber and Faber, pp. v–xiii.
—2010[1997], "My Son the Fanatic," in *Collected Stories*. London: Faber and Faber, pp. 16–127.
—(2011), *Collected Essays*. London: Faber and Faber.

Secondary reading

Bakhtin, M. (2004[1965]), "Rabelais and His World," in J. Rivkin and M. Ryan (eds), *Literary Theory: An Anthology*, 2nd edition. Malden, MA: Blackwell, pp. 686–92.

Chambers, C. (2011a), "A Comparative Approach to Pakistani Fiction in English," *Journal of Postcolonial Writing*, 47 (2), 122–34.

—(2011b), "Hanif Kureishi," in *British Muslim Fictions: Interviews with Contemporary Writers*. London: Palgrave Macmillan, pp. 226–42.

Fischer, S. A. (2014), "Embracing Uncertainty: Hanif Kureishi's *The Buddha of Suburbia* and *The Black Album*," in N. Allen and D. Simmons (eds), *Reassessing the Twentieth Century Canon: From Joseph Conrad to Zadie Smith*. London: Palgrave, pp. 281–93.

Ghose, S. (2007), "Brit Bomber: The Fundamentalist Trope in Hanif Kureishi's *The Black Album* and 'My Son the Fanatic,'" in G. MacPhee and P. Poddar (eds), *Empire and After: Englishness in Postcolonial Perspective*. New York: Berghahn Books, pp. 121–38.

MacCabe, C. (1999), "Hanif Kureishi on London," *Critical Quarterly*, 41 (3), 37–56.

Malik, K. (2009), "Kureishi on the Rushdie Affair," April, http://www.kenanmalik.com/essays/prospect_kureishi.html [accessed April 10, 2012].

Needham, A. D. (2000). "'A New Way of Being British': Hanif Kureishi's (Necessary) Defense of Mixtures and Heterogeneity," in *Using the Master's Tools: Resistance and the Literature of the African and South-Asian Diasporas*. New York: St. Martin's Press, pp. 111–28.

O'Shea-Meddour, W. (2007), "Deconstructing Fundamentalisms in Hanif Kureishi's *The Black Album*," in C. Pesso-Miquel and K. Stierstorfer (eds), *Fundamentalism and Literature*. London: Palgrave Macmillan, pp. 81–100.

Perfect, M. (2015), "The Enigma of Abandonment: Re-thinking Hanif Kureishi's Importance for Multiculturalism," in S. A. Fischer (ed.), *Hanif Kureishi: Contemporary Critical Perspectives*. London: Bloomsbury, pp. 7–20.

Ranasinha, R. (2002), *Hanif Kureishi*. London: Northcote House.

Ross, M. L. (2006), "'A Funny Kind of Englishman': Hanif Kureishi's Carnival of Ethnicities," in *Race Riots: Comedy and Ethnicity in Modern British Fiction*. Montreal: McGill-Queen's University Press, pp. 228–47.

Rushdie, S. (1988), *The Satanic Verses*. London: Penguin.

Sandhu, S. (2003), *London Calling: How Black and Asian Writers Imagined a City*. New York: HarperCollins.

Thomas, S. (2005a), "Literary Apartheid in the Post-War London Novel: Finding the Middle Ground," *Changing English: Studies in Culture and Education*, 12 (2), 309–25.

—(ed.) (2005b), *Hanif Kureishi: A Reader's Guide to Essential Criticism*. Houndsmills: Palgrave Macmillan.

—(2009), "After the Fatwa," *Changing English: Studies in Culture and Education*, 16 (4), 365–83.

—(2011), "Hanif Kureishi—'The Buddha of Suburbia'—1990," in A. Whitehead, *London Fictions*, February, http://www.londonfictions.com/hanif-kureishi-thebuddha-of-suburbia.html [accessed February 13, 2012].

Upstone, S. (2006), "A Question of Black or White: Returning to Hanif Kureishi's," *The Black Album, Postcolonial Text*, 4 (1), 1–24, http://www.google.com/url?sa=t&rct=j&q=&esrc=s&source=web&cd=1&ved=0CCAQFjAA&url=http%3A%2F%2Fwww.postcolonial.org%2Findex.php%2Fpct%2Farticle%2Fdownload%2F6

79%2F518&ei=oaQ5VMShNYP5yASjyoG4Dw&usg=AFQjCNEG8RqKPnNgMEQ dFCeib9NjPAQjBA&bvm=bv.77161500,d.aWw [accessed September 28, 2013].
—(2010), "Hanif Kureishi," in *British Asian Fiction: Twenty-First Century Voices*. Manchester: Manchester University Press, pp. 37–61.
Waraich, O. (2006), "When Bombs Speak Louder than Words," *First Jordan*, February 6, http://www.1stjordan.net/actuuk/archivesuk/resultat. php?id=1017&debut=0 [accessed February 25, 2011].
Wright, M. J. (2006), "My Son the Fanatic (Udayan Prasad, 1997)," in *Religion and Film: An Introduction*. London: I. B. Tauris, pp. 107–27.

Chapter 6: The parallax of aging: Hanif Kureishi's *The Body*, Jago Morrison

Works by Hanif Kureishi

Kureishi, H. (1985), *My Beautiful Laundrette*. Dir. Stephen Frears. Channel Four Films.
—(1987), *Sammy and Rosie Get Laid*. Dir. Stephen Frears. Channel Four Films.
—(1990), *The Buddha of Suburbia*. London: Faber and Faber.
—(1995), *The Black Album*. London: Faber and Faber.
—(1997), *My Son the Fanatic*. Dir. Udayan Prasad. Arts Council of England.
—(2001), *Gabriel's Gift*. London: Faber and Faber.
—(2002), *The Body and Seven Stories*. London: Faber and Faber.

Secondary reading

Bühler-Dietrich, A. (2006), "Technologies in Hanif Kureishi's 'The Body,'" in W. Goebel and S. Schabio (eds), *Beyond the Black Atlantic: Relocating Modernization and Technology*. London: Routledge, pp. 168–83.
Çelicel, M. A. (2009), "Representation of Body and Identity in Kureishi's *The Body*," *Interactions*, 18 (2), 51–9.
Cowley, J. (2002), "You're as Young as You Feel …," *The Observer*. November 2, http://www.theguardian.com/books/2002/nov/03/fiction.hanifkureishi [accessed October 11, 2014].
Gullette, M. M. (2004), *Aged by Culture*. Chicago: University of Chicago Press.
Kaleta, K. C. (1998), *Hanif Kureishi: Postcolonial Storyteller*. Austin: University of Texas Press.
Kunkel, B. (2004), "You've Got to Have Pecs," *New York Times Book Review*, 153, http://www.nytimes.com/2004/02/29/books/you-ve-got-to-have-pecs.html [accessed October 11, 2014].
Mellard, J. (2010), "The Jews of Ruby, Oklahoma: Politics, Parallax, and Ideological Fantasy in Toni Morrison's *Paradise*," *Modern Fiction Studies*, 56 (2), 349–77.
Moore-Gilbert, B. (2001), *Hanif Kureishi*. Manchester: Manchester University Press.

Žižek, S. (2004), "The Parallax View," *New Left Review*, 25 (January–February), 121–34.
—(2006), *The Parallax View*. Cambridge, MA: MIT Press.
—(2008), *Violence: Six Sideways Reflections*. London: Profile.

Chapter 7: The other Kureishi: A psychoanalytic reading of *Something to Tell You*, Geoff Boucher

Works by Hanif Kureishi

Kureishi, H. (1990), *The Buddha of Suburbia*. London: Faber and Faber.
—(1995), *The Black Album*. London: Faber and Faber.
—(1997), *Love in a Blue Time*. London: Faber and Faber.
—(1998), *Intimacy*. London: Faber and Faber.
—(2008), *Something to Tell You*. New York: Scribner.

Secondary reading

Adorno, T. and Horkheimer, M. (2002[1947]), *Dialectic of Enlightenment: Philosophical Fragments*. Stanford: Stanford University Press.
Buchanan, B. (2007), *Hanif Kureishi*. London: Palgrave Macmillan.
Cohn, D. (1978), *Transparent Minds. Narrative Modes for Presenting Consciousness in Fiction*. Princeton: Princeton University Press.
Freud, S. (1913–14), *The Standard Edition of the Complete Psychological Works of Sigmund Freud, Vol. XIII (1913-1914): Totem and Taboo and Other Works*. London: The Hogarth Press. Print.
—(1921), "Group Psychology and the Analysis of the Ego," in J. Strachey (ed.), *The Standard Edition of the Complete Psychological Works of Sigmund Freud, Volume XVIII: Beyond the Pleasure Principle, Group Psychology and other Works*. London: The Hogarth Press, pp. 65–144.
—(1923–5), *The Standard Edition of the Complete Psychological Works of Sigmund Freud. Vol. XIX (1923-1925): The Ego and the Id and Other Works*. London: The Hogarth Press.
—(1924), "The Dissolution of the Oedipus Complex," in J. Strachey (ed.), *The Standard Edition of the Complete Psychological Works of Sigmund Freud, Volume XIX: The Ego and the Id and Other Works*. London: The Hogarth Press, pp. 171–80.
—(1927–33), *The Standard Edition of the Complete Psychological Works of Sigmund Freud. Vol. XXI (1927-1931): The Future of an Illusion, Civilization and its Discontents, and Other Works*. London: The Hogarth Press.
—(1930), "Civilization and Its Discontents," in J. Strachey (ed.), *The Standard Edition of the Complete Psychological Works of Sigmund Freud, Volume XXI (1927-1931): The Future of an Illusion, Civilization and its Discontents, and Other Works*. London: The Hogarth Press, pp. 57–146.

REFERENCES

—(1933), "New Introductory Lectures on Psycho-Analysis," in J. Strachey (ed.), *The Standard Edition of the Complete Psychological Works of Sigmund Freud, Volume XXII (1932-1936): New Introductory Lectures on Psycho-Analysis and Other Works*. London: The Hogarth Press, pp. 1–182.

—(1937–9), *The Standard Edition of the Complete Psychological Works of Sigmund Freud, Vol. XXIII (1937-1939): Moses and Monotheism, An Outline of Psycho-Analysis and Other Works*. London: The Hogarth Press.

Lacan, J. (1994), *Le séminaire de Jacques Lacan, Livre IV: La relation d'objet*. Paris: Seuil.

Moore-Gilbert, B. (2001), *Hanif Kureishi*. Manchester: Manchester University Press.

Ranasinha, R. (2002), *Hanif Kureishi*. London: Northcote House.

Thomas, S. (ed.) (2005), *Hanif Kureishi: A Reader's Guide to Essential Criticism*. Basingstoke: Palgrave Macmillan.

Chapter 8: *The Last Word* on Hanif Kureishi, Susie Thomas

Works by Hanif Kureishi

Kureishi, H. (1990), *The Buddha of Suburbia*. London: Faber and Faber.

—(1995), *The Black Album*. London: Faber and Faber.

—(2002[1986]), "The Rainbow Sign," in *Dreaming and Scheming: Reflections on Writing and Politics*. London: Faber and Faber, pp. 25–56.

—(2002), *The Body and Seven Stories*. London: Faber and Faber.

—(2004), *My Ear at His Heart: Reading My Father*. London: Faber and Faber.

—(2005), "The Arduous Conversation Will Continue," in *The Word and the Bomb*. London: Faber and Faber, pp. 90–3.

—(2008), *Something to Tell You*. London: Faber and Faber.

—(2014), *The Last Word*. London: Faber and Faber.

Secondary reading

Appignanesi, L. (2008), "All in the Mind," *The Guardian*. February 15, http://www.guardian.co.uk/books/2008/feb/16/featuresreviews.guardianreview2 [accessed November 2, 2013].

Boucher, G. (2015), "The Other Kureishi: A Psychoanalytic Reading of *Something to Tell You*," in S. A. Fischer (ed.), *Hanif Kureishi: Contemporary Critical Perspectives*. London: Bloomsbury, pp. 99–113.

Brook, S. (2005), "Hedgemony?: Suburban Space in *The Buddha of Suburbia*," in N. Bentley (ed.), *British Fiction of the 1990s*. London: Routledge, pp. 209–25.

Dickens, C. (1996[1861]), *Great Expectations: Case Studies in Contemporary Fiction*, ed. J. Carlisle. Boston: Bedford Books of St. Martin's Press.

Eagleton, T. (1983), *Literary Theory: An Introduction*. Oxford: Blackwell.

REFERENCES

Head, D. (2002), *The Cambridge Introduction to Modern British Fiction, 1950–2000*. Cambridge: Cambridge University Press.

Kermode, F. (1983[1975]), *The Classic: Literary Images of Permanence and Change: T. S. Eliot Memorial Lectures at the University of Kent, 1974*. Cambridge, MA: Harvard University Press.

Kuchta, T. (2010), *Semi-Detached Empire: Suburbia and the Colonization of Britain, 1880 to the Present*. Charlottesville: University of Virginia Press.

Moore-Gilbert, B. (2012), "From 'the Politics of Recognition' to 'the Policing of Recognition': Writing Islam in Hanif Kureishi and Mohsin Hamid," in R. Ahmed, P. Morey and A. Yaqin (eds), *Culture, Diaspora, and Modernity in Muslim Writing*. London: Routledge, pp. 183–99.

Naipaul, V. S. (1967), *The Mimic Men*. New York: Macmillan.

Orwell, G. (2000[1939]), "Charles Dickens," in B. Crick (ed.), *George Orwell: Essays*, Penguin Modern Classics. London: Penguin, 2000, pp. 35–78.

—(2000[1946]), "Why I Write," in B. Crick (ed.), *George Orwell: Essays*, Penguin Modern Classics. London: Penguin, pp. 1–7.

O'Shea-Meddour, W. (2008), "The Politics of Imagining the Other in Hanif Kureishi's *The Buddha of Suburbia*," in N. Murphy and W.-C. Sim (eds), *British Asian Fiction: Framing the Contemporary*. Amherst: Cambria Press, pp. 33–51.

Sandhu, S. (2000), "Paradise Syndrome," *London Review of Books*, 22 (10), May 18, http://www.lrb.co.uk/v22/n10/sukhdev-sandhu/paradise-syndrome [accessed October 11, 2014].

Schoene, B. (1998), "Herald of Hybridity: The Emancipation of Difference in Hanif Kureishi's *The Buddha of Suburbia*," *International Journal of Cultural Studies*, 1 (1), 109–27.

Smith, Z. (2000), *White Teeth*. London: Penguin.

Stein, M. (2004), "Of Aunties and Elephants–Kureishi's Aesthetics of Postethnicity," in *Black British Literature: Novels of Transformation*. Columbus: Ohio State University Press, pp. 108–42.

Su, J. J. (2011), *Imagination and the Contemporary Novel*. Cambridge: Cambridge University Press.

Thomas, S. (ed.) (2005), *Hanif Kureishi: A Reader's Guide to Essential Criticism*. Basingstoke: Palgrave Macmillan.

—(2009), "After the Fatwa," *Changing English: Studies in Culture and Education*, 16 (4), 365–83.

—(2013), "Hanif Kureishi: *The Buddha of Suburbia*," in A. Whitehead and J. White (eds), *London Fictions*. Nottingham: Five Leaves, pp. 201–9.

Yassin-Kassab, R. (2008), *The Road to Damascus*. London: Hamish Hamilton.

Further reading

I: Selected works by Hanif Kureishi

Novels

Kureishi, H. (1990), *The Buddha of Suburbia*. London: Faber and Faber.
—(1995), *The Black Album*. London: Faber and Faber.
—(1998), *Intimacy*. London: Faber and Faber.
—(2001), *Gabriel's Gift*. London: Faber and Faber.
—(2008), *Something To Tell You*. London: Faber and Faber.
—(2014), *The Last Word*. London: Faber and Faber.

Other fiction and nonfiction

Kureishi, H. (1986), "A Feast of Words," *New Republic*, 195 (5), 40–1.
—(1988), "Behind the Veils: Notes on Pakistan," *Utne Reader*, 87500256 (28), 84.
—(1988), "England Bloody England," *The Guardian*. January 15.
—(1989), "Esther," *Atlantic* 02769077, 263 (5), 56.
—(1995), *The Faber Book of Pop*, ed. with Jon Savage. London: Faber and Faber.
—(1997), *Love in a Blue Time*. London: Faber and Faber.
—(1998), "Intimacy," *New Yorker*, 74 (11), 90.
—(1999), "Ladybirds for Lunch (Short story)," *Modern Painters*, 12 (4), 36–40.
—(1999), *Midnight All Day*. London: Faber and Faber.
—(2002), *The Body and Seven Stories*. London: Faber and Faber.
—(2002), *Dreaming and Scheming: Reflections of Writing and Politics*. London: Faber and Faber.
—(2003), "Loose Tongues and Liberty," *The Guardian*. June 7, http://www.theguardian.com/books/2003/jun/07/hayfestival2003.hayfestival [accessed October 14, 2014].
—(2004), "Kicking against the Pricks," *Modern Painters*, 17 (4), 34–6.
—(2004), *My Ear at His Heart: Reading My Father*. London: Faber and Faber.
—(2005), *The Word and the Bomb*. London: Faber and Faber, 2005.
—(2006), "The Drift Generation," *New Statesman*, 135 (4789), 48–9.
—(2006), "End notes," *New Statesman*, 135 (4794), 52–3.
—(2006), "Fear and Paranoia," *The Guardian*. April 21, http://www.theguardian.com/stage/2006/apr/22/theatre.hanifkureishi [accessed October 14, 2014].

—(2006), "Reaping the Harvest of our Self-Disgust," *The Guardian*. September 29, http://www.theguardian.com/commentisfree/2006/sep/30/comment.mainsection2 [accessed October 14, 2014].
—(2006), "The Writing Cure," *New Statesman*, 135 (4798), 64–5.
—(2007), "Best of British," *New Statesman*, 136 (4836), 40–1.
—(2008), "Race Ahead," *The Guardian*. January 25, http://www.theguardian.com/books/2008/jan/26/4 [accessed October 14, 2014].
—(2008), "The Sadness Epidemic," *New Statesman*, 137 (4885), 54.
—(2008), "Something to Tell You," *Critical Quarterly*, 50 (1/2), 43–60.
—(2008), "The Whole Person," *New Statesman*, 137 (4881), 54.
—(2010), *Collected Stories*. London: Faber and Faber.
—(2011), *Collected Prose*. London: Faber and Faber.
—(2011), "It's a Sin: The Kama Sutra and the Search for Pleasure," *Critical Quarterly*, 53 (1), 1–5.
—(2012), "The Art of Distraction," *The New York Times*. February 18, http://www.nytimes.com/2012/02/19/opinion/sunday/the-art-of-distraction.html?pagewanted=all&_r=0 [accessed October 14, 2014].
—(2013), "In Praise of Adultery," *The Guardian*. October 4, http://www.theguardian.com/books/2013/oct/04/hanif-kureishi-praise-adultery-week-end [accessed October 14, 2014].
—(2013), "The Racer," *New Statesman*, 142 (5168), 78–9.
—(2014), "The Migrant has No Face, Status or Story," *The Guardian*. May 30, http://www.theguardian.com/books/2014/may/30/hanif-kureishi-migrant-immigration-1 [accessed October 11, 2014].

Drama

Kureishi, H. (1992), *Outskirts and Other Plays*. London: Faber and Faber.
—(1999), *Sleep with Me*. London: Faber and Faber.
—(2004), *When Night Begins*. London: Faber and Faber.
—(2009), *The Black Album: Adapted for the Stage*. London: Faber and Faber.

Screenplays

Kureishi, H. (1986), *My Beautiful Laundrette and The Rainbow Sign*. London: Faber and Faber.
—(1988), *"Sammy and Rosie Get Laid": The Script and The Diary*. London: Faber and Faber.
—(1992), *London Kills Me: Three Screenplays and Four Essays*. New York: Penguin.
—(2002), *Collected Screenplays, vol. 1*. London: Faber and Faber.
—(2003), *The Mother*. London: Faber and Faber.
—(2006), *Venus*. London: Faber and Faber.
—(2013), *Le Week-End*. London: Faber and Faber.

Films and adaptations of the author's work

My Beautiful Laundrette (1985). Dir. Stephen Frears. Channel Four Films.
Sammy and Rosie Get Laid (1987). Dir. Stephen Frears. Channel Four Films.
London Kills Me (1991). Dir. Hanif Kureishi. Channel Four Films.
Buddha of Suburbia (1993). Dir. Roger Michell. BBC.
My Son the Fanatic (1997). Dir. Udayan Prasad. Arts Council of England.
Intimacy (2001). Dir. Patrice Chéreau. Empire Pictures.
The Mother (2003). Dir. Roger Michell. BBC Films.
Venus (2006). Dir. Roger Michell. Miramax.
Le Week-End (2013). Dir. Roger Michell. Film Four.

II: Selected critical material

Book-length studies (dedicated solely to Kureishi's work)

Buchanan, B. (2007), *Hanif Kureishi*. London. Palgrave Macmillan.
Geraghty, C. (2005), *My Beautiful Laundrette*. London: I. B. Tauris.
Kaleta, K. C. (1998), *Hanif Kureishi: Postcolonial Storyteller*. Austin: University of Texas Press.
Moore-Gilbert, B. (2001), *Hanif Kureishi*. Manchester: Manchester University Press.
Ranasinha, R. (2002), *Hanif Kureishi*. London: Northcote House.
Thomas, S. (ed.) (2005), *Hanif Kureishi: A Reader's Guide to Essential Criticism*. Basingstoke: Palgrave Macmillan.

Book chapters

Brook, S. (2005), "Hedgemony? Suburban Space in *The Buddha of Suburbia*," in N. Bentley (ed.), *British Fiction of the 1990s*. London: Routledge, pp. 209–25.
Bühler-Dietrich, A. (2006), "Technologies in Hanif Kureishi's 'The Body,'" in W. Goebel and S. Schabio (eds), *Beyond the Black Atlantic: Relocating Modernization and Technology*. London: Routledge, pp. 168–83.
Fine Romanow, R. (2006), "Embracing Maturity: Hanif Kureishi's *Sammy and Rosie Get Laid*," in *Postcolonial Body in Queer Space and Time*. Newcastle-upon-Tyne: Cambridge Scholars Publishing, pp. 102–33.
—(2006), "Remapping Time and Space: The Body's 'Anthropological Exodus' in Kureishi's *The Buddha of Suburbia*," in *Postcolonial Body in Queer Space and Time*. Newcastle-upon-Tyne: Cambridge Scholars Publishing, pp. 70–101.
Fischer, S. A. (2014), "Embracing Uncertainty: Hanif Kureishi's *The Buddha of Suburbia* and *The Black Album*," in N. Allen and D. Simmons (eds), *Reassessing the Twentieth Century Canon: From Joseph Conrad to Zadie Smith*. London: Palgrave, pp. 281–93.

Ghose, S. (2007), "Brit Bomber: The Fundamentalist Trope in Hanif Kureishi's *The Black Album* and 'My Son the Fanatic,'" in G. MacPhee and P. Poddar (eds), *Empire and After: Englishness in Postcolonial Perspective*. New York: Berghahn Books, pp. 121–38.

Ilona, A. (2003), "Hanif Kureishi's *The Buddha of Suburbia*," in R. J. Lane, R. Mengham and P. Tew (eds), *Contemporary British Fiction*. Malden, MA: Polity Press, pp. 87–105.

Moore-Gilbert, B. (2012), "From 'the Politics of Recognition' to 'the Policing of Recognition': Writing Islam in Hanif Kureishi and Mohsin Hamid," in R. Ahmed, P. Morey and A. Yaqin (eds), *Culture, Diaspora, and Modernity in Muslim Writing*. London: Routledge, pp. 183–99.

Needham, A. D. (2000), "'A New Way of Being British': Hanif Kureishi's (Necessary) Defense of Mixtures and Heterogeneity," in *Using the Master's Tools: Resistance and the Literature of the African and South-Asian Diasporas*. New York: St. Martin's Press, pp. 111–28.

O'Shea-Meddour, W. (2007), "Deconstructing Fundamentalisms in Hanif Kureishi's *The Black Album*," in C. Pesso-Miquel and K. Stierstorfer (eds), *Fundamentalism and Literature*. London: Palgrave Macmillan, pp. 81–100.

—(2008), "The Politics of Imagining the Other in Hanif Kureishi's *The Buddha of Suburbia*," in N. Murphy and W.-C. Sim (eds), *British Asian Fiction: Framing the Contemporary*. Amherst: Cambria Press, pp. 33–51.

Ranasinha, R. (2007), "Cultural Difference: Cultural Translation and the Politics of Representation: Hanif Kureishi and Meera Syal," in *South Asian Writers in Twentieth-Century Britain: Culture in Translation*. Oxford: Oxford University Press, pp. 221–65.

Ross, M. L. (2006), "'A Funny Kind of Englishman': Hanif Kureishi's Carnival of Ethnicities," in *Race Riots: Comedy and Ethnicity in Modern British Fiction*. Montreal: McGill-Queen's University Press, pp. 228–47.

Stein, M. (2004), "Of Aunties and Elephants–Kureishi's Aesthetics of Postethnicity," in *Black British Literature: Novels of Transformation*. Columbus: Ohio State University Press, pp. 108–42.

Thomas, S. (2013), "Hanif Kureishi: *The Buddha of Suburbia*," in A. Whitehead and J. White (eds), *London Fictions*. Nottingham: Five Leaves Publications, pp. 201–9.

Upstone, S. (2010), "Hanif Kureishi," in *British Asian Fiction: Twenty-First Century Voices*. Manchester: Manchester University Press, pp. 37–61.

Winkgens, M. (2011), "Cultural Hybridity and Fluid Masculinities in the Postcolonial Metropolis: Individualized Gender Identities in Hanif Kureishi's *The Buddha of Suburbia* and *The Black Album*," in S. Horlacher (ed.), *Constructions of Masculinity in British Literature from the Middle Ages to the Present*. New York: Palgrave Macmillan, pp. 229–45.

Wright, M. J. (2006), "My Son the Fanatic (Udayan Prasad, 1997)," in *Religion and Film: An Introduction*. London: I. B. Tauris, pp. 107–27.

Journal articles

Ahmed, R. (2009), "Occluding Race in Selected Short Fiction by Hanif Kureishi," *Wasafiri: The Magazine of International Contemporary Writing*, 24 (2) [58], 27–34.

FURTHER READING

Allen, C. (2008), "Young Protagonists in the Contemporary London Novel: Hanif Kureishi and Rupert Thomson," *Literary London: Interdisciplinary Studies in the Representation of London*, 6 (2), http://www.literarylondon.org/london-journal/september2008/allen.html [accessed October 14, 2014].

Ball, J. C. (1996), "The Semi-Detached Metropolis: Hanif Kureishi's London," *ARIEL: A Review of International English Literature*, 27 (4), 7–27.

Çelicel, M. A. (2009), "Representation of Body and Identity in Kureishi's *The Body*," *Interactions*, 18 (2), 51–9.

Chalupský, P. (2011), "Prick Lit or Naked Hope? Self-Exposure in Hanif Kureishi's *Intimacy*," *Brno Studies in English*, 37 (2), 61–78.

Chambers, C. (2011), "A Comparative Approach to Pakistani Fiction in English," *Journal of Postcolonial Writing*, 47 (2), 122–34.

Degabriele, M. (1999), "Prince of Darkness Meets Priestess of Porn: Sexual and Political Identities in Hanif Kureishi's *The Black Album*," *Intersections: Gender, History, and Culture in the Asian Context*, 2, 29–40.

Dyer, R. (2002), "Dirty Work, Asian Entrepreneurship, and Labors of Love in Hanif Kureishi's *My Beautiful Laundrette*," *Critical Sense: A Journal of Political and Cultural Theory*, 10 (1), 59–86.

Ferretter, L. (2003), "Hanif Kureishi and the Politics of Comedy," *Sydney Studies in English*, 29, 87–102.

Gairola, R. K. (2011), "A Critique of Thatcherism and the Queering of Home in *Sammy and Rosie Get Laid*," *South Asian Review*, 32 (3), 123–37, 250.

Gilman, S. L. (2006), "The Fanatic: Philip Roth and Hanif Kureishi Confront Success," *Comparative Literature*, 58 (2), 153–69.

Godlasky, R. S. (2006), "Revising Englishness: Embracing Hybridity in Hanif Kureishi's *The Black Album*," *Journal of Commonwealth and Postcolonial Studies*, 13 (1), 1–16.

Holmes, F. M. (2001), "The Postcolonial Subject divided between East and West: Kureishi's *The Black Album* as an Intertext of Rushdie's *The Satanic Verses*," *Papers on Language and Literature*, 37 (3), 296–314.

Juhász, T. (2011), "Back to Normal: Manhood and Displacement in Hanif Kureishi's *Intimacy*," *South Asian Review*, 32 (2), 223–39, 328.

MacCabe, C. (1999), "Hanif Kureishi on London," *Critical Quarterly*, 41 (3), 37–56.

Malik, K. (2009), "Kureishi on the Rushdie Affair," April, http://www.kenanmalik.com/essays/prospect_kureishi.html [accessed April 10, 2012].

Maxey, R. (2006), "'Life in the Diaspora is Often Held in a Strange Suspension': First-Generation Self-Fashioning in Hanif Kureishi's Narratives of Home and Return," *Journal of Commonwealth Literature*, 41 (3), 5–25.

Moore-Gilbert, B. (1997), "Hanif Kureishi's *The Buddha of Suburbia*: Hybridity in Contemporary Cultural Theory and Artistic Practice," *Q/W/E/R/T/Y*, 7, 191–207.

—(2001), "Justice and Morality in the Plays of Hanif Kureishi," *European Studies: A Journal of European Culture, History, and Politics*, 17, 241–53.

Morrison, J. (2003), "After 'Race': Hanif Kureishi's Writing," *Contemporary Fiction*, 179–90.

O'Reilly, N. (2009), "Embracing Suburbia: Breaking Tradition and Accepting the Self in Hanif Kureishi's *The Buddha of Suburbia*," *Literary London: Interdisciplinary Studies in the Representation of London*, 7 (2), http://www.literarylondon.org/london-journal/september2009/oreilly.html [accessed October 14, 2014].

Redhead, S. (2008), "Hanif Kureishi: A Life in Accelerated Popular Culture," *English Language Notes*, 46 (1), 179–91.

Romanow, R. (2011), "The Refusal of Migrant Subjectivity: Queer Times and Spaces in Hanif Kureishi's *The Buddha of Suburbia*," *Thamyris/Intersecting: Place, Sex & Race*, 22 (1), 143–59.

Sağlam, B. (2014), "Rocking London: Youth Culture as Commodity in *The Buddha of Suburbia*," *Journal of Popular Culture*, 47 (3), 554–70.

Sandhu, S. (1999), "Pop Goes the Centre: Hanif Kureishi's London," *Essays & Studies*, 133–54.

Sarkar, P. (2013), "London is [Not] the Place for Me: The Failure of the Immigrant Dream in Hanif Kureishi's *The Buddha of Suburbia*," *Journal of Commonwealth and Postcolonial Studies*, 1 (2), 39–60.

Schoene, B. (1998), "Herald of Hybridity: The Emancipation of Difference in Hanif Kureishi's *The Buddha of Suburbia*," *International Journal of Cultural Studies*, 1 (1), 109–28.

Schötz, B. (2013), "The Exploration of Community in Hanif Kureishi's Short Fiction," *The Literary London Journal*, 10 (2), http://www.literarylondon.org/london-journal/autumn2013/schotz.html [accessed October 14, 2014].

Sen, A. (2000), "Re-Writing History: Hanif Kureishi and the Politics of Black Britain," *Passages: A Journal of Transnational & Transcultural Studies*, 2 (1), 61–80.

Thomas, S. (2006), "Hanif Kureishi's *My Ear at His Heart*: 'When a Writer is Born a Family Dies'," *Changing English: Studies in Culture and Education*, 13 (2), 185–96.

—(2006), "Zadie Smith's False Teeth: The Marketing of Multiculturalism," *Literary London: Interdisciplinary Studies in the Representation of London*, 4 (1), http://www.literarylondon.org/london-journal/march2006/thomas.html [accessed October 14, 2014].

—(2009), "After the Fatwa," *Changing English: Studies in Culture and Education*, 16 (4), 365–83.

—(2011), "Hanif Kureishi—'The Buddha of Suburbia'—1990," in A. Whitehead, *London Fictions*, February, http://www.londonfictions.com/hanif-kureishi-thebuddha-of-suburbia.html [accessed February 13, 2012].

Upstone, S. (2006), "A Question of Black or White: Returning to Hanif Kureishi's," *The Black Album*, *Postcolonial Text*, 4 (1), 1–24, http://www.google.com/url?sa=t&rct=j&q=&esrc=s&source=web&cd=1&ved=0CCAQFjAA&url=http%3A%2F%2Fwww.postcolonial.org%2Findex.php%2Fpct%2Farticle%2Fdownload%2F679%2F518&ei=oaQ5VMShNYP5yASjyoG4Dw&usg=AFQjCNEG8RqKPnNgMEQdFCeib9NjPAQjBA&bvm=bv.77161500,d.aWw [accessed September 28, 2013].

III: Selected reviews, interviews, and profiles

Anthony, A. (2008), "A Chronicler of Pain and Pleasure," *The Guardian*. February 16, http://www.theguardian.com/books/2008/feb/17/fiction.hanifkureishi [accessed October 14, 2014].

Appignanesi, L. (2008), "All in the Mind," *The Guardian*. February 15, http://www.theguardian.com/books/2008/feb/16/featuresreviews.guardianreview2 [accessed November 2, 2013].

FURTHER READING

Birne, E. (2005), "His Big Typewriter," *London Review of Books*, 27 (1), 26–7.
Brown, M. (2014), "Hanif Kureishi's Archive Acquired by British Library," *The Guardian*. January 22, http://www.theguardian.com/books/2014/jan/22/hanif-kureishi-archive-acquired-british-library [accessed October 14, 2014].
Chambers, C. (2011), "Hanif Kureishi," in *British Muslim Fictions: Interviews with Contemporary Writers*. London: Palgrave Macmillan, pp. 226–42.
Clark, A. (2001), "Mood Swings," *The Guardian*. March 3, http://www.theguardian.com/books/2001/mar/03/fiction.hanifkureishi [accessed October 14, 2014].
Cowley, J. (2002), "You're as Young as You Feel…," *The Observer*. November 2, http://www.theguardian.com/books/2002/nov/03/fiction.hanifkureishi [accessed October 11, 2014].
Donadio, R. (2008), "My Beautiful London," *The New York Times*. August 8, http://www.nytimes.com/2008/08/10/magazine/10kureishi-t.html?pagewanted=all&_r=0 [accessed October 14, 2014].
Edemariam, A. (2008), "The Pleasure Seeker," *The Guardian*. February 29, http://www.theguardian.com/books/2008/mar/01/fiction.hanifkureishi [accessed October 14, 2014].
King, B. (2001), "Midnight All Day (Book Review)," *World Literature Today*, 75 (2), 332–3.
Kopkind, A. (1986), "Films," *Nation*, 242 (15), 560.
Kumar, A. (2000), "A Bang and a Whimper: A Conversation with Hanif Kureishi," *Transition: An International Review*, 1 (4) [88], 114–31.
Kunkel, B. (2004), "You've Got to Have Pecs," *New York Times Book Review*, 153, http://www.nytimes.com/2004/02/29/books/you-ve-got-to-have-pecs.html [accessed October 11, 2014].
Lawson, M. (2014), "The Last Word by Hanif Kureishi–review," *The Guardian*. January 29, http://www.theguardian.com/books/2014/jan/29/last-word-hanif-kureishi-review-lawson [accessed October 14, 2014].
MacCabe, C. (1999), "Hanif Kureishi on London," *Critical Quarterly*, 41 (3), 37–56.
MacInnes, C. (1998), "Review of *Intimacy*," *The Independent on Sunday*. May 3.
Malik, K. (1998), "Hanif Kureishi *Intimacy*," *Independent on Sunday*. May 3, http://www.kenanmalik.com/reviews/kureishi.html [accessed October 11, 2014].
Mars-Jones, A. (2008), "True Tales from the Couch" (Review of *Something to Tell You*), *The Observer*. February 23, http://www.guardian.co.uk/books/2008/feb/24/fiction.hanifkureishi [accessed June 14, 2012].
McCrum, R. (2014), "Hanif Kureishi Interview: 'Every 10 Years You Become Someone Else,'" *The Guardian*. January 18, http://www.theguardian.com/books/2014/jan/19/hanif-kureishi-interview-last-word [accessed October 14, 2014].
Mishra, P. (2008), "Listen without Prejudice," *The Guardian*. March 7, http://www.theguardian.com/books/2008/mar/08/fiction.hanifkureishi [accessed October 14, 2014].
Nasta, S. (2006), "Writing a Life: Hanif Kureishi and Blake Morrison in Conversation," *Wasafiri: The Transnational Journal of International Writing*, 48 (Summer), 19–26.
Prodger, M. (2014), "His Master's Voice," *New Statesman*, 143 (5197), 48.
Taylor, C. (2006), "Collected Stories by Hanif Kureishi," *The Guardian*. March 5, http://www.theguardian.com/books/2010/mar/06/hanif-kureishi-collected-stories-tayler [accessed October 14, 2014].

Taylor, D. J. (2014), "Can't Writers Make Anything Up?," *The Guardian*. February 7, http://www.theguardian.com/books/2014/feb/07/hanif-kureishi-real-people-books [accessed October 14, 2014].

Thomas, S. (2007), "Something to Ask You: A Conversation with Hanif Kureishi," *Changing English: Studies In Culture and Education*, 14 (1), 3–16.

—(2008), "Review of Hanif Kureishi, *Something to Tell You*," *Literary London: Interdisciplinary Studies in the Representation of London*, 8 (1), http://www.literarylondon.org/london-journal/march2008/thomas.html [accessed October 14, 2014].

Updike, J. (2004), "Mind/Body Problems," *The New Yorker*, 79 (44), 90–5.

Wachtel, E. (2006), "Interview with Hanif Kureishi," *The Arts Today*, CBC Radio One, September 11.

Waraich, O. (2006), "When Bombs Speak Louder than Words," *First Jordan*. February 6, http://www.1stjordan.net/actuuk/archivesuk/resultat.php?id=1017&debut=0 [accessed February 25, 2011].

Yelland, D. (2010), "Rich Man, Poor Man," *New Statesman*, 139 (4993), 54–5.

IV: Websites

http://www.hanifkureishi.co.uk [This is the author's official website. It contains information about the author and his work, links to recent writing and interviews and recent tweets.]

http://literature.britishcouncil.org/hanif-kureishi [This contains biographical and bibliographical information, as well as an interview.]

http://www.imdb.com/name/nm0475659/ [This contains the author's film credits as writer, director, producer, actor.]

Index

abandonment   4, 7–20, 73
aesthetics   10, 21, 23, 24, 42, 56, 117
aging   2, 4, 16, 32, 85–97
Andrew, Dudley   24, 25
Appignanesi, Lisa   125
Arnold, Matthew   35, 41, 47, 48
Asian   vii, 2, 3, 7, 8, 10, 12, 22, 27, 39, 40, 44, 69, 70, 72, 73, 74, 75, 77, 79, 116, 141, 148
Austen, Jane   127
authoritarian populism   37, 46
Ayer, A. J.   125

Bakhtin, Mikhail   71
Barber, Frances   42
Bazin, Andre   21, 22, 25, 30, 31, 33
Beckett, Samuel   140–1
Benjamin, Walter   26, 27, 28, 29
Bhabha, Homi   41, 117
Bildungsroman   12, 89, 116
biography   117, 126 128
black
   culture   55, 143
   people   viii, 43, 44, 56, 57, 70, 123, 124, 126
   politics   121, 143
Bloom, Claire   42
Britain, British(ness)   1, 3, 4, 5, 7, 8, 10, 11, 21, 22, 23, 24, 25, 26, 27, 29, 32, 37, 38, 39, 40, 41, 42, 43, 46, 47, 48, 51, 52, 53, 54, 55, 56, 57, 60, 62, 66, 69, 70, 71, 72, 73, 74, 75, 77, 78, 79, 80, 81, 83, 89, 92, 100, 111, 112, 113, 115, 116, 117, 120, 124, 141, 142, 147, 148
Brontes   127
Brook, Susan   65, 117
"brown man's burden"   24
Brunsdon, Charlotte   29

Buchanan, Bradley   100
Burgess, Anthony   125

Camus, Albert   126
capitalism   4, 22, 39, 69, 74, 77, 78, 79, 80, 81, 100, 140
carnival   70, 71, 73, 74, 83
Chambers, Claire   76, 83
city   4, 10, 12, 29, 32, 35–49, 51–2, 55–60, 63–7, 77, 79, 81, 107, 119
class   1, 2, 17, 21, 22, 23, 24, 30, 32, 36, 38, 39, 41, 44, 47, 53, 58, 59, 60, 64, 66, 71, 72, 75, 79, 81, 87, 89, 111, 112, 117, 119, 123, 127, 142, 143
Cohn, Dorrit   104
collage   21, 23, 24, 104
colonial(ism)   1, 19, 26, 29, 38, 45, 46, 47, 72, 73, 89
commodity   88, 89, 95, 96,
cultural hybridity   26, 39, 49, 117, 118

Davis, Angela   122
Day-Lewis, Daniel   23, 28, 142, 147, 148
de Beauvoir, Simone   126, 127
Dennis, Nigel   53
dialectic   27, 30, 87, 101, 104
Dickens   119, 126
disguise   16, 86, 89, 102, 115, 116, 119, 126, 127, 129
Disraeli, Benjamin   36, 48, 49
Doyle, Arthur Conan   122

Eagleton, Terry   47, 126
Eliot, George   54, 127
Eliot, T. S.   47
   The Waste Land   47, 105
Emecheta, Buchi   54, 60

INDEX

English(ness) 1, 3, 4, 17, 21, 23, 24, 28, 36, 37, 38, 39, 40, 41, 46, 51, 52, 56, 57, 58, 60, 63, 66, 75, 77, 79, 87, 117, 118, 121, 125, 127, 142, 149
Epicureanism 100, 113
ethnicity 2, 3, 7, 8, 9, 11, 12, 17, 19, 37, 42, 46, 51, 62, 71, 141

family vii, 2, 12, 13–17, 32, 55, 59, 60, 62, 64, 72, 75, 77, 79, 81, 89, 100, 101, 103, 107, 110, 115, 116, 117, 126, 142, 144, 146
fatwa 9, 69, 72, 116, 134, 142, 144
femininity 107
feminism, feminist 9, 76, 118, 127
Fischer, Susan Alice 71, 74, 83
focalization 119
Forster, E. M. 23, 53, 125
Frears, Stephen xi, xii, xiv, xv, 3, 18, 21–3, 27, 28, 29, 35, 39–42, 44, 46, 145–9
Freud, Sigmund 99, 101, 102, 106, 108–11, 127, 138, 139
  "Civilization and Its Discontents" 101, 104, 112, 113
  "Moses and Monotheism" 112
  "New Introductory Lectures on Psycho-Analysis" 109, 113
  "Totem and Taboo" 112

gay 23, 24, 131, 139, 142
Gazelle, Wendy 42
gender 2, 8, 71, 90, 111, 127
Geraghty, Christine 23, 28, 29
Ghose, Sheila 76, 82
Gift, Roland 42
Gill, Eric 126
Godard, Jean-Luc 21, 25, 27, 29
Gogol, Nikolai
  "The Nose" 3
Golding, William 125
Greater London Council (GLC) 39, 49
Green, Henry 125
Greene, Graham 125
Groce, Dorothy ("Cherry") 43
Guardian, The 23
Gullette, Margaret Morganroth 85, 86

Hall, Stuart 37
Hartley, L. P. 53
Hellman, Lillian 126, 127
heterosexual 2
hierarchy 24, 46, 71, 115, 116
Hill, John 23, 26, 28, 29
hospitality 54, 55, 57
Hughes, Ted 122, 126
Huxley, Aldous 125

identity 3, 4, 8, 18, 22, 36, 37, 40, 41, 52, 53, 54, 55, 56, 63, 72, 89, 91, 100, 101, 102, 111, 112, 115, 117, 124
  national identity 3, 22, 24, 25, 36, 51, 52, 54, 116, 118, 124
ideology 4, 13, 22, 23, 37, 38, 40, 47, 48, 57, 71, 74, 77, 80, 100, 118
immigration 27, 54, 60, 146
India 11, 32, 37, 45, 54, 62, 63
  Indian(ness) 11, 16, 17, 23, 42, 63, 64, 83, 89, 107, 117, 118, 121, 123, 142
Ishiguro, Kazuo 53
Islam 69, 71, 72, 82, 103, 110, 111, 112, 113, 120, 124, 134
  Islamism, Radical Islam 13, 72, 73, 75, 77, 116, 117, 138, 139
Islamophobia 83, 112, 115

Jaffrey, Saeed 23
juxtaposition 23, 87, 102, 104, 105

Kaleta, Kenneth C. 9, 36, 90
Kapoor, Shashi 42
Khan, Massud 124
Khan-Din, Ayub 42, 43
King, Stephen
  The Shining 126
Kipling, Rudyard 9, 10, 89
Kuchta, Todd 117
Kureishi, Hanif
  "Arduous Conversation Will Continue, The" 71, 73, 83, 84, 129–30
  "Art of Distraction, The" 2, 132
  Birds of Passage xiv

Black Album, The xv, 1, 4, 9, 10, 13, 14, 17, 18, 39, 65–6, 69, 72, 74, 75–7, 82–4, 90, 96, 99, 100, 111, 116, 119, 120, 121, 122, 124, 125, 143
Black Album, The: Adapted for the Stage xv, 3, 12, 19, 39, 69, 72, 83
Body, The xvi, 2, 4, 14, 15, 17, 85–97, 119
Borderline xiv
"Bradford" 72
Buddha of Suburbia, The xv, 1, 4, 5, 8, 9, 12, 14, 18, 39, 51–67, 71, 82, 89, 96, 100, 101, 116, 117, 118, 119, 120, 121, 122, 123, 124, 125, 127, 137–8, 143
   BBC production of vii, viii, xv, 65
"The Carnival of Culture" 70, 71, 73, 74, 83
Dreaming and Scheming xvi
"Four Blue Chairs" 2
Gabriel's Gift xv, 2, 12, 14, 19, 97
"Hullabaloo in the Tree" 2
Intimacy xv, 9, 11, 12, 13, 14, 15, 16, 100
   film xv, 19
Last Word, The xvi, 3, 4, 5, 9, 12, 18, 115–30
Le Week-End ix, xvi, 3, 5, 12
London Kills Me viii, xv, xvi, 18, 39, 48, 71
"Loose Tongues and Liberty" 36
Love in a Blue Time xv, 101
Mother, The ix, xiii, xiv, xvi, 2, 9, 12, 16, 19
Mother Country, The xiv
My Beautiful Laundrette xii, xiv, xv, xvi, 1, 4, 8, 21–33, 39, 40, 41, 45, 49, 71, 72, 75, 89, 96, 139, 142, 145–9
My Ear at His Heart xvi, 2, 12, 16, 17, 19, 126
My Son the Fanatic
   Film xv, xvi, 1, 4, 19, 69, 70, 72, 74, 75, 76, 77–84, 97
   Short story ("My Son the Fanatic") xv, 19, 69, 81
"Newness In The World" 27

Outskirts xiv, xv, 2
"Penis, The" 3
"Rainbow Sign, The" xiv, 22, 39, 72, 120–21
"Road Exactly, The" 72
Sammy and Rosie Get Laid xii, xv, xvi, 1, 4, 18, 35–49, 70, 71, 89, 133, 135, 145, 147–8
"Sex and Secularity" 83
Sleep with Me xv, 2, 76
Soaking the Heat xiv
Something to Tell You xvi, 2, 5, 9, 12, 17, 18, 83, 99–113, 119, 120, 121, 122, 124, 125, 126, 127, 136, 138, 139
"Tale of the Turd, The" 2
Tomorrow Today! xiv
Venus ix, xiii, xvi, 2, 4, 9, 12, 19, 21, 30–3
"We're Not Jews" 2
"Weddings and Beheadings" xvi, 2
When Night Begins xvi, 3
"With Your Tongue Down My Throat" 2, 3
Word and the Bomb, The xvi, 1, 2, 4, 69–73, 83, 84
You Can't Go Home xiv

Lacan, Jacques 99, 102, 109, 110, 111, 140
   dead father 104, 109, 112
   Seminar IV 109
   Symbolic father 109, 110, 113
Lamming, George 53, 54, 55, 66
language 3, 11, 23, 27, 52, 58, 63, 87, 109, 110, 116, 119, 136, 147
Larkin, Philip 126
Lawrence, D. H. 125
Leader, Darian 124
literary apartheid 71
Livingstone, Ken 39
London xiv, xvi, 4, 12–3, 15–6, 18, 22, 23, 25–6, 27, 29, 30, 31–2, 35–49, 51–61, 64–7, 70, 75, 83, 86, 94, 107, 117, 119, 121, 124, 128, 131, 135, 145, 147, 148
London bombings (7/7) 2, 73, 83, 101

love 1, 3, 4, 17, 18, 45, 59, 66, 69, 74–5, 76, 77, 81, 82, 84, 88, 90, 92, 93, 101, 102, 103, 104, 105, 107, 108, 109, 110, 113, 137, 139, 149

MacCabe, Colin 25, 26, 59, 73
MacInnes, Colin 54, 60, 64
magical realism 10, 40, 116
Mailer, Norman 126
Malik, Art 43
Malik, Kenan 9, 70, 72, 74
Marx, Karl 88, 95, 110, 124
   Marxist, Marxism 76, 87, 88, 95
masculinity 9, 31, 97, 100, 107
masquerade 89, 95
metafiction 115, 116, 117, 122, 124
metropolitan 4, 11, 23, 24, 51–3, 55–56, 58, 60, 62, 66
Michell, Roger vii–ix, xi, xiii, xv, xvi, 3, 16, 30, 31
middle-age 2, 3, 15, 18, 102, 122, 133
monoculturalism 19, 25, 73, 134
Moore-Gilbert, Bart 9, 37, 89, 100, 116
multiculturalism 4, 7–9, 11, 12, 19, 20, 39, 51, 52, 55, 60, 73, 100, 101, 124
Murdoch, Iris 127
Muslim 1, 62, 72, 74, 75, 79, 82, 83, 117, 120, 134

Naipaul, V. S. 9, 54, 117, 121
narrative space 21, 25, 28, 29
narrator 17, 18, 91, 99, 101, 102, 105, 115, 116, 118, 119, 120, 121, 124, 125, 126, 127
National Union of Mineworkers 38
Needham, Anuradha Dingwaney 74

Oedipal, Oedipus Complex 101, 102, 104, 106–9, 111, 113, 117
optical unconscious 27, 28
optique 24, 25
Orwell, George 118, 125, 129
O'Shea-Meddour, Wendy 82, 119, 120, 123
O'Toole, Peter 30, 31, 32, 137

Pakistan 17, 37, 77, 78, 79, 81, 82, 134, 135, 138, 139
   Pakistani 24, 26, 28, 70, 75, 79, 81, 121, 124, 139, 141, 142, 146
parallax 4, 85–97
pen 93, 116, 122, 126
performance 58, 63, 64, 66, 85, 89, 90, 91, 148
Phillips, Adam 124
Plath, Sylvia 127
pleasure 15, 26, 28, 31, 32, 43, 64, 72, 75, 77, 78, 79, 86, 88, 89, 90, 91, 92, 94, 95, 96, 100, 101, 104, 105, 108, 111, 112, 117, 139, 140
political correctness 32, 42, 118
politics xvi, 4, 22, 24, 27, 31, 35, 36, 41, 46, 52, 74, 76, 85, 87, 91, 99, 100, 101, 110, 113, 117, 118, 119, 147
pornography 79, 90, 91, 93
positive images 70, 82
postcolonialism, postcoloniality 1, 3, 7–12, 19, 35, 36, 37, 39, 42, 46, 47, 49, 56, 71, 100, 116, 117, 124, 141
postethnicity 3, 7, 8, 11, 12, 19
Powell, Anthony 125
Prasad, Udayan xv, 19, 77
prose viii, xvi, 89, 115, 116, 117, 128
Proust, Marcel 110, 124, 126
psychoanalysis 2, 5, 18, 27, 43, 99–113, 121, 124, 125, 126, 136, 142

queer 117

race 1, 17, 22, 30, 37, 38, 41, 42, 43, 44, 52, 57, 63, 65, 71, 72, 75, 110, 111, 119, 147, 149
   racism 1, 2, 22, 27, 39, 44, 46, 58, 61, 64, 72, 73, 75, 77, 82, 89, 115, 116, 118, 120, 142
Ranasinha, Ruvani 82, 100, 101
religion 1, 4, 10, 69–81, 99–101, 103, 111–13
representation 4, 7, 8, 10, 11, 21, 22, 23, 24, 25, 30, 31, 33, 35, 40, 43, 70, 89, 102, 105, 107, 127, 141, 142

INDEX

Rhys, Jean 122, 127
Ricardo, David 88
Ross, Michael L. 71, 83
Royal Court Theatre vii, xiv, 132, 140, 141
Rushdie, Salman 1, 2, 4, 9, 10, 11, 60, 74, 79, 83, 116, 134, 142
  The Satanic Verses 9, 10, 40, 54, 55, 69, 72, 75, 124
  Midnight's Children 134
Russell, Bertrand 125

Salinger, J. D. 126
Sandhu, Sukhdev 21, 23, 24, 29, 40, 48, 70, 116
Saroyan, William 126
Sartre, Jean-Paul 126
Schoene, Berthold 117
Schopenhauer, Arthur 113
Selvon, Sam 53, 54, 55, 56, 60, 61, 64, 66
  The Lonely Londoners 54, 55, 61
sentence(s) 5, 115, 116, 118, 119, 128, 129, 130
sexuality 1, 2, 16, 22, 30, 51, 70, 71, 72, 73, 90, 108, 112, 115, 116, 128
Smith, Adam 88
Smith, Zadie 118, 129
Sontag, Susan 24
Specials, The 38
storytelling 37, 115, 116, 123
Streep, Meryl 22, 133
style 3, 5, 16, 24, 42, 57, 62, 115–9, 129, 147
Styron, William 126
Su, John 117
suburbia, suburbs 4, 10, 12, 13, 16, 17, 19, 25, 39, 51–67, 75, 117, 119, 123
subversion 5, 10, 14, 25, 33, 46, 71, 74, 77, 83, 115, 116, 118, 119, 128, 133, 134
Suez Crisis (1956) 38

Tanizaki, Junichiro
  Diary of A Mad Old Man 21, 30, 31

Thatcher, Margaret 4, 22–25, 33, 35–49, 65, 70, 74, 133
  Iron Lady, The 22, 49
  Thatcherism 1, 21, 35–49, 71, 133, 146
Thomas, Susie 2, 5, 56, 71, 73, 74, 76, 82, 101, 116, 120, 124, 126, 127
transplant 15, 85, 86, 95

Upstone, Sara 82
urban 35, 36, 37, 39, 51, 52, 54, 55, 56, 63, 124, 143

voyeurism 91, 93, 94

Waraich, Omar 73
Warnecke, Gordon 28
War on Terror 83, 101, 111
Waugh, Evelyn 53, 125
Wells, H. G. 59
Whittaker, Jodie 30
white (characters, culture, people) 2, 3, 22, 24, 26, 27, 28, 37, 41, 70, 71, 72, 73, 75, 77, 79, 86, 95, 96, 120, 124, 142, 143, 149
Williams, Raymond 21, 22, 23, 52
Winnicott, D. W. 124
Wodehouse, P. G. 126, 141
woman(hood), women 2, 16, 22, 32, 33, 43, 44, 70, 80, 86, 91, 92, 93, 104, 106, 107, 108, 120, 122, 123, 124, 127, 128, 129, 141
Woolf, Virginia 43, 127
World War II 26, 38, 53
Wright, Melanie J. 82
writer-as-Great-Man 115, 116, 122, 126, 128, 129

Yassin-Kassab, Robin 118
youth 2, 4, 15, 17, 26, 48, 57, 73, 77, 78, 85, 91, 92, 96, 97, 147

Žižek, Slavoj 4, 85, 87–8, 94, 95, 96

www.ingramcontent.com/pod-product-compliance
Ingram Content Group UK Ltd.
Pitfield, Milton Keynes, MK11 3LW, UK
UKHW021840220426
470268UK00007B/285